T0196215

MY FOOTPRINTS
ON THE SANDS
OF HISTORY

Looking in the Rearview
Mirror of Nostalgia

MOHAMMAD OBEDUR RAHMAN

authorHOUSE®

AuthorHouse™
1663 Liberty Drive
Bloomington, IN 47403
www.authorhouse.com
Phone: 1 (800) 839-8640

© 2017 Mohammad Obedur Rahman. All rights reserved.

No part of this book may be reproduced, stored in a retrieval system, or transmitted by any means without the written permission of the author.

Published by AuthorHouse   05/16/2017

ISBN: 978-1-5246-5985-1 (sc)
ISBN: 978-1-5246-5984-4 (e)

Library of Congress Control Number: 2017900530

Print information available on the last page.

Any people depicted in stock imagery provided by Thinkstock are models, and such images are being used for illustrative purposes only. Certain stock imagery © Thinkstock.

This book is printed on acid-free paper.

Because of the dynamic nature of the Internet, any web addresses or links contained in this book may have changed since publication and may no longer be valid. The views expressed in this work are solely those of the author and do not necessarily reflect the views of the publisher, and the publisher hereby disclaims any responsibility for them.

CONTENTS

DEDICATION

I want to dedicate this book to my Past,
Present and Future well wishers

PREFACE

I want to record the events in my life so that the younger generation, in my family and outside of it, can learn from my failures and my successes. I have been a law-abiding, tax-paying citizen in this country and have tried to maintain a reasonably high standard for myself and my family. In doing so, I have tried to do the best for myself and my family. My career as an engineer spanned more than forty years, some of it in India. One of my ambitions in my early twenties was to go abroad to the United States or Germany to pursue higher education and become successful in life. At the age of twenty-nine, I had the opportunity to apply to some universities in the United States. During this period, some concrete things happened in my life: I earned my bachelor's degree in engineering—which was my dream—from a premier college in Bangalore, India; I got married; and I moved to the United States. At times, I branded myself a professional student. In 1956, I earned my bachelor's in science, but it wasn't until 1964 that I graduated from engineering college.

I want the younger generation to learn from the events of my life. The decisions in my life were largely made by my dad, as we lost my mom when I was eleven years old. Dad had his own way of doing things—he thought engineering was not appropriate. He believed that first of all, one should get a basic degree, and then he or she should go on to do what he or she wanted. So although I had a good chance of getting into an engineering college, my dad stopped me from applying and pushed me to earn the basic bachelor's degree. Anyway, today I am a successful retired professional and registered engineer in the United States.

I use conversational English throughout this book because I want my readers to easily grasp what I'm trying to say. By no means is this book meant to be considered one of the greatest work of literature—I want it to be simple and approachable. When I started writing this book, I looked at different ramifications, such as the amount of time, energy, and effort it would take, plus quite a lot of recollections and walking through memory lane. I first prepared an outline of the chapters, but things were fluid as I progressed through the chapters. My recollections led me to capture the most important events in my life. There were a few twists and turns as I went through memories of my young student life and my career days. I sometimes felt as though something else were running my life: circumstance.

I hope that as a whole, my life itself has a message for my young readers. I hope they will learn to make every effort to follow their hearts. I think there is a lot of motivation in designing your own life and not letting circumstance suppress your inner urges or desires.

Writing this book has been like a journey from my childhood for me. I didn't receive much love from my mom, because I was only eleven years old when she passed away. I missed my mom's love throughout my life. I wished to stay under her wings for a much longer time. I could only include in this book a few incidents that readers might identify with and learn from. I take responsibility for any shortcomings in this book and hope you take pleasure in reading this humble book and learn from it.

ACKNOWLEDGEMENTS

I wish to express my gratitude to all the people involved in the writing of this book, especially my younger brothers Mohammad Ataur Rahman, Mohammad Ziaur Rahman, Mohammad Sanaur Rahman and Aftab Ahmad who were very generous in sharing their time and knowledge with me. My sincere thanks also go to my wife for her tough comments together with her gentle support.

It has been a pleasure to work with Author House publications staff including the coordinators, customer support, editorial and production staff. They had critical as well as very helpful suggestions throughout the project.

There are many other fine people including the photographers, and English major graduate and other students who shared their valuable time.

And finally my deepest gratitude to my son. Shakeeb M. Rahman and daughter Farah Deeba Walls for their untiring emotional support during the writing of this book, and because I seek in them that unshakable attitude towards life which I admire and cherish and hopefully this book will project and reflect.

INTRODUCTION

This book is released at a time when terrorism is a major issue in many democracies around the world. Whichever country the terrorism takes place, the first thought or general view is that some Muslims may be. But this is not the case all the time. There are some Americans who are terrorists-like Timothy McVeigh. But the news media do not call them Terrorists, they are extremists.

The tragedy of Sept.11, changed the lives of many Americans and particularly the Muslim population in U.S. as well as other countries. Since that time Muslim communities remain vulnerable to extreme anger and threats. Some Muslim women in hijab (head scarf) have been harassed, their hijabs yanked out etc. Sikhs with turbans have been mistaken to be Muslims and have been shot at. American people made it very clear that the attackers must be subjected to justice.

In this book I have discussed some events of my life as a Muslim immigrant to U.S in early 60's. Things were very quiet then. Everything was so peaceful and serene during that era. There were no suicide bombers, no truck drivers who drove into crowds, No pressure cooker type bombs etc. Most of the people had peaceful objectives in life. I have been subjected to cyber fraud also.

I think my life is full of twists, turns and suspense. When I first started reminiscing about my life, I found out that the events of my child hood came to mind very vividly. Also, it is very clear that however much you plan your life, God takes your life through the path that he has chosen for you. The circumstances dictate which route needs to be taken and at what time. In this book I have given the historical events which influenced the decisions I took. I have given the important events in my life in the back ground of Historical events if you will.

It has been my sincere attempt to record those events which the reader can identify with and learn from it. My sincere thoughts are to narrate those events that can influence your learning process to a great extent.

Finally, I decided to mention those individuals who had a vast influence on my life. This book is also a way of expression of my sincere thanks, therefore, to my parents and immediate family, and to the teachers and inspirers, I was fortunate to have had, both as a student and in my professional life.

Each individual creature on this fabulous planet is created by God to fulfill an important role. Whatever I have accomplished in life is definitely through His help. He showered his grace and mercy on me through some outstanding teachers and colleagues. When I mention those persons, I am only praising His glory. If I have contributed even a smidgen of goodness to this world by this humble book, my efforts are paid off enormously and I will be more than satisfied.

May God bless you.
Mohammad O. Rahman

CHAPTER 1

My Humble Beginnings

The background of my life begins with my grandfather Moulvi Gulam Ahmad, who was a schoolteacher as well as a *moulvi fazil*, someone either educated in advanced Islamic studies or is a cleric. He must have been born in the late 1860s or early 1870s. I once asked my dad about the ancestry of his father, and he told me about his grandparents' lives, but I lost or misplaced my notes. Apparently, my grandparents were all in respectable professions and lived comfortable and good lives. In other words, my roots are honorable and respectable.

The name Gulam Ahmad, or Gulam-e-Ahmad, means "servant of the prophet Mohammad." It is an appropriate name that my great-grandparents gave to my grandfather. He lived up to it. He was indeed a servant of God as well as of the prophet throughout his life. A man of great principles, firm and strict about his convictions, he balanced his obligations to work, family, and religion; acted responsibly toward his children; and commanded respect from his contemporaries as well as his relations and friends. Moulvi Gulam-e-Ahmad fathered seven children—five girls and two boys. The girls' names are Najmunnissa, Mehrunnissa, Tajunnissa, Rahmat-Unnissa, and Taherunnissa, and the boys are M. Abdul Aziz, my dad, and G. Abdul Basith. All the women except Taherunnissa and Rahmat-Unnissa were teachers—good ones who valued and respected education, pursuing it with zeal even into their later years by continuing to study and attend school. Aunt Rahmat-Unnissa went to a middle school in Sheshadripuram, a suburb of Bangalore City, which was not far from my own middle school in Sheshadripuram. The example of my aunts had a strong influence on me. In those days, women, particularly in India, spent most of their time in the kitchen—their main tasks were to cook and feed the family, keep the house clean, and raise the children. That was their duty. I am proud that through their pursuit of education, my ancestors were ahead of the game. Even my grandmother Amir Bi worked as a schoolteacher while taking care of her children.

In those days in India, a bachelor of arts was one of the highest degrees a person could receive. It was rare—in some circles, if a man had a bachelor's degree, he was nicknamed BA So-and-So. Of course, there were also exceptional people who were moulvi fazils, barristers and lawyers, and so on, and some daring and exceptional people, such as Sir Mohammad Iqbal, Mahatma Gandhi, and Qaide-Azam Mohammad Ali Jinnah, had advanced and foreign degrees, especially from England. My father studied for a Master's Degree after his bachelor's. He also achieved high marks in Farsi and earned a gold medal from the University of Mysore. Dad started as a clerk in the state government of Mysore, and over the years, because of his hard work and dedication, he earned promotions and retired as assistant director of industries and commerce with the state. He was a tahsildar or amaldar for several years in the revenue department; it was a prestigious job in the taluk headquarter town in a given district of Mysore State, which is nowadays called Karnataka State. Every three years or so, my dad used to be transferred from one taluk to another in a different district. When my siblings and I were young, it was exciting to go to a different town every now and then. We were able to see quite a bit of Karnataka. Such a move meant a new school, new people, a new house, and a new environment for my younger brothers and me.

That is a little bit of my father's background. Now for my mother's story. My mom, Amina Begum, was a nice, hardworking person with firm principles of her own. She was nice to people and naturally expected the same in return. Sometimes people did not return the same respect she showed to them. However, she was not the kind of person who would take mistreatment silently. She would fight for her rights and try to get even or at least get matters in the right order. She was an excellent mother and took care of her kids in the best possible manner.

My maternal grandfather's name was Qazi Mohammad Hussain. He held a prestigious job, I think, as a superintendent of police. I must have been young, maybe two years or so, when he passed away at the Chamaraj Pet house in Bangalore, which he owned. I had four maternal uncles: Mohammad Ahmad, Khader Mohiyouddin, Mohammad Yakoob, and K. Ahmadullah. I also had two maternal aunts: Fatima Begum and Ayesha Begum. Fatima Begum, whom we used to call Ammi Khala, was married to Anwar Ali. His ancestors were from Iran. He had a government job in Tamil Nadu. So my *khala*, my aunt, raised her family in various cities in Tamil Nadu. She was the author of some books in Urdu and received awards from various governments. My nana was originally from Kolar. My uncle Anwar Ali and aunt used to come visit their brother Mamujan, who stayed in Bangalore for most of his government service. My uncle Mohammad Ahmad held high jobs in the state government service in Karnataka. He had a bachelor of arts degree, as my dad did. He was an ambitious person. They told me that when my mom passed away in Bangalore in 1946, on her deathbed, she asked my uncle to take care of her kids. He kept his promise until the end. He made sure we all got good educations and were healthy. All my uncles and aunts received good educations. I will say more about my uncles and aunts later. Another uncle of mine took a keen interest in helping us out. He invited us to his house every now and then. He also loved his sister, my mom, dearly. At this time, however, I would like to pose a question to pick your brains a little bit. Are you ready?

What was the most important news or event that took place in late 1933 or early 1934?

1. Alcatraz officially became a federal prison.
2. An 8.4 earthquake hit Nepal, resulting in the deaths of thousands.
3. Adolf Hitler merged the offices of chancellor and president, declaring himself the supreme leader.
4. The family of my *dada sab* and the family of my *nana jan* met at Lal Bagh, Red Gardens, Bangalore, India.

If you chose one, two, or three, you are partially correct. However, number four is the best answer. So the story goes. My cousin Dr. Ather Ali told me once that the families of my maternal and paternal grandparents met in Lal Bagh, which is one of the most beautiful botanical gardens. There was nothing red about this botanical garden. Deevaan (Chief Minister) Sir Mirza Ismail named it Lal Bagh, or "favorite and beloved gardens."

These gardens stretch over several acres of land and are maintained well. The purpose of this meeting was to show my young dad his potential bride, my mom. The two families did not actually meet but were at different spots close enough but still not within the range of being able to talk with each other. My dad liked my mom and agreed to marry her. This is one way arranged marriages happened in those days.

Another interesting matter happened at that meeting. Another young man from my nana's family took a liking to a woman, Taherunnisa, in my dada sab's family. Thus, two beautiful marriages evolved at that time. I don't know all the details, but a daughter of one family went to the other family and vice versa. My dad and my uncle were about two years apart in age, with my uncle being older. Both were in government service.

The men liking the respective women wasn't enough; the families must have talked to each other and come to an agreement. I am not sure about the date of the weddings. It seems both weddings took place at the same time. Sir Mirza Ismail, the deewan—chief minister—of Mysore, attended the wedding ceremony. What an exciting time it would have been, with two weddings, the union of two families, the exchange of daughters, and so on. My dad and uncle Mohammad Ahmad had some similarities. Both had bachelor's degrees, were starting spectacular careers in the state government, and became a significant part of each other's family. My dada sab was fair, and his daughters were fair also. Anyway, the two families got along well in the following years. My uncle Mohammad Ahmad had four children: two girls and two boys. The eldest daughter is Yasmin, Khutaijatul Kubra, and the younger sister is Nargis, Fatima Sogra. The name of the older son is Kishwar, Sadiq Hussain, and the younger brother's name is Iqbal Hussain. All are well settled in their respective lives. Except for Yasmin, all of my uncle's children are living in the United States. I am fortunate to have cousins like them. Even Yasmin and her husband, Dr. Noor-Uddin, have been in service outside of India from time to time.

So far, I've brought up the names of some of my family members to give you the flavor and some background of my family and my roots. I would like to again bring up those relatives and friends who have touched my life one way or another as I continue my story. I will not be doing justice here if I do not bring up the name of a formidable and famous ruler of Mysore. His famous saying was "To live like a lion for one day is far better than to live like a fox for one hundred years." His name was Tippu Sultan, son of Haider Ali, who was the ruler of Mysore before Tippu Sultan, of course. Tippu Sultan never compromised his ideals, always stuck to his goals, and never submitted to the supremacy of a foreign power, such as the British. He was always concerned with the well-being of the people, and he realized that the freedom of Indian people was at stake due to the cunning nature and diplomatic and military skills of the British. He built an exceedingly efficient system of administration. He built factories in different parts of the state of Mysore, thus providing jobs and improving the living standards of people. His attention to the details of the governmental system and promotion of agriculture made Mysore a prosperous and progressive state on the continent during the eighteenth century.

In this paragraph, again, I would like to challenge you with a question. I will give you multiple-choice answers, and you need to select the most important and appropriate answer.

What was the most important event that took place early in the year 1935?

1. Airplanes were no longer permitted to fly over the White House in Washington, DC.
2. A boy was born in the family of M. Abdul Aziz and Amina Begum in Bangalore, India.
3. President Mustafa Kamal Pasha named himself Ata Turk, or Father of Turkey.

If you picked number two, you are right on the money. I was born in the early part of 1935. One small piece of paper my mom saved says I was born on February 11, 1935. However, my high school certificate says my date of birth was March 6 of that year. Anyway, to be consistent, I kept the latter as my birth date. In India as well as in Karnataka (then Mysore State), the high school certificate, or marks card, was an important document. It was used as a birth certificate as well as proof of passing high school requirements. At the time of this writing, my elders are not here to verify, but I think I was born in Bangalore (Chamaraj Pet), India, in my nana Jan's house. The house was named, as was tradition in those days, Dar-us-Salam (Abode of Peace). It was a beautiful bungalow in a suburb of Bangalore. At that time, across from the house, there was nothing but a jungle with large trees. One of my uncles, Mr. Khadar Mohiyoddin, had a camera and used to take pictures of the family. My cousins and I used to call him Bucchane. The land in front of the house was cleared by felling the trees. Big trees came crashing down, and it was a thrill to see for me. I might have been a child a year or two old. I have seen a picture of myself and my brother Asif descending the front steps of my nana Jan's house. We were two cute little guys wearing knickers (maybe there were suspenders), and the knickers did not have zippers. Zippers were invented much later. An entry gate and small compound were in front of the house. I remember my youngest uncle cycling back into the front yard when he returned from college. His name is Ahmadulla. He became a successful lawyer in Bangalore. His means of transportation in those days was a bicycle. K. Ahmadulla was a man with a great sense of humor, always cracking jokes and doing small stunts. All brothers gathered in the hall of the house for namaz (prayers). Uncle Khadar Mohiyoddin gave azan loudly, and all brothers performed the namaz. I do not recall who led the prayers. It was probably the oldest brother, Mohammad Ahmad, whom we called Mamujan. I do not recall what each of the brothers was doing at that time. They spent quite a bit of time in the kitchen. There was a jackfruit tree in the backyard. The jackfruit is a large green fruit with several yellow *gareas* (baby fruits) inside, which are sweet and tender to eat. This fruit is popular in India. There are large seeds inside these yellow eatables, which are also used for cooking in curries and are delicious. Except for the shell, every part of the jackfruit is edible. On the shell are thorny growths that are pretty to look at. I recall a picture of myself and Asif climbing down or standing on the front steps of the bungalow, and it seems I had to shake the dew of my little lily. I was a few steps up, and he was a few steps below me. The picture was small, and I don't know whether I performed the act or not. I do not know whether we were living there at Dar-us-Salam or just visiting. I remember when my nana jan passed away. I was just a little kid.

My nani (Imam Unnisa) passed away after three years. My nana's family were all qazis (imams) in the masjid. They were kind of community leaders also. He had a high post in the police department. My nani jan was buried next to the grave of Nana Jan Qazi Mohammad Hussain.

My dada sab's house was in Malleshwaram, Mohammadan Block, Bangalore, India. It was a neat little community in the city center. The residential streets were called First Crossroad, Second Crossroad, etc. The house was rented and was a pretty big house with a big hall, my dad's room in the front portion of the house, my chacha's room in the front on the opposite side of the house, a kitchen, a bathroom, and a toilet way in the back. I think there was no running water at that time in the house. I do not recall a public tap on the street corner either. Eventually, there was running water in the house. New taps were installed in the house wherever it was practical.

There was a place with a faucet of running water by the kitchen, with a curb around it to contain the water when washing dishes. This was the equivalent of a modern sink. It was about six by five feet, with granite flooring so water could flow toward the drain. There was no hot water available readily. Water needed to be heated with wood and then poured into buckets, and there was a tumbler to put water on your head and wash your body. There were no overhead showers. There were two kinds of soap. The one for washing clothes had no aroma and was yellowish in color. The other was usually Lux soap, which was aromatic and expensive. The yellow laundry soap came in bars that almost looked like cheese bars.

My dada sab was a religious man and used to go to the mosque for namaz frequently. We had a place in the front yard that was the urinal. It was a squat type of urinal. The urine went into a big, trapezoidal over-the-ground channel that was constructed at the edge of the front doors of the houses and the road. At the front door, it was covered by a rectangular, thin stone about three feet wide and five feet or so long, which formed a ramp to the road level. Dada sab, when he passed his urine in the designated place, used to dry the urine by holding a mud cake, which looked like a cookie specially made for this purpose. He used to walk back and forth on the private front porch until the mud cake had almost dried. That was his routine. Remember, running water was not available, and purification (*taharat*) was important.

All the mosques in those days used to have plenty of mud cookies available for use. That was the custom for men, but please don't ask me how women purified themselves!

The Lux soap was a luxury to some people, including me as I was growing up. We spent time at Nana's house as well as my dada's house in Bangalore. As I recall, my dad took us to a town called Pavagardh in Tumkur District. In that little town with a mountain not too distant behind our house, my mom raised us. The house had a little *aangan* (yard) space in the back.

Imagine a small town of Karnataka State in the mid-1930s. My dad was a high-level officer with servants in the house and in the office. We could see the mountain from the backyard of the house. It was beautiful. There was hardly anything on the road, only an occasional car, buses, and lorries. I am bringing this up to convey to you how peaceful it was in those days and how serene life used to be. Look it up on Google Maps; it is interesting to observe life in a small town in rural India in the late '30s.

Even though my father had a high post in the state government, he was a frugal man. My mom did namazas (prayers) on time. I do not know if she had access to a clock or not; she used to estimate the time by the length of the shadow of her palm on the ground.

There was lots of sunshine in the yard, and I remember her measuring or estimating the time that way. Those were my toddler days. She used to make meals for me. Asif was about two years younger than I. He used to bother me by trying to get some food from my plate. Mom used to put me on the windowsill so Asif, even when standing up, could not reach my plate. I recall the street in front of our house. I don't think there was electricity or running water in the house. After Pavagardh, Dad took us to Nelamangala in Bangalore District. I do not recall much about that taluk headquarter town. All I know is that it was close to Bangalore. Therefore, as kids, we spent a lot of time in Malleshwaram, where my dada's house was. While my dad, Bawajan, was busy making his career in the government service, Mom was busy raising the family. She used to sew our clothes on a Singer machine. Bangalore is relatively cold, so she sewed us caps that covered our ears. In Bangalore, a city about three thousand feet above sea level, it gets cold in the mornings, especially in January and February. It does not mean much to you to read the names of all these small towns where my dad worked. I'm telling you just for the record, and also, it will serve the purpose of letting you know where I lived as well as how simple and peaceful life was for me in those days.

It's time for some questions at this juncture. I think you are getting better at these pop quizzes. Keep up the good work, as there will be a big test at the end.

What world events happened between 1936 and 1939?

1. A successful first helicopter flight was made.
2. A war between China and Japan began.
3. Asif, my brother, was born in May 1937.
4. An earthquake in Chile killed thirty thousand people.
5. The Golden Gate Bridge in San Francisco opened.
6. An American company, DuPont, began commercial production of nylon toothbrush bristles.
7. My dad took us to which town in Chitradurga District.
8. A third child was born in the Aziz family. I will tell you his name in a little bit.
9. The Second World War began.

If you answered "All of the above," you are correct. I will tell you the answers to the above questions as I go. Asif, my second younger brother, was born in the family. I have mentioned him in previous pages a little bit. Mom used to say that when born, he weighed close to ten pounds or so. I do not recall where he was born—maybe in Bangalore. We were both growing up in Bangalore as well as the little towns my dad took the family to. Mostly, we wore knickers or shorts with suspenders in those days. I do not recall any underwear that we used. As I said, my Dad was a frugal man. He kept a record of all his expenditures, both big and small, in detail. Budgeting every item was his favorite thing to do. Every penny spent had to be justified.

I think he trained my mom to do the same. Both my mom and dad came from families who earned money the hard way. They respected each other in this effort of being frugal. He kept control of money always. I do not know to what extent my mom had authority to spend family budget independently or even if she had any access to the funds of the family.

The taluk headquarter town my dad was transferred to was Challakere in the Chitradurga District. It was a little town. When we first moved into the house after our bus journey, my mom sat down on the floor in the middle of the hall of the house to feed the little one—maybe it was Altaf, the third son. As soon as she settled down with the bottle of milk for the young one, there was a rattling noise on the tile roof above her, and a live snake fell down not far from her. Mom started screaming and running away from the snake, which started crawling on the floor. My dad and I were both around. We started panicking and trying to help Mom get away from the snake. There were servants around also. They took care of the snake, which could have been a cobra. I was about four and a half or five at that time. There was no ceiling in the room, and the house might not have been checked or cleaned before we came in. I do not know how we disposed of the snake, but that was an excitement for all of us. We were fearful, but we all pitched in together to face and resolve the crisis.

I have a lot of memories of that town. I started my primary school education there. I walked to school, which was not far from our house. One time, the teacher changed my clothes to a Boy Scout uniform and sent me home with the uniform to show it to my mom and dad. There were exciting times at the school. I think it was Urdu primary school. During class, one older kid used to go to the teacher and raise his hand with all the fingers folded down and the little finger raised up. He used to do this quite a bit, maybe every hour or so. I watched him. This happened during the beginning of the school year, when I first started school. I could not figure out what that gesture meant. Finally, after a couple of days, I found out that the fellow was asking the teacher for a break to go to the bathroom. This is how I faced the world and started my educational journey.

One time, there was a big excitement in the town: the viceroy of India, who is a dignitary, came to Chellakere. My dad, being the tahsildar, was right in front with him. There was a big *pendal* (a temporary shelter), and hundreds of people came to see the distinguished visitor. Also, I recall a competition to select the best baby boy among several entries. The Viceroy was a top government official in the British government. Of course, my mom entered baby Altaf as one of the contenders in the competition.

Altaf was selected by the judges as one of the best babies. We were told that the viceroy, after congratulating my dad and baby Altaf, held a silver cup, first prize, on his palm in front of Altaf. Altaf, who was about a year and a half at that time, picked up the cup with his little hand to applause and cheers from the crowd. My dad and mom were proud of that moment for quite some time. My little brother Altaf, at that time, did not know what was going on.

I remember very little about the teachers at the Urdu primary school I attended in Challakere. I vaguely recall that a teacher of mine was fond of soccer and used to play in a nearby field often. It could have been the year 1940 or so.

Now, let me ask you: What world events took place in 1940?

1. Pan Am's first flight took place from the United States to England.
2. The first air-conditioned automobile was exhibited in Chicago.
3. Yours truly became a full-fledged primary school student.

Obviously, all three answers are correct. From Chellakere, my dad was transferred to Chennaraya Patna, which was in Hassan District. There, I had some friends, and one of them was a little girl. I do not remember her name. She lived near our home. There were some boys also. In that town, we had a big tree in front of our house, and the bus stand was within our view. I used to learn the names of the buses' brands, such as Ford and Dodge, from the shape of the engine or front of the bus. In other words, I became interested in the automobiles somewhat. There were not many cars in those days in India, especially in that town. Mom fasted during Ramadan, and I told her I wanted to fast. She said, "Arif, you are too little yet, and you do not have to keep *roza* or fast until you are seven." At that time, I might have been only six. However, I was adamant, and I went without eating all morning. I went outside the house and sat under the big tree. Mom kept calling me to come eat, but I was determined to continue my fasting. However, after a while, in the early afternoon, I broke my fast, and Mom and I were both happy. I do not remember my school. Mom used to tell stories to us. Mom used to beat or spank us once in a while, and I don't think my dad did that unless he had to. One time, while Dad was in his home office, I slowly closed the door of the office, latched it from outside, and secured it with a stick so he could not open the door from inside.

After a while, he came to the door. "Open the door. Who locked it?" he said. He started rapping on the door. I kept quiet, and finally, after a while, laughingly, I opened the door. That time, he spanked me hard. I do not know where my mom was during that horseplay of mine. If she had seen it, she would have stopped it, I am sure.

My mom gave birth to twins: Ashraf was a boy, and Musharraf was a girl. Both passed away when they were about a year old. Both of them had the same disease. We had a veranda in front of the house, where we used to spend quite a bit of time sitting around.

India was under British rule at that time. Mahatma Gandhi was fighting for the freedom of India. His approach was nonviolence. My dad had a lot of stories about how people hated the English. My dad, being a tahsildar (head of the revenue department) in the taluk, had to face violence of people, as he was working for the British. The nonviolence movement consisted of breaking the railroad tracks and streetlights, etc.

That was just the beginning of the fight for freedom from the British. The Second World War was in full swing, with various countries joining the war at different times. In our dada sab's house, where we grew up, we talked about digging a bomb shelter in the alley that was the access to the back of the house. The alley was about four feet wide and ran along the depth of the lot, which was about a hundred yards or so. I sometimes used to see a bunch of airplanes flying over our area, and everybody got scared that the German planes could drop bombs. However, we did not go any further on the thought of the bomb shelter, which was supposed to be a hole in the ground. It never did materialize. We spent our lives in Bangalore whenever Dad was transferred from one place to another and was in the process of settling the family in the new place.

What events took place between 1941 and 1945?

1. The Japanese bombed Pearl Harbor.
2. After fourteen years, drilling was completed on Mount Rushmore.
3. Germany and Italy declared war on the United States.
4. Life went on without any major events in the Aziz family.
5. The United States dropped bombs on Hiroshima and Nagasaki.
6. The M. Abdul Aziz family moved to Korategere in Tumkur District.

If your answer was "All of the above," you were correct. Korategere was a small town, and of course, it was the taluk headquarters. There were lots of wild monkeys in town. They used to snatch food from helpless kids. Also, the monkeys used to come onto the lean-to roofs of the little shops, bend down, and steel bananas from the clusters hanging under the awnings in front of the shops. They roamed around freely in front of the houses. They were not afraid of people. In the Hindu religion, Hanuman was considered to be the god of strength. On a certain occasion, he carried a whole mountain from one place to another. I have seen photos of Hanuman carrying the mountain in his palm. This is according to Hindu mythology. As far as my schooling was concerned, there was a problem in that town. I will talk about it a little later. Asif and I used to play in front of our two-story house. One time, we were playing on a bullock cart parked in front of our house. Asif fell down and was hurt badly. The injury resulted in a lot of bleeding. Some kind of a screw or something from the cart frame pierced his neck when he fell. One of the peons saw this and quickly acted. He collected the blood as it drained out of one of Asif's arteries in a small bucket and rushed to the hospital. We all worried about Asif; however, I do not remember the details. Asif was lucky to get quick attention from one of our peons. He recovered fully after that.

Needless to say, I was in a complete panic. I must have acted quickly in letting someone know about the incident. God saved us from that crisis.

There was a river near our house within walking distance down the road. Quite a few ladies came to the river to fetch drinking water. There was a technique to make sure the water was clean. The river was not a fully flowing type of river. There were lots of watery holes as well as sandy patches in the shallow river. The ladies used to make circular, shallow pits with their feet in the sandy patches; the water would filter into them; and they used to fill their containers with the water in those pits. Asif and I used to play in the shallow river. There were small fish in the watery parts of the river. Asif and I used to catch them by throwing water with the fish onto the banks. They were small fish. One time, I do not know if a dam upstream somewhere broke or what happened, but there was a big flood in the river. The river surged, and there was a tremendous flow of water, which we had never seen, almost like a little tsunami. I heard that trees and bullock carts were washed away into the river. Water reached over the banks. It looked like it came all of a sudden. There were no warnings, I believe. I have not heard of any causalities. Lucky for us, we were not playing in the river at the time. Our relatives, including my *phuppa* (uncle) Moulvi Zahiruddin, lived in a town that was only about ten to twelve miles from Korategere.

As I mentioned before, my schooling was a problem in Korategere. The problem was that there was no middle school in town. My parents solved the problem by sending me to Madhugiri every week and bringing me back home on the weekends. Thus, my middle school studies took place in Madhugiri. I missed my mom and the family very much, but I had to get my education. The arrangement worked out well. My aunt Phuppi Jan took care of me well.

My cousins Saleem, Khaisar, Fairoz, Dilshad, Mumtaz, and Fiaz were good company for me. I hopped on the bus every Monday morning, went to school, and came back on Friday to Korategere. This routine went on for a while. The conductor of the bus did not like my riding the bus for free as the son of a tahsildar. My phuppa Saab was also a moulvi and a teacher. There were many kids in their house (Masha-Allah). There was a big mountain in the town. Another kid and I climbed the mountain for fun once. We believed a tiger lived on the mountain. We'd heard stories about how the tiger came into town and one time came into the yard of one of our neighbors. That summer, some people were sleeping in the yard of the house. The tiger made its way into our neighbor's yard, and the guy who related the story said he saw the tiger come in through the door and walk around the yard. Tigers are known to prey on live animals and humans. The guy told us that after he saw the tiger trespassing in the yard, he held his breath and froze, and lucky for him, in a few moments, the tiger was gone. When my friend and I went up the mountain, we were cautious. My friend told me that normally, we'd smell the tiger if he was present within a certain distance.

My uncle and cousins went swimming in a pond once. I did not know how to swim. I went along with them, and Saleem told me to try swimming. I hesitated at first. As I saw them swimming, I went with Saleem into deeper water, and I almost drowned. I think Saleem saved me from drowning.

One time, my mom came to Madhugiri. I felt happy and secure at seeing her there. I used to watch military vehicles go by through town. I was told that the military soldiers kidnapped young girls. Not knowing much, I believed whatever I heard without arguing much.

In Bangalore, we used to see films with fighting scenes in them. We saw pictures in which a woman with a turkey cap used to be a fighter. I think her name was Nadia. This was in a theater called Paramount Talkies near the city market.

From Korategere, I think we moved to Saklespur, which is in Hassan District. I remember our house in Saklespur vividly. It was built on a ridge. The doors were uniquely built—not in the center wall of the room but kind of in the corner position. There was a hall, as usual. There was a big yard, and the restroom was way back in the backyard. There was no underground system or flush system. The refuse had to be removed manually. There were lots of cobras and other snakes in that town. I was about eleven years old. My grandpa visited the town. Since it was a Malnad town, it was cooler than usual. My dad ordered a thick mattress filled with dry hay for my dada sab to sleep on. My dad took care of his dad's health. In those days, there were no *khats*, or beds with legs, mattresses, and box springs. It was common to sleep on the floor. At least the elevated beds were not common in our circle of life. Nowadays, Saklespur is referred to as "poor man's Ooty." Ooty is a famous hill station in southern India. Malnad districts were also known for malaria due to the abundance of mosquitoes. Sleeping with mosquito curtains was common. We were all cautious about that.

The doctors performed circumcisions on all three brothers. Anwar was too young at the time and was excused. The circumcision was hardest for me, as I was eleven years old. The best time to do the procedure is when you are young or even right after birth, as they do it nowadays. Anyway, we recovered from the circumcisions slowly but surely in time. Since we lost lots of blood during the operations, our parents decided to raise some chickens to feed us. This was supposed to help us gain strength. It was believed the young chicken was the best. I had seen as a little boy that young chicks, as they were grazing, were sometimes preyed on by eagles. The chicks were beautiful. I hated the eagles doing that to the chicks. You might have seen on television or otherwise how they dive down from their flight and skillfully pick up their prey live. I found a solution to the problem. I found a big bamboo stick and tried to save the chicks from being picked up by the cruel eagles. I held the stick way up in the air and walked along with the young ones wherever they freely moved. There were no more attacks on the young chicks. This was in the summertime, so there was no school, and I spent several hours a day doing this. My parents might have told me not to do it. However, I mentioned to them what I was doing, and I did not have anything else to do anyway. Hence, they let me be the shepherd for the chickens that summer. My brothers and I regained our strength. We had several peons in the house. They used to tell us the mythological stories of Mahabharat and Ramayana. We were interested in listening to those stories. The servant who told us the stories was a good storyteller, and he gave lots of details.

In front of the house was a big field. Sometimes the peons helped us make kites and fly them. It was lots of fun. The kites were handmade. The peons used to take us for a walk in the evenings. One day we saw a snake crossing the road. There wasn't even a Snake Crossing sign over there! I wanted to do something. However, our Hindu peon told us not to do anything. Hindus used to consider the snake, especially a cobra, a God.

When I was about ten, I contracted typhoid and got very ill. I dropped out or missed school so much that in my second year of middle school, I was asked to repeat the year. Thus, I lost one year of time. My dad gave the news of my staying in the same class to my mom in front of me in our Saklespur house. I could not understand the seriousness of the situation. We were tossed between Bangalore and the other places where my dad was working.

Several of our relatives visited our house in Saklespur. Among them were Mr. Yakoob, one of our maternal uncles; our aunt Chan Chichani (Saleemunnissa), wife of G. Abdul Basith; and, of course, Pyari Apa (Tajunnissa). The town had rainy weather. I think they were monsoon rains. People used to put burlap bags folded in a certain way on their heads and backs as rain coats.

Do I have an exciting snake story to tell you about? Yes, I do indeed. One early afternoon, one of our peons was walking along the bushes in the yard. It was a warm day, and he was wearing shorts, as usual. I was playing around close by. I heard the noise of a clap, like striking the hands together, loudly near him. All of a sudden, the peon was stunned, and he withdrew his leg quickly and grabbed the snake's body a little below its head. He quickly found a burlap bag, put the snake in it, closed the mouth of the bag, and started beating the bag on the ground by hurling it in the air. He did this vigorously several times. I was awestruck by this. Those snakes are poisonous, and we had heard several cases of fingers having to be cut off after a snakebite to save the life of the victims. All this happened so quickly that I had to ask the guy what had happened.

He said, "The snake struck me on my foot. As soon as I was struck, I knew it had to be a snake, and I withdrew my foot before the snake injected his venom." I learned that when a cobra strikes, first it makes a wound, and then it injects the venom. If you move quickly after the strike and withdraw, you will be saved. To make a long story short, the guy hit the snake in the burlap bag hard on the ground and eventually killed the snake that way. The guy must have been trained to do so. Amazing.

A government official like my dad was supposed to spend some part of his service in a Malnad area. Saklespur is a Malnad area. It had lots of rain and rough weather. Anyway, that town happened to be the last town where my Mom lived as the tahsidar's wife. I think she enjoyed life as much as she could. One day we heard that a nun from a convent had died in a bus accident My sister Gulzar had passed away at the age of five. My dad loved her very much. I think she had typhoid. As she was a girl after several boys, my parents liked her very much. My dad even took her to a Hakim—a doctor who practices Homeopathic medicine, I guess.

It's time to play Q and A. What world events took place in 1946?

1.   There was an addition to the Aziz family.
2.   The Philippines gained independence from the United States.
3.   The first meeting of the UN General Assembly opened in London.
4.   A big tragedy happened.

The last child born to my Mom was Amjad and he lived only for about four or five days. My mom became ill. She was bleeding a lot. She became weak and was not able to walk. I do not know what really happened. The doctors in the town told Dad to take her to a better and more well-equipped hospital. Mom had to be carried to a vehicle while wrapped in a blanket. There was no driveway up to the house. The vehicle was parked a little ways away down below. Our peons helped Dad take her to the vehicle.

We had a special bogie in the train reserved, and we were on our way to Bangalore. We brought a woman attendant for my mom from Saklespur to Bangalore.

My mother was admitted to the Victoria Hospital in Bangalore. The doctors tried to treat her. However, the situation was serious. Her health had deteriorated beyond cure. She had lost too much blood. My uncle Mohammad Ahmad was in Bangalore at the time. He came to see her in the hospital. We kids were brought to the hospital to Mom. Not knowing the seriousness of the situation, we were running up and down the stairs and playing in the hospital. The next morning, the attendant who was with Mom that night in the hospital was in the house. That meant she had left the hospital without my mom.

I asked her, "How come you are here and not with Mom in the hospital?"

She replied, "She does not need me anymore." I knew that something was wrong. Something must have happened to my mother. I judged the matter in my own young mind. After a while, it became clear. Her body was brought home from the hospital; she had passed away that night. That was one of the biggest and most unexpected blows of my life. I had not yet completely felt the warmth of a mother's love, and she'd slipped away from us. We three bothers cried like babies. They took her body to the graveyard on Mysore Road. The Mysore Road graveyard had a dedicated family space from the days of my nana jan for the close deceased members of the family. All the family elders are buried in there. All the close relatives came over to say good-bye to my mom and pay last respects. My mom's elder sister, Fatima Begum (Ammi Khala), also came over to the graveyard.

We did not realize at the time how big a void her death created in our lives. An Urdu poet put it beautifully:

Agar mujh se koi pooche keh maa'n hoti to kya kehta,
Na hota kufr duniya mein to main maa'n ko khuda kehta.

The meaning is as follows:

> If somebody asks me what I would say to my mom if she were around,
> I will say that if I did not believe in one God, I would say my mom is God.

Life after my mom was different. We missed her very much. We were four youngsters who had to be taken care of. Some relatives felt sorry for us. Our aunt Pyari Apa, Akhil's mom, took care of all of us, as did our dadi jan. We learned to take care of ourselves too.

During his service for the state government, Dad had to travel and visit other towns under his jurisdiction. The roads were not good in some areas or townships. At one time, he owned a horse, which he used to ride. My dad was not a tall man. He used to put a chair next to the horse and asked a peon to help him get on the horse's back. He used to go to various towns riding on the horse.

My dad had to take a certification exam or something in Tumkur. We were in Korategere, and he missed the bus, so he had to go by bicycle a distance of seventeen miles or so. He was a dedicated and responsible person. My mom had told my uncle that when she died, she wanted to be taken to her husband's house. She wanted to depart on her last journey from her husband's house. Therefore, even though it was closer to the Mysore Road graveyard from my nana's house, she was brought to Malleshwaram, where her last rights were performed. Malleswaram was my dad's home.

When Mom passed away, Dad secluded himself in his room for almost two months. He was only forty at the time. Talk started about his marriage. My aunt Ammi Khala used to tell us, "Tell your dad not to get married. It will not be good for you at all." We did not know the depth of all this. I kind of knew, that pleading my father not to get married was not going to be of any use. What my aunt said made a lot of sense, though. But who is to bell the cat?

Are you curious to know which of the following events took place in 1946 and 1947?

1. Syria gained independence from France.
2. Nehru formed a new government in India.
3. A patent was filed in the United States for the hydrogen bomb.
4. Amina Begum (my mother) passed away in Bangalore.
5. World War II ended.

Yes, the correct answer is "All of the above." After my mom passed away, as I was the oldest brother, the burden fell on my shoulders to take care of my younger brothers. However, both my aunt and grandma took care of us well. In the meantime, arrangements were made regarding my dad's marriage. I remember some of the young women from the extended family who contested for the position of my second mom. However, Dad had his eye on a girl whom he had seen a long time back in Kunigal as a little girl. The usual talks took place, and marriage was supposed to take place in that town. All the relatives came to the wedding. My second mom's name was Rahmat-Unnissa. She was the daughter of one Nawab Jan. I am not sure if it was a coincidence or what. Mr. Nawab Jan was looking for a home where the man was mature and had lost his first wife. All his daughters were married to such men. My dad qualified, and the wedding took place. I was strongly opposed to the wedding in my mind, but I was helpless. Anyway, the first home she came to in our family was Hiriyur. Hiriyur was a small town. There was no electricity in the house or on the streets. A guy used to light the kerosene lamps on the streets every evening. There was no running water either. Water had to be heated in big containers and then put in buckets, and a tumbler had to be used to put water on your head and body. In other words, there were no showers per se.

What did we use to write with? We had pencils. However, if something had to be written in ink, we'd use an inkpot (a little bottle filled with ink) and a pen with an attached nib. The nib, once it was worn out, could be replaced. We used to dip the nib in the inkpot to get some ink adhered to the nib and then start writing on paper. As soon as you wrote something, maybe just a line, the ink on the nib would dry out. You'd have to dip the nib into the bottle again and again until you were done with the writing. In the middle of the writing process, if you were negligent, you could have the unpleasant experience of dropping the bottle and the ink on papers, the mat you were sitting on, or your clothes. I am telling you this to illustrate the old and simple ways we used to have. Sometimes the ink flow from the nib was too much, and we needed to control or clean it up. The cure for this was a blotting paper, which was a thicker pink-colored paper with tremendous absorption qualities. Wherever there was an excessive ink drop on paper, we blotted it with the blotting paper. The problem was solved this way. As time passed, the pen became much improved. Somebody invented a small tube barrel with threads so that the nib head could be screwed onto the pen barrel. This eliminated the dipping of the pen nib into the bottle of ink. The ink bottle kind of got attached to the pen nib, and we could write without any interruption for quite a while. There was another problem: as the threads wore out, sometimes you painted your coat pocket and fingers with ink. Most ink was black or blue, but red ink was available too. When we were serious about a certain issue, we used to write with red ink, as if writing with blood. Before this, somebody also cleverly invented a bottle design wherein the ink would not be able to get out of the bottle if the bottle was dropped onto its side. Then came a real high-tech pen: the ballpoint pen. It involved no ink barrel, threads, leaks, smears, or blotting paper. A click from the top of the pen or a twist of the cap made the ball point protrude or retract into the main housing of the pen. There are several variations of the ballpoint pen, but today this is the kind of pen we all use.

Now I will tell you who passed away in our family in 1947. He was sick with a stroke for more than a year. One side of his body was paralyzed. As time went on, he became bed ridden. My aunt Salim Unnissa took care of him a lot. Dadi Jan took care of him quite a bit too. I don't think he was able to talk either. My dada, after a long illness, passed away.

We were in Hiriyur. My dad was playing songs on his seventy-eight-rpm His Master's Voice gramophone. A gramophone is a boxlike device on which you put a record. You wind the machine up, and it turns the record. A needle runs over the small grooves on the record and produces sound and plays songs. A handle just like the handle we used to have to turn the driveshaft of an automobile engine to start a car did the winding. As he was playing the songs, we received a telegram from Bangalore. My dad immediately turned off the gramophone and quietly walked into his room. He came out after a while and declared with a choked voice that Grandpa had passed away. This was a big blow for the family. My dada Ji was a pious man with high regard to life matters, such as health, family responsibility, etc. He took us for long walks sometimes, and he himself used to walk to the mosque and other errands. When he took us on walks, he used to kick any stones from the road, and he told us, "I do this to save other people from getting hurt." Even today I appreciate what he did in those days. Back then, the roads were unpaved in India, and quite a few pebbles and stones were on the road.

In 1947, a big thing happened to India: it became independent from the British. The efforts of Mahatma Gandhi, Nehru, and others worked out. There was joy in the streets, with people dancing and cars and buses blowing their horns. I think we were in Hiriyur. I remember my middle school there. There was an attraction in town we used to go to a lot and enjoy: the tent cinema. The picture was shown on a big screen inside a large tent. The cinema guys used to play a patriotic Kannada song every evening, such as "Udaya Wagali Namma." The speakers were loud. We used to frequent the cinema and watch movies. There was an irrigation canal in town that we used to frequent as well. The peons of our house used to swim and take baths there. There was a doctor not far from our house—named Ranga, I think. He became a family friend.

One time in Hiriyur, while I was taking a bath, I could not stand well or walk. I slowly dried myself and came into the main hall of the house. My right leg and foot were shaking uncontrollably. After trying to control myself, I fell unconscious. My aunt Pyari Apa was there, and she took care of me. The doctors diagnosed it as Fitz syndrome. It was bothersome for me for a while. I thought it was being caused by a cold or something, so I took care of myself by staying warm. By God's grace, it has not repeated again. It was a form of seizure, I guess.

In the meantime, we were in Bangalore often. I remember seeing the Hindi film *Chandni Raat* starring Naseem Banu, Saira Banu's mother and Dilip Saheb's mother-in-law. One of her songs, "Zindagi ka Saz Bhi Kya

Saaz Hai," became famous, and Dad used to play it on his gramophone a lot.

In Bangalore, our middle school was by the masjid in Sheshadripuram. I admired one teacher very much. His name was Aziz Saab. Aziz Saab was a good teacher and also strict. Even though we moved so much with my dad, he was particular about our education, and we did not lose any schooling time. Our uncle Chamu Ameer Ahmad took care of us, along with our mamujan, Mohammad Ahmad. Chamu did not have any children of his own. We spent quite a bit of time with Chamu, who was in a high post in the police department. He was highly educated and had been trained at Scotland Yard in fingerprint technology. He was instrumental in solving a murder case that happened in Bangalore. It had national attention, perhaps even international. The whole family of a famous lawyer, Belur Srinivasa Iyengar, was brutally murdered in his house in Gandhi Nagar, Bangalore, in 1956. I do not recall the whole case in detail. My uncle was involved in the case, and the media covered the case extensively. The murder case shook up the whole state of Mysore and the country. Graphic descriptions were published in the newspapers. I did not follow the case in detail. I do not remember who the suspect was or what the motive was; the details can be looked up on the Internet. After everything settled down, the bungalow was converted into a restaurant.

Like I said, my uncle Chamu took care of us from our middle school days. He used to invite us to his place in Bangalore often. Mamujan used to pick us up in his car, and we'd have a get-together at his place. His wife, Auntie, was also a generous person, and she loved us all. I think for a while, my cousin Naseer stayed in their house while he was a student of engineering. Mamujan had a good relationship with Chamu. Chamu was concerned about my engineering education as well as about my career in general. Our auntie's nephew or some relative was in the air force or some military branch. My elders talked about enrolling me in the army or air force. At that time, I used to have a hairdo like an actor. We all, in our younger days, wanted to look like one famous and good-looking actor or another. Some of us, including me, wanted to be like the famous actor Dev Anand. Auntie's relative once told me, pointing to my head, "This actor-like puffy hairdo has to go if you want to pursue a career in military service." Also, there was talk about me becoming a doctor—an LMP, or licentiate in medical practice, which is like a physician's assistant. I do not think there was a physician's assistant position in those days, at least in India. Anyway, joining the air force or becoming an LMP doctor did not work for me. I did not want to give up my actor haircut for nothing. (I am just kidding.)

I used to go to Chamu's office in Bangalore quite a bit for help of some kind. Chamu was taking precaution with food because of his high blood pressure and other health problems. One day while I was busy with my engineering courses in 1963 or so, I heard that my uncle was in the hospital in Shivaji Nagar, Bangalore. I owe him a big debt of gratitude. Since the time I heard he was in the hospital, I wanted to go see him. I did not find time between my studies and other useless activities. I had the bad habit of smoking cigarettes. I always found myself broke. I borrowed money from most of my relatives. I was in a bad situation.

You might be wondering what else happened in the world in 1947. Right? Here we go!

The sequence in my writing might not be in order.

1. The subcontinent was divided into Hindu India and the Muslim state of Pakistan.
2. Hundreds of thousands died in communal bloodshed after the partition.
3. The transistor was invented in Bell labs.
4. A two-term limitation was confirmed on the presidency of the United States.
5. Moulvi Gulam e Ahmad passed away.

I touched upon some of these events earlier. My grandpa was buried in Rajaji Nagar, which is a community near Malleshwaram, where he passed away. I do not recall attending the funeral. Like I said, we were in Hiriyur. One of my aunts, Bee Apa, became a widow. My grandma gave particular attention to her. She was working as a teacher in Anekal. Dadi Jan went to Anekal a lot to visit her widowed daughter, Mehrunnissa. Mehrunnissa had a daughter named Iqbal. Dadi Jan took care of both. I remember the days when Dadi Jan was a primary school teacher in Malleshwaram. Dadi Jan gave lots of time to her daughters' well-being. There were problems with Rahmat Apa's first marriage. She also had some problems with her second marriage. She was married to a doctor named Mr. Yunus. He was a Punjabi guy.

Pyari Apa was also a widow for a long time. Dadi Jan loved all her children very much. She took it upon herself to solve all their problems while she took care of us too. Our dad took care of her and some of his sisters financially. As an elder brother, he fulfilled his duties well. He was a compassionate man.

Among all the cousins, I think Bilqees was the oldest. She was the daughter of Bee Apa (Mehrunnissa). Unfortunately, she fell sick when she was still a youth. It was a terminal sickness. In those days, they did not even know the disease by its name. It was a strange disease. It could have been tuberculosis. It could have been cancer. Nobody knows. Anyway, during her last days, they dressed her up like a bride to fulfill her and everybody's wishes. It must have been emotional. I think her dad's name was Alauddin. He passed away due to heart failure at a rather young age. Iqbal, my cousin, became an orphan.

Allauddin had a second marriage. I do not know much about the woman he married or if they had any kids. For Bee Apa and also my grandparents, it was a bad feeling. It was all legal and probably affordable, so nobody could do anything about it.

Communal fights took place all over the country following the partition. There was lots of tension. We were in a cinema once, and when we left, there were communal clashes on the streets. Cha Cha, our uncle, protected us. In those days, it was customary to wear caps on our heads as Muslim boys. When we came out of the theater, Uncle Basith asked us to hide our caps so that people could not tell we were Muslims. Also, he told us, "If somebody asks you for your name, make up a Hindu name." We were lucky that we reached home without being caught in the clashes going on. We heard about lots of incidents in which Muslims killed Hindus and vice versa. Our uncle Basith used to go outside with a two-by-four stick in his hand. On our street, the majority of people were Muslims, and that's why it used to be named Mohammadan Block. This communal crisis lasted for quite a few months. There was a lot of tension. Hindus wanted all Muslims to move or shift to Pakistan. For a short while, I think our elders were thinking of shifting to Pakistan. We loved the newborn nation called Pakistan, a Muslim nation, so much that we used to write in our books, "Long live Pakistan." Quite a few families moved to Pakistan. However, Dada Saab and other elders decided against it.

I want to come back to Rahmat-Unnissa now. She divorced one Mr. Syed Ahmad. He was a learned man and well respected. It seems from day one of her marriage, Syed Ahmad was not interested in my aunt. As far as I know, she was a beautiful woman. We found out Syed Ahmad was not interested in women at all. That's the reason Aunt Apa divorced him. She used to sing a song with the lyrics *Mere liye Jahan mein chayn na kharar hai"* (I am restless in this world). I think that song became an echo of her life. She gave birth to some children after she got married to Dr. Yunus. The kids moved to Karim Nagar in Andhra State. The doctor was a womanizer. My aunt used to visit us in Bangalore quite a bit and stay for long periods. This might have had something to do with my uncle, her husband, starting to look elsewhere. The story I am talking about happened several years after the late 1940s. I got carried away with my rambling.

There were no serious problems with Rahmat-Unnissa's health, but she was depressed quite a bit of the time. She had some beautiful children from her second marriage. First was a girl named Parveen. Second was a boy named Naim. Naim was born with weak legs, so he moved by crawling on his knees. At the time of this writing, though, I heard he is able to walk and is married and leading his life in a normal fashion.

Once, when my aunt was visiting Bangalore from Andhra, she wanted to visit her elder sister's house in Mysore.

Time for a pop quiz again. What important events happened in 1948?

1. Gandhi was assassinated by Nathuram Godse.
2. Pakistani leader Mohammad Ali Jinnah passed away.
3. The Indian army invaded Hyderabad State.
4. The Aziz family purchased a house in Bangalore.

"All of the above" is the correct answer. East and West Pakistan were formed in the north, based on the majority Muslim population. Kashmir in the north was undecided, and a portion of it went with India, while a certain portion went with Pakistan. It is a complicated situation. Part of Kashmir is claimed by China. No solution is acceptable to any of the countries. Several people have lost their lives in the conflict.

We were also confronted with a deadly epidemic in parts of Bangalore. It was called a plague in those days. The disease was called bubonic plague. Dada Saab decided to move out of Malleshwaram and stayed with Uncle Mamujan for a while. We had some trying times.

The lesson I want readers to learn here is that if you have good and strong family ties, family members will help each other and support each other. There is a beautiful bond and selfless tie between the members of the family. There is no value for this. I was blessed to have good relationships with the elders of my mother's and father's families. When my mother passed away, my aunt Pyari Apa took care of all of the brothers. This was a selfless act from my aunt. May Allah bless her soul and place her in Jannah. All my elders and family members will always be in my thoughts and prayers. Always appreciate and cherish the moments when the elders are with you for love, advice, and guidance. Sometimes, in trying to guide you, the elders might seem to go overboard, but this is for your own good. At times, I became angry with my mom as I took her beatings or spanking. My mom was a woman of high principles. She was a woman who would not give any chance to others to complain about anything she did. In other words, she performed her duties in a flawless manner. She was conscientious of what was expected of her. She respected everybody in the family and expected the same respect in return from all.

I have included a copy of a letter she wrote to my dad when Asif was a little child.

CHAPTER 2

Our Big Move

My dad purchased a house in Palace Guttahalli, a suburb of Bangalore. It was a modest one-story house. After a few years, we constructed a second story for more accommodation. I had started my high school education. The school was a stone-block building. We used to walk to school. I felt proud of myself for being a high school student. I think I completed only a year or so at that school, and then we had to move to Mysore. My dad took a job as the director of a sanatorium or a tuberculosis hospital. I went to a school called St. Philomena's High School. I studied with lots of interest. It was a Christian school. The principal was a Jesuit priest. There were some good teachers in the school. One geography teacher used to talk in a low and soft voice and whispered when he talked about where gold was found or where there were gold mines. He used to talk about Coolgardie and Kalgoorlie in Australia and whispered about gold findings there, lest people go there and try to steal it. It was funny.

Rabello, our English teacher, was a good man. His advice to us was to make full use of all the help we could get and try to excel in our subject. He always referred to the glossary at the end of the chapter to improve our vocabulary. His advice was right on, and I appreciated it. I do not remember the names of many of my classmates. I still remember some faces, though.

I was not much of a sports guy. I played soccer or football once in a while prior to high school. We used to go to the sports field in Malleshwaram to play soccer. I remember my first experience with a bicycle in that field. We rented a bicycle from a local shop and tried riding it in the field. I balanced the bike well the first time. The only trouble I had was in turning, which improved over time. Akhil and I took the bicycle to the field. I also played with glass marbles and used to roll a bicycle rim with a specially bent, thin rod. In Mysore, we had a good life. We had good neighbors, including Inspector Yousuf Saheb, Umar and Akhtar Hussain, and Bashir. My second mother's dad lived not far from our house. My stepmother used to visit her dad's place a lot. No telephone was in our house in those days, and Dad used to ask us to go ask her to come back home. As exams were approaching, I was supposed to be glued to the books and study hard, but one day I decided to go to the movies. I argued with myself that a little bit of enjoyment and relaxation would freshen up my mind, and I could get back to my studies with more intensity. So I chose a movie and went to the cheapest seat in the front, close to the screen. In those days, the cheapest seats were in the front, and as you went back farther away from the screen, the ticket prices were higher. At the intermission, the auditorium lights were switched on. When I turned back, I was awestruck at what I saw. My dad was in the theater. I suddenly sat back in the seat and bowed my head so he would not see me. Not everybody leaves the theater during the intermission. I was praying for the lights to be shut off again and the movie to start. I hoped he had left. My dad, as I have mentioned earlier, was a strict guy. He taught a lot of discipline to us and exercised a lot of control on us. He made sure we got a good education in school. Anyway, the lights went off, and the movie started again. Needless to say, the rest of the movie was ruined for me. I was thinking of getting up and going home right there and then, but my money would be wasted. Therefore, I thought of staying in the theater and watching the movie to the best of my circumstances. I made plans to leave the theater just before the movie ended and run home. My dad rode a bicycle in those days. I had to outrun him, and before he made it to the house, I had to get home and open up my books. You should have seen me run from the theater to my home as fast as I could. By golly, I made it home before he bicycled home. I thanked God that I was saved that time.

I think our uncle was in Mysore also at that time. He used to come take us to the movies. He was the deputy commissioner of Mysore District. In Mysore, after passing my high school secondary school leaving certificate (SSLC), I started college. I was keen on going to medical school. I was kind of inspired by my cousin Firoze, who was in medical school in Mysore. In those days, you needed to pick your major subjects right after high school to go into whatever field of study you would pursue in the upcoming years. My enthusiasm knew no bounds that I was at Yuvaraja's College in Mysore, pursuing my intermediate studies with chemistry, botany, and zoology as the majors.

While I was enjoying pursuing my plans of study, a twist came up, and my dreams of becoming a doctor were shattered.

My dad was transferred to Alur in Hassan District. The whole course of my life had to be changed. The college at Hassan did not have my current majors as an option. Hence, I was forced to switch to physics, chemistry, and Mathematics. My father did not think of other options, such as my staying at a hostel. I was disappointed. When you have a certain mind-set and have found your path, it is hard to change. Life was interesting in Mysore. There were quite a few relatives there. That was the town where my dad grew up. His name, M. Abdul Aziz, symbolizes his affiliation with Mysore. I do not know many details of his era in Mysore. In Mysore, I developed an affinity for Urdu poetry. The teacher of Urdu at the school made it interesting, I guess. I started writing Urdu poetry in my school notebook. It was all romantic, as influenced by the poets I read in my textbook. The Urdu language became interesting to me. It made sense to me and gave me a way to express my feelings.

Well, guess what? Time for a history quiz! What world events happened in 1949?

1. The first commercial jet was unveiled.
2. The Soviets detonated an atom bomb.
3. Nonstop around-the-world flight happened. The US Army's Boeing 50-A made a flight around the world, a total of ninety-four hours. It refueled in the air four times.

4. I was in Mysore.

5. The People's Republic of China proclaimed Peking as the capital.

There was no coed schooling in those days, and I went to an all-boys high school. Please pardon my overlapping of events a little bit. Walking through memory lanes that far back is kind of hard, if you can understand and appreciate.

By the way, you passed the quiz if you said, "All of the above." I should have graduated from high school in 1950. However, as I mentioned earlier, I lost one year, my second year in middle school. I graduated high school with high second class, just eleven marks short of first class. I was happy. In Alur, there was no intermediate college, so I was put in a Muslim hostel in Hassan. I used to come home every weekend to Alur. Alur was a one-street town in those days. Therefore, I enjoyed living in Hassan. I made quite a list of friends in Hassan. Hassan was an interesting town for me. There were two theaters in town. It was bigger than Alur for sure. My dad used to send Asif and Altaf to Hassan for me to take them to the movies and then bus them back to Alur. They used to wait for me by the bus stand. My responsibility was to safely take them to the movies and send them back to Alur by bus. I think Anwar stayed at home, as he was too little, maybe about six or seven years old. Pyari Apa (Tajunnissa) took care of him a lot. One time, Mamujan and family visited us in Alur. We used to go out for a walk. The Alur house was pretty big. We brothers had one room. Our stepmother and her small kids had a large room. My dad had an office room at home. Akhil used to visit Hassan and Alur quite a bit. Akhil stayed in the Muslim hostel for a while too. I recall Mokhtar, Jabbar, Moula, Naaza'n, Ghouse, Ghalib, and Jaleel as some of the hostel mates. Moula is in Bangalore now. He was our physics professor. That was his first lecturer job. He was so nervous that he could not speak properly when he was lecturing in the class. He gradually regained confidence and did well later on. He took care of me quite a bit and became a good friend. I took keen interest in Urdu poetry and never missed a class of Urdu literature. Our Urdu professor, Ahmad, lived not far from the Muslim hostel where I lived. A teacher—I believe his name was Haneef Kaleem—told us in a speech, "This young man Obaidur Rahman is going to be a great poet and will shine our names. He has great promise." One of his *shers* (verses) goes as follows:

Nikala patti you'n se rus, badi takleef kee tum ne
Hamare khoon se mehendi banaleate tou kya jata

It translates as follows: a man is talking to his beloved, saying, "You took so much trouble by grinding and crushing the leaves of the plant to extract *mehendi* from them. It would have been much easier if you had used my blood for hinna or mehendi" Hinna is kind of a red polish equivalent for the nails. This was the only way to make hinna or mehendi in those days. Many a young woman used to apply this process to color their nails red.

There was a field in front of the Muslim hostel where I stayed. We played football sometimes. We had our good friend Sayeed across from the hostel, and we used to go to his bungalow quite a bit. My friend Gaffar, who still lives in Hassan, was related to Sayeed. Unfortunately, Sayeed got killed in a motorcycle accident a few years later in Mangalore, India.

There was another poet and teacher I used to know. His name was Fayyaz Belgodi. He sometimes listened to my poetry and gave me suggestions. Gaffar and I were best friends. Also, Hasan Pasha used to be one of our good friends. Gaffar used to write poetry, and his pen name was Soaz. We used to have small get-togethers at the hostel and recite our poetry. From the intermediate college at Hassan, I shifted to the intermediate college in Bangalore around 1950 or so. I did not do well and had to write the exam again. Dad put me in a tutorial institute called City Tutorial College in Mysore. I think Mamujan (Mohammad Ahmad) happened to be in Mysore at the time.

Oh, wait! I forgot to tell you the story of how we made money while I was in Hassan. With my dad, there was no concept of giving us pocket money. All our needs were met, though. Bawajan used to come to the hostel where I was staying and clear up my bills for food and lodging. In that hostel, everybody took turns being the food prefect, whose responsibility was to schedule the menu for daily food, get the groceries, etc., for all the residents at the dorm. Once in a while, I was a food prefect, which was an honorary job. My dad used to give us six annas each for bus charges from Hassan to Alur. We decided we would walk a distance of eight or nine miles and save the bus charges he gave us. I don't think he checked the timings closely. We did this several times and saved quite a bit of change for going to cinema, etc. If we ever reached the town earlier than the bus arrival time, we waited or hid a little ways away from the house until the bus came and then arrived to the house. The bus station was next to the house. While going to Hassan from Alur, we had no choice but to board the bus. You had to work hard and be innovative to make a penny, right?

When we were in Alur, an accident happened to Mamujan in Mysore. During the annual Dasara procession, in which he was riding, his horse started acting up. The horse became unruly, and my uncle could not control the horse. Mind you, these are big horses. He was displaced from the saddle, and one of his feet got caught in the stirrup. Horses are sometimes aggressive. My uncle's head hit the ground, and he started bleeding. There must have been a big turmoil during the ceremonies. In the middle of the procession, this accident happened to a high-level state officer. Everybody panicked over what happened to my uncle. The news spread all over the state. The maharaja of Mysore participates in the Dasara procession and usually rides on an elephant. Obviously, this accident had a big impact on the festivities. The news may have said, "Mohammad Ahmad, deputy commissioner, fell off his horse during the Mysore Dasara procession." I had no time to read the newspaper. I do not know even if there was a newspaper in Alur in those days. My uncle might have been in Alur not long before this incident. I had limited means, but I managed to take time to catch the bus to Mysore to see him. Thank God it was not as bad as they'd made it sound. I visited him in the hospital. He embraced his children often from his hospital bed. He welcomed and thanked me a lot for coming. It looked as if he had lost lots of blood. He was weak and uneasy. He had a big plaster on one of his legs.

The news must have made the maharaja worried. He came to visit my uncle in the hospital. This was a great honor unparalleled to anything else. The king of the state had come to see him. The monarchy was at its height in those days yet. Later on, in independent India, it started losing its influence.

When in Mysore, while going to the City Tutorial College, I stayed with Phuppi Jan. One thing that impressed me was that Firoze used to write on the floor while studying for his medical studies. He wrote with chalk on the mosaic floor, and it worked well. Also, writing information while studying instills it in your mind, which comes in handy at the time of an exam or test. The only drawback is that you need lots of floor space, and also, your knees should be good and flexible for you to sit on your feet while doing this. I started doing the same when I came to Bangalore. I started writing on the floor. There might have been other ways of doing the same thing; however, that worked for me and produced good results.

It has been awhile. Let us take a quiz break. What events happened in 1950 and 1951?

1. I started intermediate college in Hassan.
2. North Korea invaded South Korea, capturing Seoul.
3. President Truman approved manufacturing a hydrogen bomb.
4. Gasoline was eighteen cents per gallon, and the average cost of a new car was $1,510.

"All of the above" is the right answer again. I have given an account of the intermediate college in Hassan. I did not do well. I was distracted due to Urdu poetry and girls. There was no TV at that time that I knew of. There were demonstrations of TVs in exhibitions. I might have gotten ahead of myself earlier. Anyway, after much effort and hard studies, I passed intermediate college. My cousin Naseer was in the government engineering college in Bangalore at that time.

Now my elders were thinking of different options for my future. Joining the military was one of the considerations. I was selected for National Cadet Core at Yuvaraja's College in Mysore. It interested me a somewhat but did not fascinate me too much. My Uncle Chamu's wife, Auntie, asked me to meet her relative who was in the military. When I met him, he said, pointing to my hairdo, "This hero haircut has to go." He meant that my haircut had to be shortened to a military style. Anyway, it did not interest me. Then they slated me to go into pursuing studies to become a Licentiate Medical Practitioner (LMP) doctor. That did not materialize either. While all this was happening, my uncle Mamujan recommended I try engineering. I applied at the government engineering college and got an interview. Since Mamujan was in a high post, it was certain that I would be selected. During the interview, to my disappointment, they showed me a letter from my dad that said he couldn't afford to send me to engineering college. He believed in his son pursuing a basic degree first, such as a bachelor of science. In my heart, I cried like a baby, as my dreams were shattered. I respected my dad and did not create a federal case out of this. My dad had said not a word before the interview. I felt angry. I was caught by surprise.

Hence, there was no other course for me but to go for a bachelor of science degree with physics, chemistry, and math as majors. Yes, a person had to select three majors in those days. It was a heavy load. In my central college studies, I was awarded a scholarship in such a way that I did not have to pay the tuition fee. In those days, I picked up the bad habit of smoking bidis and cigarettes. I think I was getting some pocket money from Dad. My poetry craze had not dwindled. I used to attend *mushairas* and other literary events regularly. My dadi used to say, "Everything seems to be okay with our boy. But this love of poetry is ruining him. Look at him." There was a general belief that poets were not going to do well in life. "He will be a loser and good-for-nothing person."

In those days, the mushairas were conducted at a hall called Eajman Mohammad Ali Hall in the Lashkar (Cantonment) area of Bangalore. At times, they were conducted in an open area with just the stage part in a cover or shelter. In those days, in Bangalore, some of the poets were Shakir Bangalori, Hazrat Zaiq, Hazrat Shouq, Syed Ali, and Hazrat Mushtaq. I used to show my writings to Hazrat Zaiq Saheb. He was nice to me. He taught me a lot about Urdu poetry.

I enjoyed that era. In those days, we had several friends. I cannot forget Basheer, who lived only a few houses down from ours. We used to go into an abandoned building in a nearby park and sing songs from the films *Nagin*, *Amar*, and *Baiju Bawra*. My favorite singer used to be Mohammad Rafi. We used to sing the songs of Talat Mahmood, Mukesh, Kishore Kumar and also some others. Wherever songs were played on the loudspeakers, I used to tell the organizers that I'd like to sing a song or two. One time, in a suburb of Bangalore, Sheshadripuram, there was a function going on, and a loudspeaker was playing Bollywood Hindi songs. I looked for the organizers and told them I would like to sing some songs if they would like. They let me do it. I started with the *Nagin* picture song.

"Oonchi oonchi duniya ki deewarien sa'nyaa'n toar ke ji, toar ke ji."

When I started leaving, the guy in charge said, "Where are you going, sir? Please continue. There is a swarm of people gathered outside to listen to you. You are doing very well." I was encouraged and rendered two or three more songs before I left. In the same way, I continued to sing songs for friends and at functions, and people liked it. Even though I was interested in Urdu poetry, I did not pay much attention to the song lyrics at the time. We usually sang famous, light songs. This way, I goofed around a little bit along with completing my studies.

Now let's examine what happened in 1952 and 1953.

1. Joseph Stalin passed away.
2. The world population hit 2.68 billion.
3. Dwight D. Eisenhower became president of the United States.
4. Edmund Hillary of New Zealand and Tenzing Norgay of Nepal reached the top of Mount Everest.
5. I was about to begin studies in central college.
6. We used to hear the *Binaca Geetmala* radio program of top Hindi Bollywood songs on the radio, hosted by Ameen Sayani every weekend.

I covered my central college studies a little bit already. I had some friends from engineering college also. Sometimes we used to meet near Cubbon Park. I remember. I used to know Shafi, I do not know where he is now. Also, I remember Aleem. During the years 1954 through 1956, I was busy with my studies. I participated in Urdu debates and the recitation of

Urdu poetry. I goofed around a lot also. I used to go to the exhibitions quite a bit. I enjoyed athletic events at the Kanteerava Stadium in Bangalore. There was an athlete named C. M. Muthiah at the central college in those days. I enjoyed watching soccer. Firoze and Mumtaz, my cousins, were good soccer players. I think both of them became varsity star players and were team captains. I saw a film called *Davedas* with Dilip Kumar and could not sleep properly for three nights, as the picture had a tragic story.

In those days, I was always broke. I had no job or any way of earning money. I owe deep gratitude to my brothers Asif and Altaf, who helped me while I was a student. They met my needs, along with my dad giving me some pocket money. Asif and Altaf both started pretty early in their job careers. To meet my needs, I even borrowed money from my uncle Basith sometimes.

One time, Cha Cha, my uncle, wanted to buy a radio. This was a high-tech thing, at least in our household. He asked me and my cousin Akhil to go shop for a good radio. We went to South Parade and purchased a radio for him. Prior to that, we were only familiar with the gramophone. The radios were pretty big and bulky in those days, like boxes with knobs. There used to be an aerial, or antenna, for reception. It was hard to catch a good station to listen properly. There were all kinds of noises, as if from outer space, while you were turning the knob to get good reception. Anyway, this was a high-tech addition to our house, which was owned by my uncle. I think after a certain time, my dad also bought a radio. Like I said, I had not seen a television at that time, but they used to demonstrate TVs at exhibitions or fairs. It was amazing to me how an object could be transferred to the screen right there and then live. In those days, at least in our circles, even a camera was a luxury. The film in the form of a cartridge or a roll had to be installed inside a camera, and we had to be careful not to expose the film roll to light. If you exposed the film to light, there was a possibility of losing the pictures. I myself never owned a camera at that time. Some of our friends had cameras, and they were in high demand, of course. In colleges, sometimes group pictures were taken by a professional photographer. I hid in a closet or dark place to replace the film in a camera. The idea was not to expose the film to light.

Let's enumerate important events that happened in 1956.

1. Reorganization of states in India occurred.
2. I secured first rank in part two of my bachelor of science exam for the entire state of Mysore.
3. The Suez Crisis was caused by Egyptian nationalization of the Suez Canal.
4. Actress Wahida Rahman's first Hindi film, *CID*, was released.

I did not have money to buy the textbook called *Hamari Shayeri* for my Urdu subject. I borrowed the book from my cousin Yasmin for a couple of days before the exam. I did everything right on the exam for Urdu. I felt good after the exam. I did not pass part three of the exam, which was physics, chemistry, and mathematics. I did not know that I was ranked first in languages or part two in the entire state of Mysore. Mamujan, as soon as he heard the news, made time to come to our place and congratulate me. It did not take me much effort to achieve those high marks.

However, I had to rewrite the exam and pass the rest of the subjects. I concentrated and was determined this time to do it, and I soon finished and earned the degree. Jobs were hard to find with just a basic degree. Technical education was what was needed to get employed. My future did not look bright. I was running into solid walls. I registered myself at the employment office to seek some employment. There was no luck. My brother Altaf gave me a lead about a newspaper firm. I went and applied for a job. They gave me a job, which required roaming all over Bangalore, knocking on doors of previous customers and trying to collect old bills. This was hard. Some people gave me a hard time. There was not even a contract or anything. The newspaper was *Indian Express*. Even though it was a leading newspaper, it was a second-tier paper. Then there was the challenge of getting orders from new customers to start the delivery of papers to their homes. This gave me experience in salesmanship. This paper was not as popular as the other paper in town, *Deccan Herald*. Anyway, I traveled around Bangalore quite a bit and worked as a bill collector. The manager was a fellow from Kerala, I believe, and he liked me. After a few months, he promoted me to advertisement clerk. My job was to collect advertisements and coordinate publication of the same. The manager trusted me. However, I was not going to make that job my career. It was just an interim job for me. For what it was worth, I enjoyed it, and there was something of value to be learned from it.

However, my inclination in life still was to become an engineer. Therefore, I joined the AMIE, Associate Membership of Institution of Engineers in India, an organization that prepares a person to be an engineer. This was an alternative to getting a bachelor of engineering degree. It was considered equivalent to a BE degree from the university. The advantage was that you could be working full-time and still pursue this curriculum. I worked hard in my studies and passed one subject—maybe it was physics or mathematics. The same exam was given throughout India, and it was a tough competition. I think it was tougher than getting a BE. However, I was busy with this for a year and a half or so. I tried again to get admission into engineering. I applied at BMS Engineering College and tried to get the recommendations of some selection committee members. Akhil, my cousin, had completed his bachelor's degree by then. Mamujan again bestowed his blessings on me, and I got accepted at the college. I had graduated from central college almost two years ago. Both Akhil and I wanted to get admission at BMS Engineering College in Basavanagudi, Bangalore.

Some of my friends asked me, "What are you going to do? Are you still going to pursue engineering studies? What are your plans?"

I told them, "This is the opportunity of my life. I cannot forgo it, and I will do it. It is my dream come true. Better late than never." I was on top of the world. My happiness knew no bounds. I thought my uncle Mamujan was going to help me pay for my education. There was no scholarship award or anything, sadly.

Here are some of the major events that happened in 1957 and 1958.

1. The first electric typewriter was placed on sale.
2. The Suez Canal reopened.

3. US president Eisenhower apologized to a minister of Ghana, Komla Agbeli, after he was refused service in a restaurant in Delaware.
4. The film *The Bridge on the River Kwai* was awarded the Best Picture of the Year.
5. I started engineering studies at the University of Mysore.
6. Madonna, the songwriter and actress, was born.
7. Michael Jackson was born.
8. The Soviets launched *Sputnik 3*.

I was excited to start my engineering studies at BMS Engineering College in Basawan Gudi, Bangalore. I hauled myself on a bicycle a distance of six miles one way every day. Many students at BMS had to pay donations to get admission at the college. I was lucky. I think Mamujan's recommendation helped too. Anyway, the first two years were smooth sailing, I think. Engineering was respected a lot in India. I had a little bit of exposure to engineering subjects with my AMIE studies. My cousin Naseer had been doing civil or structural engineering at the government engineering college. When taking courses for the AMIE curriculum, I chose mechanical engineering courses.

The engineering studies became my first priority in my life. I purchased a slide rule, which was a tool for doing calculations. There were no calculators at the time. Most of the engineering students were supposed to be equipped with a good slide rule. Learning the slide rule itself was like taking another course for most of the students. I requested the help of some friends in learning it. I also bought a drawing board and drawing tools, such as a T square. We spent quite a bit of time on the drawing board, developing drawings of houses, valves, and other objects.

In a way, I became a professional student. In my mind, I felt guilty. I was learning but not putting to use what I had learned. Anyway, my goal was to complete engineering studies and become an engineer. Every year in engineering, there was a public exam, unlike in intermediate and bachelor of science courses, in which the first year did not involve a public exam. I felt I'd accomplished something big by passing the two years successfully. The 1960–61 academic year did not prove so lucky for me. The years, as we progressed, became tougher. At least that's what I believed. I did not do well in my third year. I had to redo the exam in some subjects.

Let's take time to review what happened in those years.

1. My third year in engineering proved to be tougher for me.
2. The Cold War continued to become colder as the two sides distrusted each other more.
3. OPEC (Organization of Petroleum Exporting Countries) was formed in a meeting in Iraq.
4. John F. Kennedy won the US presidential election, defeating Richard Nixon.
5. I pledged to myself that before I was thirty, I would leave India and go abroad.
6. Yuri Gagarin was the first human in space.

I am not making excuses, but in front of our house, there was a grinding mill for crushing paddy and removing the shell out of it and also making flour out of wheat. When it started, it made a loud noise that deafened you. When I was trying to concentrate, the mill made a deafening noise that was disturbing and annoying. All my books and notes were in my room. It was not practical for me to go to the library or someplace else to study. Sometimes I went to a park, found a private or secluded place, and studied there. All during my engineering studies, I had to wrestle with that noise. But I was determined. If you have desire, determination, and drive, you can overcome any obstacle that gets in your way.

Asif and Altaf were outside in a rental room. I used to go study there once in a while. I watched few movies in those days. I saw *Psycho* and *Guns of Navarone.* I did not follow news closely either. Sometimes a friend of mine, Kuppa Swamy, and I went to study in a park not far from our house. I stayed away from Urdu poetry as much as possible so I could focus more on my studies. Sadat Ullah was a good friend of mine at BMS. He and I were smoking buddies too. He lived with his brother Mr. Safi Ullah, who had a high post as an engineer. Sadath Ullah was a good student. He went into electrical engineering, and I went into mechanical engineering. We had our own routes to follow, but we kept our friendship. I went to his house in Shanti Nagar (Double Road). Shabbir Hassan Macci and Anwar Pasha were also in college with me. I think that for a while, my cousin Fiaz also was at BMS. He eventually graduated from the government engineering college.

In the third year of engineering, it was customary to take the students for a tour of India so they could get exposure to the industry in various parts of the country. I think my cousin Sageer, who attended BMS College of Engineering, and some of my friends went along. This would have been a valuable experience for me, but I stayed back because I was not able to afford it. I was hoping to go for the tour in the final year. Did I get to go with the tour in the final year of engineering? I will tell you in the following pages.

In the year 1961–62, I tried to pass the third year of engineering and finally passed it. There were some issues, such as lack of funds. I was ashamed to ask for money from my uncles and brothers. After all, who will bet money on a horse that has shown no promise? I used to go to Vidhana Soudha (the state parliament building), the corporation office, and the inspector general of police office to see my uncles for tuition fees and money. I rarely saw my uncle Khadar Mohiyuddin, who was also working at the government office building. My youngest uncle, K. Ahmadullah, was working as a lawyer in Bangalore, and I seldom saw him.

Asif and Altaf were both working at the time. The constant worries about my financial difficulties forced me to seek a job with the state government. I took the examination for first division clerk as well as second division clerk so I could cover all bases. A funny thing happened: I received a letter from the State Department of Transportation saying that I had failed the second division clerk exam but passed the first division clerk exam. Having secured a job with much difficulty and having seen my brothers happily settled in their jobs, I accepted the job at the department. I thought I would work for a while and then save some money and finalize my engineering. Government jobs were hard to come by. I felt satisfied and thought this was a God-given solution for my financial dependency. I started working with full enthusiasm as a case-working first division clerk. I enjoyed working there. I thought, *Things look right for me. I will take a couple of years' break from my engineering studies, save money, pay my debts, and then continue again.* I discussed the matter with my brother Asif. He was of the opinion that this was not a good idea. I thought deeply, and finally, I submitted my resignation. To my surprise, when I submitted my resignation, they would not accept the resignation at first. I was as if on a strike. I left my chair; went outside; and, under protest, stood on the veranda, demanding acceptance of my resignation. Eventually, they had to let me go.

I signed up for an apprenticeship at Bangalore Wool, Cotton, and Silk Mills Company in their machine shop. I obtained some hands-on experience of working in a factory. I learned small chores, such as grinding, drilling, repairing gear teeth, and filing.

A year or so went by in this struggle, and eventually, in the year 1962–63, I went back to school again. I had one more year left to become an engineer. I was valued in the family circle. It was great to feel that some of the girls' parents in the extended family eyed me to marry their daughters. After medical, engineering was number two in many circles in India.

Engineering commanded a lot of respect in the sense that it was considered hard to achieve, and salaries and employability were good. Time went on, and I sacrificed a lot. Sometimes we brothers all went to a movie. We enjoyed watching a movie at the late show in the evening. I felt a great sense of satisfaction in seeing a movie and having betel leaf treat (*gilori*) and a cigarette. Notice that we were not asking for much in those days. Only myself and my cousin Akhil were the smokers in the group.

Time for a pop quiz. In the period 1962–63, which of the following events happened?

1.   China attacked India over some disputed territory.
2.   US car maker Studebaker went out of business.
3.   Marilyn Monroe was found dead of an overdose of sleeping pills.
4.   President Kennedy was shot and killed in Dallas, Texas.
5.   Jack Ruby killed Lee Harvey Oswald, the man who killed John Kennedy.

6.   I was busy with my last year of engineering studies.

"All of the above" is the correct answer. Some of my classmates in engineering would not take the forthcoming final exam. They would postpone till the next exam, which was usually almost six months away. Their reason was to study thoroughly and achieve first class. Finishing first class had its advantages, such as getting a better job and going abroad for studies. In my case, I tried hard and passed in January of 1964.

Three major things happened in my life in 1964: I got married to Shakeera Begum, daughter of Haji A. R. Abdul Aziz of Munireddy Palyam, Bangalore; I completed my bachelor of engineering degree; and I came to the United States for higher studies in engineering.

Like most marriages in those days, mine was arranged. By the way, I did not go for the all-India tour in my final year, again because of lack of funds. Nobody sponsored me.

I stayed with my new bride in Bangalore for only about five months or so. I had a job as a junior engineer in Bantwal, Hassan District. The use of maps was not common in those days. At least I was not aware of any maps, as we have today. Bantwal is about 206 miles from Bangalore. Mangalore was about eighteen miles from Bantwal. Whenever I had some time, I used to go to Mangalore and stay in a hotel there for the week end etc.

Meanwhile, in Bangalore, preparations were going on for my move to the USA. My passport was the first step. My brother-in-law, Dr. Ismail Shariff, was doing his PhD in economics at the University of Wisconsin, Madison. Nasir Ali and Nargis, my cousins, were in New York, where they'd arrived about three to five years prior to 1964, I believe. Nasir's adventure of going abroad instigated me to plan to go abroad also. My uncle, Nasir's father-in-law, used to talk about Nasir's life in New York.

My father-in-law, Haji A. R. Abdul Aziz, worked hard to get my passport. Ismail Shariff, my brother-in-law, made efforts to get me admission at the University of Wisconsin. Some of the fellows I knew in those days went to Germany to obtain higher education. There was one drawback, though: you had to learn the German language before you could pursue your higher studies. Therefore, it made sense to go to America to pursue higher education. Also, before that era, quite a few people went to the UK for studies. Rafeeq, my cousin Akhil's stepbrother, went to England for higher studies. My cousin Dr. Athar Ali went to Canada in 1956 or so; he is now living a retired life in Montreal, Canada. My old teacher Nazir Ahmad (Akhil's brother-in-law), who had completed his law degree, went to England and settled there. Once everything was coming to a close, a lot of my friends gave me a send-off at Bangalore. It was hard to get separated from the family, especially since I'd just married months ago. However, the excitement of going abroad for higher studies and improving my life kept me going. I wished things could have been a little different. I went to Madras and secured my visa. I also faced an English exam that I needed to pass before everything was confirmed. I felt confident about the exam and passed it. Shakeera and I knew that the separation was coming soon. We talked about it a lot. We wished we were going to America together. However, it was not a possibility. My visa was strictly based on my admission to the university and my continued studies there. As you can see, there was a lot of pressure on me.

At that juncture of my life, I was so busy that I did not have time to watch the news about the rest of the world. Radio and newspapers were my main, source of news; there was no TV during that period. Which of the following events happened in 1964?

1. Lyndon Johnson, president of the United States, declared war on poverty.
2. Cassius Clay (Muhammad Ali) became a black Muslim.
3. Lal Bahadur Shastri was elected prime minister of India.
4. China became the world's fifth largest nuclear power.
5. In August of that year I came to United States for higher studies in Engineering.
6. Shakeera Begum and I got married in Bangalore, India

All of the above is the right answer.

In the meantime, I was finishing up my work at Bantwal's assistant engineer's office in the public works department. Most of our work involved surveying for future roads. All my engineer friends there congratulated me. They gave me a befitting send-off party.

I want to say a few things about Bantwal. It was a small town with a beautiful river. The climate was warm. I stayed in an apartment with some roommates. When we went surveying in the rural areas, we saw a snake or two on the trees. The roads we traveled on to Bantwal by bus were called the Western Ghats. Being hilly, the roads were narrow and dangerous. The bus drivers had to be careful on the roads, as they were passing lots of valleys and canyons.

The languages spoken were Kannada and Tulu. I went to Friday prayers, and the sermon was in Kannada. It felt strange. We usually went home for lunch, ate a lot, and even had a good nap before we returned to the office. The salary for engineers was meek and was paid in cash.

There were no checks or closed envelopes. The paymaster would give you your salary in cash, and you needed to sign a register. Primitive, right? That's the way it was in those days. We have come a long way, I tell you! I resigned from that job and returned to Bangalore. Telephones were not common in India at that time. Mail was the most common way to reach people from other towns. Prior to this, there were messengers or postmen who would ride on horseback or bicycles to deliver messages. Further back in history, a letter was tied to the neck or foot of a dove that would carry it to the proper destination. Amazing, isn't it?

The takeaway for you here is that whatever you do, you need to apply yourself properly. You've got to insert yourself fully. There are no two ways about it. There are no halfway attempts. You are in it to win it. You must have the end result in your mind. This way, you will motivate yourself and see that you are hitting the target and on the way to achieving the goal. You'll feel a sense of self-fulfillment that will encourage you to do bigger and better things.

CHAPTER 3

Migration and Beyond

It was an exciting time for me. My dream seemed to be coming true. I started to get ready for my big journey. My father-in-law arranged to have some warm clothes tailored for me. I think I even had a blanket in my luggage. Until that time in my life, I did not brush my teeth with a regular toothbrush. My brush was my index finger, and I rubbed wood coal powder over my teeth with a stroking motion. That was how I cleaned my teeth every morning. That was the only known way in those days. Somebody—I think Fatima Ahmad, my wife's cousin—told us about getting a brush and using it. She'd been in America for a few years and was visiting Bangalore when I was about to leave for the United States. She gave us lots of tips about American life. Shakeera's cousin Zahir Ahmad also visited us. He showed a movie in the open front yard of my father-in-law's house. It was a homemade movie and was well done. I am sure it was in black and white. In those days, photos and films were only available in black and white. As you are aware, in India, the cow population is high. It was common to see cow dung cakes made by women and tacked on the walls of the house. Once the cakes were dried out by sunlight, they were taken out and used as a supplement to the wood fuel they used to cook food at home.

By the way, did you know that the first color film in Hindi was made in 1937, and the name of the film was *Kisan Kanya*? Also, the first

Bollywood film with sound was *Alam Ara* in 1931. Color films did not become popular until the late fifties.

Anyway, the day of my journey to the USA came. Several friends and relatives came to the airport. The modern airport that we have now was not there. I had to walk up to the plane and climb up the stairs to the seats. There were no jetways. This was the first time I'd ever embarked on a plane, and I was nervous and excited at the same time. I was thinking about all the brothers, sisters, and parents and, most of all, my newlywed wife I left behind. I had plans of doing my master's in engineering. There was an insert in the local *Deccan Herald* about my sojourn to the United States. Everybody was emotional. There were lots of embraces, handshakes, and tears. There were no cameras or videos—nothing like that.

I want to share a couplet from a famous Urdu poet:

Lehro'n se ghabra kar naau paar nahi'n hoti
Koshish karne wale ki kabhi haar nahi'n hoti

The translation is as follows: "A boat will not reach its destination if it is afraid of the waves." The person who tries hard rarely faces failure. I tried hard, and it looked like I was bound to achieve my goal.

I left Bangalore on August 19, 1964. I reached Bombay and stayed overnight at Taj Mahal Hotel. I was excited. In the hotel, it was the first time ever in my life that I saw a Western toilet. I needed to go to the bathroom, but I did not feel comfortable. All my life, I was only used to the squat position. The only way I knew to use the commode was to put my heels or feet on it. While I was trying to balance, the whole commode toppled down. Luckily, I did not get hurt. Somehow, my needs were met, and I rested well before I could catch my flight. On the airplane, they served me a pulpy yellow-colored drink. I said to the passenger next to me, "What is this? It has a different taste."

He replied, "You will get used to it. It is orange juice." I was unfamiliar with it and its strange bittersweet taste. The aircraft stopped at about six or seven airports before it reached New York. I think some of the stops were Daharan, Athens, Cairo, London, and Paris. I was overwhelmed. My family members Nasir, Zahir, and Ismail Shariff all went to the United States by ship. It took about twenty-eight days or so on the ship, and the flight took only about twenty-six hours with all the stops. I was dazzled by the brilliant lights at Kennedy Airport. I landed safely in New York. I had some time before I had to catch the flight to Madison, Wisconsin. I called Nargis and Nasir to tell them I was in the airport at New York. I think they said the airport was too far from their apartment, and the traffic would be bad. They were not able to see me at that time. Then I called Sajida, my sister-in-law, to inform her that I was in New York. My next flight was to Minneapolis on the way to Madison. As much as I like big cities, the Madison airport looked small compared to what I had seen elsewhere in my journey to the United States. I kept saying to myself, *Is this the place I dreamed about? I should be in New York or Chicago—in one of those universities.* I got disheartened a little bit. Even though the University of Wisconsin is one of the top world universities, I could not console myself enough to heighten my excitement to the next level. Anyway, Ismail Shariff showed me all the ropes and introduced me to pertinent people. He was living at the graduate student apartments at Eagle Heights, near Lake Mendota in Madison. The place was far from the university campus. I took the bus from near the house every day and most of the time returned home with him in his car.

Mansoor, a nephew of mine, was a toddler at that time. We used to say we lived in "dignified poverty" in those days. Bhai Saheb had a big circle of friends both in and outside of Eagle Heights. I also became friends with Arsalan, Saeed, Anwar, Zaheer, Aga, Ather Abdul Khader, Amaan, and Farooq. Most of them were graduate students. I went to college earnestly and wanted to make worthwhile use of my money and time. The exchange rate was four and a half rupees for one dollar. I think the fee at the university was about $300 per semester. I knew it was a hefty burden on my father-in-law's shoulders. I did not know what kind of an understanding Bhai Saheb had with my father-in-law. I will never stop appreciating the untiring help and assistance that he and Sajida Shariff provided to me in my formative years in the United States. I will touch upon some details of my plights at various junctures as I began my life in

America. In a nutshell, whatever I am today is due to the efforts, guidance, and timely help of Bhai Saheb and my sister-in-law Sajida Shariff. I owe them a great debt of gratitude.

I went through the formalities of registration. On my first day of class, all the young students looked alike to me. Everyone seemed to be an Anglo Saxon white guy. It was hard to [As a footnote, my cousin Nasir Ali passed away unexpectedly yesterday, December 20, 2014. Please say prayers for him. Ask Allah to place his soul in Jannah, and pray for his loved ones to be patient in the time of this tragic event. *Jane wale khabhi Nahi'n aate, Jane wale ki yaad aati hai* (One who passes away never returns, but his or her thoughts never leave us).] distinguish between the faces. For a while, I felt as if I were the only guy of color. I felt odd and out of place. However, as time went on, I saw some black folks who were students too. There were few, though. I met some Indians as well.

At this point, let's jog our memories and see what was happening in the world. Except the first, most of the following events happened around 1964. The first one took place as early as 1946.

1. Plans to build the World Trade Center in New York were announced.
2. I immigrated to the United States with the intention of returning after my education was completed.
3. New York's World Fair was held.
4. Pandit Jawahar Lal Nehru passed away.
5. The Civil Rights Act of 1964 was passed, abolishing racial segregation in the United States.
6. The Vishva Hindu Parishad was founded in India.
7. Lyndon Johnson defeated Republican Barry Goldwater in the US presidential race.
8. The most successful James Bond mIndia bovie, *Goldfinger*, was released in US theaters.
9. Nikita Khrushchev was deposed as leader of the Soviet Union. Brezhnue and Kosygin assumed power.
10. Cassius Clay (Muhammad Ali) beat Sonny Liston and was crowned Heavyweight Champion of the World.

As you can tell, it was a busy year. This happened to be one of the busiest years of my life too.

I needed a period of adjustment in America. I came to Madison, Wisconsin, in the middle of August, and the school year started in September. I was considered a "special student." *Special* did not refer to my distinctiveness or exclusiveness in any way. It meant they did not recognize my undergraduate degree as equivalent to the undergraduate degree of any university in the USA. Based on my marks on the BE degree exam, they could not admit me directly into the graduate program. (In India, it is called the postgraduate degree program.) Hence, they placed me on a special status. I was supposed to achieve high marks in order to be successful. The aim was to get me into the graduate school or Master's Degree program. There were lots of emotions tied in with my journey to the United States; the money problem; my father-in-law's scholarship; living with my brother-in-law, who was also a PhD student in his own formative years; and expectations from my new wife back home. I felt responsible for making use of the money, time, and support my relatives gave me. I was not doing well in school. I considered switching to material science or something. I talked to my brother-in-law, Ismail Shariff. "Considering the circumstances, I want to drop out of school at the present time," I told him.

"What is the matter?" he asked.

"I don't think I am making good use of time and money. Instead of wasting the resources, I will at least save them from going down the drain. I need time to get adjusted. I will go to school next semester."

I do not know what transpired between Bhai Saheb (Ismail Shariff) and my father-in-law.

My brother-in-law asked me, "Will you get the money back from the school?"

I found out there was still time. I finally dropped out of school

It was a hard and trying time for me. I usually consulted my brothers about my decisions. In this case, they were away, and contact was not easy in those days. A direct call to India was not possible. You would call the telephone company, and they would try to open up a line of contact and call you back when it was available. Sometimes it took a couple of days or more to get the line. You waited day and night, staying by the phone to get connected. It was a mess. Letters took about ten days to reach India. I shared all my decisions and got guidance from my brother-in-law. At one time, I think I wanted to give up the hassle of foreign education and return to India, but it was not that easy. I would have cursed myself for the rest of my life for failing to follow my dream. I will talk about the hard decisions and the results a little bit later.

Finally, the money I got back from the university was applied toward the fees for the next semester. I experienced a big change in the weather. Wisconsin is known for its harsh, cold winters. I dared through my first winter. It was hard to walk on the sidewalks when they were icy. I slowly learned the ropes, though even after fifty years, I am still not comfortable. Of course, I am talking from my perspective. Other people might see things in a different light.

There was another obvious problem I faced. The university admits foreign students based on a valid visa. The visa is only good if you are studying at the school. Therefore, dropping out of school means you can lose your visa, as the school officials are in direct contact with the Immigration and Naturalization Department. Half of my worry in those days was how to keep my visa current. I made up my mind that I would study hard in my second semester at the university. Bhai Saheb made arrangements for me to stay with a friend, Eswara from Karnataka, on the campus. It was a one-bedroom apartment with a bunk bed, near Camp Randall. All the libraries were close enough to study in. My sister-in-law Sajida Shariff used to send meals for me regularly. Also, I used to come home for supper, I believe. Ismail Shariff used to give me a ride. The semester went by without my accomplishing what they wanted from me as a special student. In other words, the bad news came that I no longer belonged to the university with the current situation. I could not get a minimum of Bs or As to get out of the special status and be selected for the graduate school. Dr. Obert wrote this order on paper and gave a copy to me. It was a cut-and-dry order. Even though I got Bs in a couple of subjects, the rest of my marks were weak. As per the orders of Dr. Obert, I did not meet the goal. I could not continue at the university. Not being at the university meant being expelled or deported from America. I applied at as many universities as possible. I made up my mind that going back to India was not an option. I wanted my wife to come to America and see the high standard of life there. I thought, *If others in the extended family can do it, I must be able to do it too. I am not any less in ability than them.* I was comparing myself to relatives who had come to the United States before me. I was determined that I was not going back. I applied to Marquette University in Milwaukee and Christian Brothers College in Memphis, Tennessee. I got rejected from various colleges and universities for obvious reasons.

I was desperate to get admission into any college in any program. Meanwhile, I wrote to my father-in-law about the situation I was facing. He did not see any promise in me. He said in a letter about me, "He is like a race horse who has not proven himself in a one-mile race. We want him to run in a three-mile race. Impossible." He gave up hope.

Ismail Shariff was getting some assurance from my father-in-law to provide financial help to me. After judging my progress, or lack of progress, I think he cut off the father-in-law scholarship. This is what I believe; I am not sure what happened. I again owe a great debt of gratitude to my brother-in-law, who pulled me through that difficult time and helped me financially and otherwise. At various universities, when I applied, they wanted the original transcripts from my studies in India. It was next to impossible in those days to accomplish that in a hurry. Time was running out. After all those rejections and disappointments, I got a letter from Christian Brothers College in Memphis, Tennessee. My happiness knew no bounds at the joyous news. My friends had a little get-together for me at Vilas Park in Madison. The next day or so, I took a Greyhound bus to Memphis. It was a long journey from Madison to Memphis. Quite a few people were traveling by bus in those days. I reported to Christian Brothers College. It was an accredited college. I went there with all sincerity to pursue my studies. Even at a small college like that, I met some Indian students. We must have paid tuition fees and all that. I took a job in the canteen, washing dishes. Christian priests ran the school, and they helped me a lot. The college authorities gave me information regarding where to rent a place to live. I rented a small mobile home in the backyard of the main house along with some other students. I did not know all the standards of housing at the time. I grabbed whatever I could get. I was satisfied that I had my own bedroom. The other students had their own bedrooms also. The place was within walking distance of the college.

By the way, let's examine what was happening in the world during the year 1965.

1. Malcolm X, black nationalist leader, was shot to death at a Harlem rally in New York.
2. I returned to Wisconsin from Memphis.
3. Black people rioted for six days in Watts, Los Angeles, resulting in thirty-four dead and more than one thousand injured.
4. There was tension between whites and blacks all over the nation.

I received the good news of my acceptance to Marquette University in Milwaukee, Wisconsin. My brother-in-law telephoned me with the good news. Marquette was a better school than the one in Memphis anyway. I thanked God for this opportunity to get back to Wisconsin. I had become familiar a little bit with the people of Wisconsin. I did not even have my feet wet at Christian Brothers. In a way, I was not happy with this little college, even though it was accredited. I wanted to graduate from a reputable university. I returned to join Marquette University. Marquette is a Jesuit school and was well known at that time for its dental school and engineering school. Anyway, my program was to take some courses at the undergraduate level. When I first arrived in Milwaukee, I stayed with some Pakistani students in an apartment building. They were helpful. One was named Baig, and I think the other guy's name was Akhtar. Ismail Shariff and another friend of ours from Pakistan came to talk to some advisers at Marquette University. One adviser looked at my transcripts and said my Indian engineering courses were far behind and outdated compared to the courses in this country. I was not admitted to the graduate school right away. One day in Memphis, I found out that I was accepted at Marquette University. I had brought my slide rule from India. I do not know if I used my slide rule at Marquette that much. I do not recall what kind of calculator there was at that time. Texas Instruments made different kinds of calculators. There were business calculators, scientific calculators, and real estate calculators. That company still makes good calculators, I suppose.

While I was an undergraduate student at Marquette University in Milwaukee, I was looking for part-time jobs to support myself. Bhai Saheb supported me to a great extent, even though my father-in-law had almost given up on me. I do not know what the deal was between Ismail Shariff and my father-in-law. In fact, at the time, I wasn't sure if there was a problem at all. Even though the discussion was about me, it was not clear to me. I know that Ismail Shariff took chances in supporting me. Like I said before, I am grateful to him. We put whatever he loaned to me in writing. I am proud to say that whatever I borrowed I was able to pay back. I wish to state that I can never pay him back for all the moral and other support I got from him. It is not easy for anybody to help someone financially while one is still a graduate student. Ismail Shariff was studying for his PhD in agricultural economics.

In those days, there was an employment company in the United States called Manpower. There might have been others, but that was the only one I knew of. I contacted them, and they referred me to a company, though they did not give me many details in the office. All they did was give me a brief description of what I needed to do and the address of the place, and they asked me to go there directly. I was not driving in those days. I took the bus to the place and contacted the person I was supposed to. When I went to the office, they directed me to the job site, where I saw a big silo about twelve to fourteen feet high and maybe about twelve feet in diameter. There was noise outside of the silo, as if some machine were running inside. There was a ladder on the outside of this concrete or metal silo, and there was a similar ladder inside to get to the bottom of the silo. The guy in charge was wearing high rubber boots. He explained to me and showed me what I was supposed to do. From a chute, fish were dumped into the well, and they were supposed to be shoveled into the center hole in the well. The bottom of the tank was sloped toward the center hole. It was slippery as hell inside the well. It looked like there was a grinder that ground up the fish underneath the bottom of the well. I was supposed to wear proper ankle boots. It was a dangerous job, as far as I could see.

I was desperate in trying to support myself but not desperate enough to put myself in harm's way. Not only was it slippery, but also, the whole tank bottom was sloped toward the center hole. After looking at all this, what do you think I should have done? The job was mine if I took it. I turned around and went home. I bet they had a hard time filling that job.

Subsequently, I kept looking for other suitable jobs. However, my primary goal was to get the degree for which I'd sacrificed so much. I was determined to be self-sufficient and support myself 100 percent. I picked up a job as a press operator. There was a company in Milwaukee called Empire Level Manufacturing, which was quite far from my apartment. In those days, my transportation was the public bus. Working on a press was dangerous. I needed to follow certain safety procedures. Both hands had to be away from the area where the holes were supposed to be punched in the aluminum level. This was a safety feature of the machine. The buttons for operating the punch were way above where the hole was to be punched. This was by design, so both hands would be forced to be out of the way and out of danger.

There was a foreman at the company who was a nice man. The foreman's son was also a worker at the company. We could work piece work, meaning the more pieces you produced, the more money you got. The regular pay would be the hourly wage regardless of the number of items you produced. People who had good speed and safety could make somewhat more money. This was an option they gave the worker. I chose to stay away from piecework.

There was a big challenge for me while I was at Marquette University. For one thing, I had to maintain my grade point average at a reasonably high standard. I wanted to be self-sufficient. I wanted to meet and beat the challenge. I worked hard. I was determined. I challenged myself by saying, "If they have done it, why can't I? I will be able to do the same." That desire and determination kept me going. I discussed the option of forgetting everything and going back to India. That would have meant shame and admitting failure. I was sensitive about that. I wanted to stay there and bring Shakeera to that country. I love her so much, and I wanted her to see the beauty and glamour of that country and experience life there. This was considered the best country to live in.

Then I took an odd job of cleaning windows and changing screens. A fifty-year-old man hired me to work on his dad's house. He told me he would pay me hourly wages of less than a dollar. By the way, in India, where I grew up, the wages are paid by the month for the salaried workers in the office. The workmen are paid by the day, I suppose even today.

I took a job with a small company called Pratt Manufacturing Company in Milwaukee. They were manufacturing and assembling surgical packaging machines. I did miscellaneous jobs, such as painting machine parts to work on lathes, milling machines, shaping, and drilling machines. There was one numerical controlled machine on the floor, but I did not have any experience working on that machine. That job, in any manner, was not supposed to advance my career. It was just a part-time job to earn some spending money. I am giving you the details here so you can understand how perseverance can help you accomplish your goals in life. At the time of this writing, many of these companies I have mentioned here might not even exist. By my giving you the details, you will get the full flavor of the story. Make sense?

Racial tension was a big factor in the country. One day, while I was at the big common wash basin at the end of the work day, another guy, who happened to be a white man, said to me, "Hey, guy, however much you wash yourself, you cannot change your color to white." I became angry but only chuckled and kept quiet. The guy was so dumb he did not even know that you wash yourself not to become white but to clean yourself. From time to time, I used to get quite a few comments like this. What could I do? White people had all the power. Even though slavery had been abolished a long time back, with some people, there was still a feeling that black people were inferior. They could never be equal in job status or any aspect of life to white people. They were expected to be in jail or in cotton fields, picking cotton.

Black people were only offered menial jobs. Most servants and maids were black. In the southern states, the matter was even worse. I am glad I did not have to stay long in Memphis, Tennessee, where I was accepted at Christian Brothers. One time, when I went to a restaurant downtown to have some snacks and coffee, the waitress served everybody who was white, even if they came after me. She kept ignoring me until I had to remind her about my turn. There was a general belief that black men were more aggressive and hostile, as if they were revolting against the way they were being treated in this country, as if they were saying, "White guys, you have taken enough advantage of us. You have subdued our lives every step of the way. Stop suppressing us this way. We have dreams too that we wish to fulfill in this world." The racial tension triggered several riots in various big cities, such as Detroit and Los Angeles. As per my nature, I get excited with big cities. I grew up in Bangalore, India, which was a pretty big city even in my days in the early sixties. I am used to the hustle and bustle of big cities. However, it was different in this country. Usually, the bigger cities have bigger problems, including racial tension. Not that the smaller rural towns do not have problems. I am generalizing a little bit here.

I took several small part-time jobs to support myself. Shakeera came to this country in 1966. As many spouses do in this country, Shakeera tried to work here and there a little bit. Her point was "If I work outside, I cannot pay full attention to the upbringing of the kids." Who could argue with that point? Therefore, while I worked outside, she stayed home and paid full attention to the upbringing of the kids.

My major aim in coming to this country was to get my graduate degree in engineering. Hence, at the bottom of my heart, that was what I longed for. While I was pursuing undergraduate courses, I had an eye on the possible opportunities to get into graduate school. The purpose was to earn some money and prove to the US immigration department that I could support myself and also support my wife. I felt a big responsibility to be able to sponsor her on my own. I was greatly challenged. The immigration department would not allow you to become a public charge. One cannot depend on government help. I understood all that to some extent. One important thing I learned is that in this country, you have to stand on your own two feet as much as possible. You will get information, guidance, and moral support from those who are near to you. However, you need to be the one to achieve it. The immigration department kept telling me, "You cannot become a public charge. That means you cannot claim handouts from the government." I did not know the full meaning of the system. One thing we found out was that health insurance is important in this country. There could be enormous expenses to go to the doctor, clinic, or hospital. I did not think about these things in India. It is your home. When you go to a foreign country, no close relatives are near you. This fact became more pronounced for me when I was ten thousand miles away from home.

In this foreign country, lonely as I was and far away from all of my relatives, I remained focused on my goals. Anurag Prakash Ray says, "Nothing can stop you from achieving your goals in life if you have the hunger and desire to achieve." Another author, Anil Sinha, says, "Desire is the key to motivation. But it is determination and commitment which enable you to reach your goal with excellence."

Time now for a pop quiz. Hope you are ready. What events occurred in 1966 and 1967?

1. I was busy seeking admission to a graduate program.
2. Heavyweight boxing champion Muhammad Ali, formerly known as Cassius Clay, declared himself a Conscientious Objector and refused to go to war.
3. Miniskirts were in fashion.
4. Indira Gandhi was elected prime minister of India.
5. *Dr. Zhivago* became a popular film.
6. Color TV became popular.

"All of the above" is the correct answer.

Professor A. F. Elkouh at Marquette University was seeking a student to help him in his research. I approached him, and he offered me the scholarship to work under his direction on a research project. After we discussed his plans, I accepted the scholarship. Until then, I'd been paying the tuition fee. I had a part-time job. I took some odd jobs to make ends meet in those days. This, along with help from Ismail Shariff, helped me to keep going. Now, with this research scholarship, I was exempt from paying the fee, and I also earned a stipend. I became an earning member, and I could sponsor Shakeera to come join me in the United States. After all the paperwork and formalities, Shakeera came to the United States at the end of 1966. I'd been separated from her for more than two years. I regretted this separation, but there was no other way. I still had my goal to complete my Master's Degree. I was thrilled that my new bride was with me in this country. We could start our lives and plan things together. When in India, Shakeera wrote me letters encouraging me in my efforts to complete my studies. It took me a little longer to do my Master's Degree, as I had to write a thesis as partial fulfillment of the requirements. I needed to support not only myself but also my wife. But my biggest challenge was to complete my studies and earn my degree. Anything short of that was not acceptable; there was no other option. I was stressed out. Usually, people came to this country to do a master's in one year and start earning. In my case, I'd already spent three years in this country and had not achieved anything. All this thought had put me behind the eight ball. I told Bhai Saheb that I would like to learn how to drive a car. He said that was not a high priority.

However, I had a strong urge to learn driving. There was a jeep at the University of Wisconsin, where I had a part-time job while I was in Madison. I used to sit in the driver's seat and play around a little bit. Anyway, I studied for the driver's test and passed the written test. I still had to take the road test to get the license. I always want to challenge myself. I purchased a car, a Chevrolet Tempest, for about $400. I did not even know there were models of cars based on the year they were made. I did not know the ins and outs of buying a car. I had a friend at Marquette University who helped me to deal and purchase the car. Shakeera and I lived in a modest apartment near the school. The engineering college was within walking distance, so the car was parked in the yard. Another friend, Mannavli from India, taught me a little bit about the car. One time, he showed me how to change a tire. Mannavli took me around to demonstrate how to drive.

Eventually, I took the road test and passed it. It was a big thrill and joy for me to be able to drive on the roads of Milwaukee.

Several times in my analysis of life, I thought, *Why should I do the Master's Degree in engineering? I could do something in other fields I am strong in, such as Urdu.*

One of the popular majors for engineers in those days was Industrial Engineering. This required time and motion study. I was interested in the core mechanical engineering subjects, such as energy sciences. Material science is another subject I thought of. Anyway, it is not an easy, clear-cut decision as to what you do in the graduate school of engineering until you explore and feel for yourself. There were lots of avenues. At this time, let's take a quick pop quiz to test where we were in world events at that time. I will make this one "Jeopardy" style. I will give the answers, and you give me the questions.

1. This South African surgeon performed the first heart transplant operation.
2. This American surgeon conducted the first heart bypass operation.
3. The USS *Pueblo*, an American intelligence gathering vessel, was captured by this country.
4. James Earl Ray was convicted of the assassination of this black civil rights leader.
5. This man was the first Muslim to become the president of India.
6. Sirhan Sirhan killed this famous politician.

The questions for the above answers are as follows:

1. Who was Dr. Christian Bernard?
2. Who was Dr. Rene Favalero?
3. What is North Korea?
4. Who was Dr. Martin Luther King?
5. Who was Dr. Zakir Hussain?
6. Who was Robert Kennedy?

I started working under Dr. Elkouh, who specialized in Fluid Mechanics subjects. The gentleman is from Egypt and was nice to me. Dr. Elkouh was a doctoral graduate of the University of Wisconsin, Madison. He offered me the research scholarship. I designed the equipment under his directions, put together the whole thing, and started taking data for my research project.

This specific topic of Research was unique and something that nobody had done before. The literature search in those days was hard. There were no computers. There was no other way but to dig through books. My professor told me that the work had to be original. There was lots of pressure. The other graduate students with me were working on their own research projects. I knew a little bit of what they were doing, but the time pressure was so much that you needed to produce a justification for every day you spent on your work. I kept seeing the professor regularly, and he gave me directions and guidance every step of the way. The major professor is like your boss at work or even more than a boss. It is in his hands whether you get the Degree or not. I had learned about this experience from other graduate students who were with Bhai Saheb and whom I knew personally.

Professor Elkouh not only guided me in completing the requirements for my Master's Degree but also instructed me on some practical life and career skills. He used to tell me that if you drag a thing too long, you will lose interest in it. Everything has to be completed in a timely manner. Also, never stop a project; keep on contributing something to it with the aim of completing it in a timely manner. Also, if I was a few minutes late for his appointments, he used to say, "If you are late like this in the Industry, you will be fired. People are very strict."

Being his research assistant, I was very much influenced by him. He told me, "I am helping you only because you are a Master's Degree candidate. If you were a Doctoral Degree person, you would work very independently. Nobody would help you." I completely got absorbed in my studies. I appreciate Shakeera's patience in those days. She worked for a woman who was a Banquet Director. Shakeera took care of her kids in her house. In other words, she was a babysitter for her. I went with Shakeera over there often. One of the requirements for me was to stay close to the school, as it should be within the walking distance.

I changed several apartments. I spent lots of time on my studies, and I had an office on campus. In those days, there were not many Indians in Milwaukee. Shakeera made friends with Shahnaz, Dr. Younus's wife. We used to go to Madison off and on to Sajida's house. Mazkoor Shariff (Mazy) was a baby then. Shakeera enjoyed taking care of him. Sajida and Bhai Saheb visited us in Milwaukee quite a bit. Shakeera naturally wanted to spend time with her sister frequently. This helped me concentrate on my studies. In the second year of my tenure as a graduate student, I lost my research assistantship. The professor said he had run out of funds and could not fund me anymore. I was lucky to get teaching assistance right away. Those were trying times for us. We were racing against time too. Assistantships are not there forever. Now I had to spend time on writing my thesis as well as teaching engineering students. I was assigned to be a Teaching Assistant for the drafting class. I worked for Professor Lonergan. He was a straightforward type of guy. He used to tell me his philosophies in giving references for his students: "I would rather not say anything instead of saying something bad about them."

Anyway, I carried on my research and started writing my Thesis. Ismail Shariff had a typewriter, and I borrowed it to start with. Eventually, I purchased an electric typewriter to work on my thesis. These typewriters were supposed to be much better than the manual ones.

There were lots of Differential Equations that I needed to solve in my thesis project. The computer rooms in those days were big. There was no access to anybody but the computer operators themselves. They are called mainframe computers, I guess. I do not claim by any measure to be a know-it-all about computers. I used to work on card-punching machines, producing sets of seven-by-three-inch cards that had tiny holes. These sets of cards were given to the computer programmer, who read them on the magnetic tapes of the machine and printed out the results or the data. It took hours or even a day or so before you got back the results. The bigger the program, the larger the number of cards and the longer the time for the computer to spit out the results. If you made a single mistake in the key-punching machine, the particular card had to be redone. I think the printout said where the mistake was. IBM was a big name in computers in those days, as it is even today. In making progress in my studies, I concentrated on both my course work and the thesis credits. The requirements were thirty credit hours, with twenty-four for course work and six for thesis. The six thesis or research credits were the hardest to earn.

While I was working to complete my degree, Shakeera and I also were planning to have children. I did well in my course work. I took advanced Mathematics, Thermodynamics, Fluid Mechanics, and heat transfer. Unlike other universities close by, Marquette had the requirement of a thesis for Master's Degree candidates. Most of the graduate students worked hard all week and took a good night's rest or break on Friday evenings. We used to enjoy a movie once in a while. Of course, in those days, there were no Bollywood movies we could watch. The word *Bollywood* had not even been coined at that time. We missed those movies and Indian culture very much. In Milwaukee, there were no stores where we could buy Indian clothes or condiments. After some time in town, we found out that there was a guy who sold Indian saris and more from his basement.

Months went by this way for a while. I was successful in completing the requirements for the degree. Shakeera was busy making our home and working outside a little bit. The TV shows were all American. Shakeera took an English course to get familiar with the American English language. The neighborhood where we rented the apartment was not the best by any measure. I had my car broken into a couple of times during the night. I was lucky that there wasn't any major damage. Ismail Shariff and Sajida Shariff gave us a lot of advice. These were our formative years. The big concern was to have a permanent visa to stay in this country. We had to stay in this country for a certain number of years before we could apply for a green card, as it is called.

Well, guess what. It is time for a break. However, during the break, we are going to have some fun by answering some questions about the historical events during the period when all this was happening in my life.

1. This team won the Super Bowl (the American professional football championship) in 1968. Vince Lombardi was the head coach.
2. This US president announced he would not seek reelection.
3. This popular weekly magazine show debuted on the CBS TV channel.
4. This member of our family was awarded a Master's Degree in engineering from Marquette University, Milwaukee, Wisconsin.
5. This popular politician from the Republican Party defeated Democrat Hubert Humphrey and Independent George Wallace for the office of president of the United States.

I will give you the answers in a little bit. Having a green card was a desirable thing for most every student. I applied for immigrant status as opposed to student status by self-sponsoring after my Master's Degree. The way it worked was that the US Labor Statistics Department checked whether an applicant would take away a job from an American citizen in his particular profession. Based on that, I was successful in getting the immigrant visa. In other words, I did not replace anybody by being a mechanical engineer with a Master's Degree. I thought it was much easier then to become an immigrant than now. I might be wrong, though. At that time, only professionals with valuable degrees were able to become immigrants. Nowadays, it is different. You know what the status is nowadays. I was relieved that my immigration problem had been solved. I felt secure. Shakeera automatically got an immigration visa as a spouse. Now I was sitting pretty except for one thing.

One hurdle before I got my degree was to defend my thesis. The process involved naming three professors who would read my thesis thoroughly. A day was set for me to present the thesis in front of these professors. These three professors evaluated the material in the thesis and made sure it was a worthy and valuable contribution to the knowledge of science. The day came when I was supposed to present my thesis and defend it. I had heard stories from other students regarding how they'd failed to prove that they had something worthwhile to contribute. The degree granting was based on this 150-page or so documentation of your work. I was a nervous wreck that day. I prayed to Allah, and I presented the thesis.

I know that Allah's blessings were with me. After I presented the material of the thesis, I would not know whether I made a meaningful contribution or not. It was a nerve-racking and stressful day for me. The three professors who examined me were Dr. John Bush, Dr. A. F. Elkouh, and Dr. James Lewis. Dr. Elkouh was the director of my work. Following the presentation, they asked me questions. Then they asked me to step out of the room and wait. They were going to discuss my work and decide whether I deserved the degree. I must have prayed in the hallway continuously during the wait period. They were making a decision on my fate. The thesis title was "Flow Development in the Entrance Region of a Radial Diffuser." I thought that was kind of a fancy name. I have to give credit to Professor Elkouh for appropriately thinking of a name like that. It looks powerful. Anyway, my wait period felt as if it was never going to end. I stood close to the room, and my eyes were glued to the door all the time. After a while, the door finally opened, and Dr. John Bush emerged, walked toward me, and said, "Congratulations. We think your thesis has made a meaningful and valuable contribution to the knowledge of science." Then the other two gentlemen congratulated me also.

I'd worked hard on my thesis, and there were not many flaws that I knew of, but when your work is critically looked upon by distinguished professors, all you have are negative thoughts. *What if they do not like my experiment? What if they do not like my presentation? What if that? What if this?* My anxiety was going through the roof. Hearing the news of my success, I let out a big sigh of relief. I thanked God. My hard work of a couple of years had paid off. I couldn't wait to tell my wife that I'd passed. That was a beautiful day for me, and I thanked God again.

I know you must be curious to know the answers to the questions I posed a little while ago. Are you ready? The answers are as follows:

1. Green Bay Packers
2. Lyndon B. Johnson
3. *Sixty Minutes*
4. Yours truly
5. Richard Nixon

At that point, I had completed the purpose of my journey to the United States. Professor Elkouh pointed out to me that I could do my PhD in engineering. However, the PhD did not tickle my fancy much. I did not see myself as a professor or a teacher. To some extent, however, I was attracted to the concept of research in the field. I always liked to come up with new and original ideas. This was a far-fetched ambition of mine anyway. Also, as you are aware, I had been a professional student for a long time. I wanted to start earning and start a family.

"I want to end my academics here and pursue normal avenues of life," I told my professor.

My next move was to find a suitable job. Dr. Elkouh agreed to be my reference, as did Mr. Lonergan, who was my supervisor while I was a Teaching Assistant. I started using both of these people as my references. I applied at local companies in Milwaukee. Milwaukee is a good industrial town. There were various companies I had my eye on. I started interviewing with some of the companies. I applied at IBM, Kodak, City of Milwaukee, National Steel, Caterpillar, and more. I got a job offer from the City of Milwaukee, but there was a condition that if they found a citizen to do the job, they would have to let me go. Then I got a job offer from National Steel Corporation. Everything looked good, and I took the job. It would have been nice if I had found a suitable job in Milwaukee itself. That way, I would not have had to move to Detroit. Just about that time, in 1967–68, there were huge riots in Detroit due to racial issues. I was fascinated by large cities. I found out that Detroit was about four times as big as Milwaukee. Anyway, I took the opportunity and accepted the job offer. They helped pay for my move from Milwaukee to Detroit. All this sounded good to me. I did not know any better. There was nothing to compare to. I was new to these things and also young and inexperienced. I had to make decisions on my own and in a quick manner. That was how I learned about the fast pace of life in this country. I did not know much about how things happened in this country. I got some guidance from my Brother-in-law I learned that you are on your own in this country. Everybody has his or her own problems. There is a famous saying: "You've got your problems. I've got mine."

Time is the most luxurious thing. People do not have enough time to tackle their own problems. In these circumstances, how can they afford to give time to others? The responsibility of the immediate family comes first. Most everybody starting here is in their formative years, which are the most challenging times in our lives. Like they say, if you pick a right path and follow it with persistence, you might end up a success. Self-help is the best help. All our lives in our country, our parents guided us. However, in this country, they were not there. Phone calls were not easy, as I have mentioned before. Therefore, we did our best in the circumstances that came our way. Most of the graduate students with me got good jobs, and a few went for PhDs.

In those days, there was a big civil rights movement in the country. There was discrimination on the basis of color, creed, religion, age, etc. I might have applied to twenty-five different companies. To tell you the truth, I did not have a vast choice. So Shakeera and I started planning to move to Detroit. We were excited. My first job after graduation would be at a well-known steel mill. The pay was good by the standards of those days. There were health benefits and other fringe benefits. The company paid for my move. When I first came to Detroit, they kept me for a while in a nice hotel until I found an apartment. My first priority at that time was to settle down in Detroit. One day I was walking down the street in Detroit, when I met with a guy from Hyderabad, India. He gave me a lead on an apartment building where he lived in Highland Park, Michigan. This gentleman's name was Abdul Ghani, and later on, we became good friends. Along with him in the apartment complex lived Allauddin, Hamid and Asif. The apartments were kind of far away from Great Lakes Steel, where I worked. For me, driving was a pleasure in those days, and it still is. I think I lived in those apartments for more than a year or so. The car used to be parked on the street near the apartments. There was a school across from the apartments.

What was happening in the world at that time? Let me inform you.

1. The Netherlands got their first color TV.
2. Christian Bernard performed the second heart transplant.

3. GM produced its one hundred millionth automobile, the Oldsmobile Toronado.
4. Arthur Ashe became the first black person to be ranked number one in tennis.
5. Intel Corporation was founded in Santa Clara, California.

I was working rotating shifts as a management trainee at the Great Lakes Steel Corporation in Ecorse, Michigan. Shakeera and I were planning to have a baby even before we left Milwaukee. Anyway, as the time passed, we started looking for a house. The condition was, of course, that it had to be close to the steel mill where I worked. I had been driving too far for too long. At work, I learned a lot about boilers, instruments, steel-making furnaces, giant steel-slab-making machines, annealing, heat treatment of steel, basic oxygen furnaces, open-hearth furnaces, and more. It was an exciting time. There was a lot to learn, and I did learn. Safety was a big concern in the mill, as gas was used as a fuel to burn the scrap in the process. We were charged with the responsibility of making sure that when we lit a furnace, it was safe for the property and also for the personnel. A combustion engineer used to go through the furnace to make sure everything was safe. There were open-hearth furnaces, eighty-inch mill furnaces, and various other furnaces that needed to be checked. Another part of our work was to troubleshoot the hydraulic, pneumatic, and electronic instruments that controlled the furnaces, including fuel distribution and optimization.

Ivan Akey, Jim Walls, and Vendal Tate were my bosses. I worked with George Eskola a lot too. George Eskola lived in Dearborn, Michigan. He made me comfortable by talking to me about simple things, such as my hobbies, in the beginning of my tenure there. I also worked for Ed Williams, who was a supervisor at the BOP plant, a brand-new Basic Oxygen plant constructed within the campus of the facility. The furnace was big, about three stories high or so. Metal scrap and iron ore were dumped into the vessel by cranes, and oxygen lances were introduced into the vessel along with the fuel, and the process started. It was more than two thousand degrees Fahrenheit in the vessel. Our department took the temperatures of the molten steel as the vessel was tilted. This was a huge operation, and I was excited to be a part of this mill and the department. The plant was alongside the Detroit River, and several thousand people worked at the plant over the three shifts. I assume it was about two miles or so long along the river. I was assigned to shift work as a Fuel Practice Engineer and Combustion Engineer. The job was kind of dirty in the sense that the atmosphere was full of the dust of iron and steel. We engineers used to wear steel-toed boots and trench coats to protect ourselves from sparks and molten iron. I was reading up a lot and learning about instrumentation, supervision, processes, pumps, boilers, fuel distribution, piping, and furnace safety. Shakeera liked to meet people from India. We made some friends, including Noor Jehan and Tufail Niazi, Mumtaz Saheb, Ather Abdul Khader, Mujtaba and Tasneem, Ghani and family, Allauddin and Atiya, and Hafiza.

My brother-in-law, Ismail Shariff, and Sajida visited us from Green Bay often. The sisters were close, and Masha-Allah, they are still close to each other. Happy news came while we were in Highland Park. Toward the end of 1968, Shakeera became pregnant with our baby boy Shakeeb. Children are God's gift. Our joy knew no bounds at this blessed news. After a long wait, we were blessed. She started seeing a doctor at the hospital not far from the apartment. It was an Osteopathic Hospital. She was under good care. Shakeera had the guidance of her sister Sajida constantly. During the birth of our baby, my sister-in-law came up to Detroit and stayed with us for the duration. This helped Shakeera and me quite a bit. When we were in the Highland Park apartment, Dildar Hussain visited us, along with the Shariffs. Dildar Hussain got sponsorship from Ismail Shariff and stayed with them. His stay in the United States was not very long. He went back to India for good. He was young at the time. I think we all did whatever was best for him.

It has been awhile since we took a Test Break. What events happened in 1969?

1. God blessed us with a baby boy.
2. Golda Meir became the first female prime minister of Israel.
3. Dwight Eisenhower, US president, died.

4. The Chappaquitick incident happened. Edward Kennedy drove off a bridge on his way home from a party on the island. Mary Jo Kopechne, a former campaign aide to Kennedy's brother, died.
5. Actress Madhubala from the Hindi film industry passed away.
6. Neil Armstrong and Edwin Aldrin took their historic walk on the moon.

"All of the above" is correct.

Continuing on the story of Dildar Hussain's return back to India, I do not know the full details about this decision. I was not completely involved in the whole thing. My father-in-law and Ismail Shariff must have discussed the move.

Shakeera and I had been actively looking to buy a house in the Downriver area of Detroit. We felt that our new arrival needed to live in a nice house. I felt that our kid deserved to live better than we did. We looked at several houses. At that time, the cost of a simple house with three bedrooms was cheaper than what we can buy a new car nowadays. The houses we looked at were simple gable-roofed ranches with three bedrooms and a one-car detached garage. This was how most people within our circles lived. Also, the people I worked with told me you could only afford to pay so much toward the monthly mortgage. One guy told me he only paid about sixty-four dollars per month on his mortgage. He said we had to have money for food and clothes, etc. I started to set my standards accordingly. It is not the luxury of living; it is just a roof over your head and a comfortable place to eat, sleep, and fulfill your needs of life. Of course, the main criteria was that the mortgage payments had to be reasonable.

After looking at different houses with a real estate agent, we decided on a house in Taylor, Michigan. It was a clean suburb in the Downriver area, about eleven miles from work. We were proud to bring our little prince home and provide him with his own room. Shakeera and I were thrilled at this property ownership in America. Even though there was a mortgage on the house, this was part of the American dream fulfilled. This was a modest and humble starter home by all measures, but it was ours. That was all that mattered for us at the time. I felt fortunate and blessed by the way things were happening. I paid full attention to my job and kept on learning new things and gained experience. At Great Lakes Steel Company, performance evaluation was an ongoing thing. They did not have a regular yearly performance evaluation. We were backed by the United Steelworkers Union, which was a strong workers' union. Therefore, we had pay raises automatically as the union pay was raised. Everything looked like smooth sailing for me, though I longed to get out of shift work. When I was getting used to one shift for about seven or eight days, it changed to another shift. I had to get used to the new shift again, and this happened over and over again. Some of the other engineers were lucky to get out of shift work and secure the day shift. I asked my bosses when I would be able to get the Day shift.

"You complete about twenty years on the job, and you will get the day shift," they said.

Like I said, shift work was getting to me, and I was getting tired and sick of it. I needed to sleep during most of the day when I was on the night shift. After the seven days of night shift, we used to get what was called a long weekend. This was kind of a compensation for not being able to sleep during the regular nighttime hours. This schedule disturbed my circadian rhythm. I could not adjust to the twenty-four-hour cycle and could not respond to changes in light and darkness in terms of the physical, mental, and behavioral aspects. This was not serious, but as you know, the night is made for sleep and rest, while the day is supposed to be for mental functioning. This is not serious or anything, but you cannot get adjusted to it at all. Hence, in my heart, I made up my mind that I should get a day job either at Great Lakes Steel or elsewhere. I took some courses to learn more at Henry Ford Community College. I earnestly studied and tried to apply the knowledge acquired at work.

At work, I got promoted to shift supervisor and was in charge of many more departments. I was supposed to run the shift and make decisions by myself. I enjoyed more challenges and responsibility. I was charged with the responsibility of inspecting various departments, making rounds, and making shift reports. When I went home after a night's work, it felt good to eat something and go to bed. This went on for a while. My prince was growing, and Mom took care of him dearly. I had real meaning now to work hard for my prince and raise him in the best possible environment and provide him with the best care possible. Everything in our lives revolved around Shakeeb. His checkups, doctor visits, and immunizations were our priority. I played with him and spent time with him as much as possible. My younger brother Anwar was also with us at the time. He loved Shakeeb and used to say, "This kid has become a citizen of this country before I could do it."

Anwar was working on his green card, or permanent residency, at that time. Anwar came to this country right around that time. He lived with us for a while, and then he lived with Ghani Saheb and other students. Anwar helped us around the house quite a bit. I used to be handy in those days. One time, we needed to replace the cement driveway, as it was all torn up and had cracks. The process was to tear up the old driveway completely. A contractor could have done it happily. In order to save money, I took it upon myself to tear up the old driveway. I had a sledgehammer, and I went to the backbreaking work of tearing the four-inch-thick driveway. The driveway was about twelve feet wide by thirty-five feet long. It was amazing how, with help from Anwar, I was able to complete this awesome job. In addition, we rented a trailer and hauled the heavy chunks of driveway to a landfill site. I could not imagine doing this kind of work now. It was heavy-duty work. People I knew used to work on their cars a lot in those days. They used to tune up their engines, change their oil, etc. I remember working on my breaks one time. In those days, if I am not mistaken, the brake pads were made out of asbestos. The awareness about asbestos came out later, and it was banned from use on different things, including brake pads.

"Do it yourself" was a motto we took pride in. We enjoyed working around the house. I replaced the old rain gutters with new ones. Anwar, my baby brother, is mechanically inclined and helped me on that project. In those days, I believed in buying good used cars. Buying a new car, I thought, was a waste of money. I bought a Chevy Caprice with a dent on the door. I thought I got a good deal. It was a big car with eight cylinders. I enjoyed driving it. With a friend of mine, I tried to get the door dent fixed.

We ended up replacing the post by the door, and I think we changed the door. One thing or another started going bad on that car. Before that, I'd had other used cars, which I'd sold for low prices. People used to buy cars for the parts too. I think I had a Buick, which I think I sold for less than one hundred dollars. The car was of no use to me. Just the tires on the car would have had more value than what I sold the car for. By the way, there used to be inner tubes in the tires. If there was a puncture, we used to find out where the puncture was and put a patch on it. At Great Lakes Steel in the late sixties and early seventies, we used to have a kit to repair the leaks in the tires. Modern-day tires have come a long way. I used to put snow tires on my vehicles during winter.

You could junk a car too, I guess. I had the car run to the ground. Then guess what. I bought another used car, which, in my judgment, had low mileage. This time, I bought a blue Dodge Polara with about twenty-four thousand miles on it. I remember the year of the model.

As I said, I used to get a long weekend because of my shift-work schedule. During these four days, we often went to Green Bay, Wisconsin, to Shariff's house. We used to informally visit each other. They used to come to our house in Taylor, Michigan, often. They liked shopping in Detroit. There was a lot of choice and availability since the stores were bigger. At that time, we did not have Targets, Walmarts, etc. There were large stores, such as Montgomery Ward and Sears, Roebuck, and Company. We still have Sears. I think Montgomery Ward has been out of business for a long time now. These big stores came by and put the little stores out of business. In other words, there was no place for mom-and-pop or family-owned businesses. That's how the times changed right before our eyes. Like I said, I liked driving so much that despite the long distance, we used to go to Green Bay quite a bit. It was a seven- or eight-hour trip, I believe. Our kid and my brother-in-law's kids were growing up together. They liked to play football and baseball. We both had open-door policies and visited each other freely. We started to have common friends also. In Detroit, we used to shop at a market where we could get a variety of veggies as well as meat products normally not available in regular stores. For example, we used to get the *boati* of the lamb (intestines and other internals of the stomach). I did not personally like that stuff; however, my in-laws and Shakeera liked it, so we used to frequent this market and bring home these specialized items. In Taylor, we were on a dead-end street. I bought the house for about $26,000. It was a neat little house. We loved it. However, eventually, I made a decision with Shakeera to move to Wisconsin, particularly to the Green Bay area.

At this point, let us take a break to complete the ritual you must have become accustomed to by now. That is, we will test ourselves on what was happening in the world at that time.

1. The world celebrated Earth Day, which is now celebrated in 192 countries each year. Worldwide support for environmental protection of the earth is demonstrated in this event.
2. Four students were killed at Kent State University during a Vietnam War protest.
3. US troops invaded Cambodia.
4. The Supreme Court ruled unanimously that the busing of students could be ordered to achieve racial desegregation.
5. An earthquake killed more than fifty thousand in Peru.
6. Egyptian president Nasser passed away and was replaced by Anwer El-Sadat.
7. IBM introduced the floppy disk.

While I was at Great Lakes Steel, we recognized that the steel coming from Japan was good in quality. The automobile companies in Detroit started buying steel from Japanese companies. We faced big competition. Japanese steel was not only cheaper but also of better quality. The steel industry in the United States was facing a big challenge. Our mill equipment was becoming obsolete, and several lines had to be phased out. We needed to invest in new state-of-the-art mills. This took lots of capital. The trade unions were strong, and they settled for good wage increases every year. This did not help the case. Therefore, it was obvious they had to lay off quite a bit of people in order to stay competitive. The government increased the tariffs for the imported steel. It still was hard for this country to keep up with the foreign imports. Ford Motor Company manufactured their own steel at the biggest industrial complex in the States, River Rouge Complex. Tours of this plant were available, and I, along with friends and relatives, was able to tour the facility. I think our company sold steel coils to General Motors. I think General Motors themselves had a plant called McLouth Steel. At that time, US Steel in Gary, Indiana, was the largest steel mill. Pittsburgh was known as the center of steel manufacturing. After US Steel, the Bethlehem Mill in Pennsylvania was the second largest. Then came the Republic Steel Mill. The steel industry was considered the backbone of the economy in the United States. For various reasons that I do not want to go through here, it started declining; lots of mills were shut down, and quite a few people were laid off. For me, that job was okay. I got along well with people. I worked reasonably well on my assignments and projects. But I also became uneasy about what was happening with the industry. As time passed, I had the urge to get out of that industry and go into something else. It looked as if I had labeled myself to be working in a manufacturing concern or a mill.

As time went on, Shakeera and I planned for more kids. We missed India. We could have a taste of India by mingling with our Indian friends and talking about home. There were some Indian restaurants and stores. We missed the Bollywood movies. Once in a while, in the Ford Auditorium, we used to see an Indian movie. This was a rare occasion. Also, one time, Mohammad Rafi came to town and gave a performance. We went to the concert. It was highly enjoyable.

At this point, I have a pop quiz for you. What world events occurred in 1972?

1. God's blessing was showered upon us in the form of a baby girl.
2. President Nixon made an unprecedented visit to Communist China and met with Mao Zedong.
3. Eleven Israeli athletes at the Olympic games in Munich were killed after eight members of an Arab terrorist group invaded the Olympic village.
4. The Academy Award for best Hollywood picture went to *The French Connection*.
5. Arthur Bremer shot Governor George Wallace at a political rally.

Yes, our princess was born on February 29, 1972. Shakeera and I prayed to God with happiness and were thankful. I think our prayers were answered, as we wanted to have a girl. In the immediate family, no baby girl had been born for a while. Sajida came to Detroit to help us, and we were grateful. Shakeeb was thrilled to have a younger sister. You should have seen the happiness on the faces of Mazy (Shariff's son) and Shakeeb when she was brought home from the hospital. It was a joyful time.

When Farah was still a baby, we planned a trip to Washington, DC. Bhai Saheb and I took turns driving and went out east for a week or so. We saw all the important landmarks of Washington, DC, and had a blast. Another time, from Detroit, we went to Niagara Falls for a short visit. We had visited Niagara Falls before with our friends Ghani, Hamid, and Alla Uddin. It is stunning to see the falls from different points. At one point, we were so close to the falls that there was an enormous mist from the falls, and sightseers were encouraged to wear raincoats and cover themselves well. There is an American side and also a Canadian side of the falls.

Whenever we went to Green Bay, I explored the possibility of getting a job at the paper mills. Wisconsin is known for its paper production. At one time, 11 percent of all the paper produced in the country was made in Wisconsin. There were famous paper companies in Green Bay. I inquired with Ismail Shariff, and he told me that American Can Company was a good company. Soon after that, I applied at American Can Company. The name was misleading. Actually, it was a paper-manufacturing company, especially toilet paper, napkins, etc. I got an interview and eventually got the job. I think Sy Hirsch and other people interviewed me. It was a day job, and there were no shifts involved. My designation was project engineer. I was supposed to come up with the design of projects, which involved capital investments either to improve the process or speed up the paper machine. The company moved me from Detroit and paid all incidentals until I got settled in Green Bay. Green Bay is a football town, and at that time, I did not know anything about American football. Our house in Taylor, Michigan, was put on sale. I made sure the house was in order and everything worked okay before we put the place on sale. We were in that house for about five years. The house did not increase in value much in those five years. I reported to duty at American Can Company. In the beginning, I stayed with my brother-in-law. I was excited to have a job as a project engineer in a well-known company. Like I said, Wisconsin is well known for its paper mills. Right next to my company was the famous Proctor and Gamble Company, which made Charmin. If you are old enough, you must have watched the famous commercial of Mr. Whipple: "Don't squeeze the Charmin." Charmin toilet paper was so soft that the store manager in the commercial could not resist his temptation to squeeze it over and over again. This commercial was a big hit in those days. We all enjoyed it. Mr. Whipple became a celebrity soon after the commercial was aired in the late sixties or early seventies.

My daughter was still a baby when we moved to Green Bay. Shakeeb was a toddler. The sisters, Sajida and Shakeera, as well as the rest of us enjoyed each other's company. In those days, we used to play cards and used to bet small amounts of money to make things interesting. Ismail Shariff and Sajida got us interested in bridge also. I played it with interest for a while, but it was not my type of game. We played rummy, which was kind of interesting. Most of the time, we played the three-card game. In our language, we used to call it *teen patti*. Most friends of ours and Shariff's were hooked on this gambling. It was our main pastime. We used to go to other close-by towns to friends' houses, and we had the same activities over there. Sometimes we played so late in the night that we slept at the friend's house and drove back to Green Bay the next day. Dr. Shah, originally from Pakistan, used to travel in his airplane to different parts of the country to meet with his friends and play cards. He was a staunch teen patti card player. The other people I remember were Nisar, Majid, and Desai. We used to have picnics and get-togethers. We had a good time. Our good friends Tufail Niazi and family visited us in Green Bay. We bought a house on a corner lot on Libal Street in Green Bay, which was not far from Shariff's house. The house we picked was being constructed and was almost done, except for the choices on the interior of the house. I advise people not to do this if they do not have much time on their hands. It is fun but also a lot of headaches. You need to pick the color of the stain and what kind of switches you want in the house. Shakeera and I kept going to the builder almost every day to pick materials for the house. This way, you can build the house per your taste. You get emotional and cannot help overspending beyond the allowance from the builder.

Shakeeb started school at Doty School, where Mazy, the second son of Shariff, was. Shakeera and I were excited to see Shakeeb join the school. Green Bay was mostly a white community at that time. I was afraid we might be isolated in the neighborhood as people of color. For a while, Shakeera got interested in an Avon business. She would go door to door to demonstrate and sell Avon cosmetic products, mainly for women. I used to drive her in the evening hours and off days. She got a discount if she bought products from Avon. She enjoyed being an Avon lady for a while. Shakeera also worked as a quality-control person in a produce company for a while.

Working outside and making a career was not the main objective in life for Shakeera. She felt that if a mother works outside, it will take away her time and energy from the children, and she cannot completely devote her time to the children. It was not right, in her mind, to do that. My thoughts were different on the matter. Anyway, after some arguments, we decided she would not work outside the house until the children were grown up a little bit. Once that happened, she would then go to work outside. I think that's when she decided to do day care. I do not know if any certification or any such thing was required for a day-care provider. There might have been such a thing, but we did not look into it. Shakeera liked babysitting, and she started spending time doing that.

I had some interesting projects at American Can Company. Since paper machines are noisy, one of my projects was to purchase and install sound booths for the operators. I had some projects in the boiler room, such as replacing all the old instrument control panels to new ones. I worked on revising the drawings on the service water lines, natural gas lines, and compressed air lines in the plant. I designed pumping systems for adding colors to some specialty papers. I did steam balance for the mill. Steam balance is a way to find out how much steam is produced in the boilers, how and where it is used, and if there is any waste. Project requests came from anywhere in the mill. Also, we were working with outside consultants at times. There were some turnkey projects, or engineering projects in which the contractor takes responsibility of the project from start to finish and keeps the engineer abreast of the different phases of the project. There were several projects in which pumping and associated piping had to be designed. John Lawson was a friend of mine and was the team leader. I learned a lot at his mill as a project engineer. I learned how important paper drying is, what defects can take place in paper, what the important properties of napkins and tissue paper are, and what the digesters are. At one time, I asked the head of the pulp mill, which is an important part of the mill, "What are my expectations when I work on projects in the pulp mill area?"

Tom McDonald, the head of the pulp mill, replied, "All you need to do is keep me smiling." Obviously, he meant to do everything right and not cause any trouble. I kind of liked the way he put it. I worked on several projects at the same time. Different projects were at different stages of completion and different magnitudes.

Jim Fox, my boss, was a hard taskmaster. He was particular about the accuracy of a given project. There were three draftsmen in the engineering department. The other engineers and I gave them a sketch of the project design, and they created detailed working drawings. Finally, the project went for the construction phase with the approval of the engineers who designed it as well as the department head who sponsored the project. This was the usual setup. The construction supervision either by the contractors or the mill craftsman was also part of my responsibility. I learned a lot in that mill about the process as well as project engineering aspects. One thing is for sure: when you are dealing with other people (project sponsors), you do not have much room for experimenting or not doing something right the first time. This was a lot of responsibility on the shoulders of the engineer. The pressure of work made me bring work home and sometimes go to the office on Saturdays and holidays.

During this time in my life, some other events happened in the world. Let me quiz you on those. If these were before your time, you can dig and learn from them.

1. Three major countries entered the European Economic Community. Name those countries.

2. A US president accepted on national TV responsibility for a scandal and accepted the resignation of his advisers. Name the president and the advisers.

3. US bombing of a country in Southeast Asia ended after twelve years of combat activity in the region. What was the name of the country?

4. _____ of Michigan was sworn in as president of the United States, and he granted full, free, and absolute pardon to an ex-president, _____. Fill in the blanks.

For answers to these questions and much more, please read the following chapters.

CHAPTER 4

Journey through God's Country

Our kids were young while we were in Green Bay. They grew up with my brother-in-law's kids. The town was good, people were nice, and my career was good. I became a citizen of this country by giving up citizenship of India. Needless to say, this was an emotional move on my part. I still had several relatives in India, and I had lots of memories. Anyway, after much debate, I chose to become a citizen. I read books on the Constitution and the form and branches of government in the United States and got well prepared for the interview. I went with two of our American friends (well, the man was originally from India, and he married an American woman) to Milwaukee, Wisconsin, and got sworn in as a citizen of the United States. While they were in the immigration office, they were interviewed separately, as was required at that time. As American citizens, they gave us a "Let them in" recommendation. We thanked this couple a lot and returned home. My friends became my references. The advantages of becoming a citizen far outweighed immigrant status. You could buy property as an immigrant, but you could not entirely benefit from the system in lots of different ways. In the beginning, for me, immigration problems were of the highest priority. It felt good and secure to be a citizen. We thought both of us should become citizens; however, my wife owned some property in India, and we were not sure if we could hold property if both of us became citizens. Therefore, only I became a citizen; she remained a citizen of India, our birth country.

When we first came to Wausau, we stayed in an apartment. There was a drive-in theater near the apartment. For those of you who do not know what a drive-in theater is, it is an outdoor theater with a big screen, and cars needed to park by a post with a speaker mounted on it. When you park your car next to this post, you take the speaker inside your car and watch the movie from your car. I think sometimes there were heaters too. However, these outdoor theaters were fun mostly in the summertime. Soon enough, it was time for us to look for a house. Our house in Green Bay was for sale, and the company that hired me in Wausau, Weyerhaeuser, took care of all the incidental expenses. The arrangement was that you'd try to sell the house on your own, and if it did not sell within a reasonable amount of time, the company would buy it for the market price. This was a fair deal for the person they wanted to hire.

Wausau is a beautiful small town in the central part of Wisconsin. Some people referred to Wausau and its surroundings as God's country. There were lots of pine trees all around. Some people said they were part of the plantations of some paper companies. There was a lot of industry in town. The paper industry thrived, as there was plenty of wood, and there was a river flowing through. Weyerhaeuser Company owned and operated a hydroelectric dam and produced electric power for use in the mill. The paper industry is an energy-intensive industry. There were several boilers, which produced steam. The steam was used to heat the plant, dry the paper being manufactured, and produce electric power using turbines.

At this point, let us address the questions presented at the end of chapter 3.

1. Great Britain, Ireland, and Denmark
2. President Nixon and advisers H. R. Haldeman and John Ehrickman
3. Cambodia
4. Gerald Ford and Richard Nixon

At Weyerhaeuser Company, I was charged with many challenging projects, including ash collection silo modification for the wood boiler, hydraulic dumping of the truck trailers for emptying the chip loads, modification of the paper machine drives, energy conservation projects, coordination of the state inspection of boilers, boiler tube repairs and replacements, and hydraulic turbine repairs. All of the projects were capital improvement projects as well as projects to maintain the functionality or increase the efficiency of mill operations. I learned a lot from handling these projects from conception to the final startup. By mentioning these projects, I want to give you a little flavor of how I spent my time at the company. This was the time when gradually, mainframe computers were being phased out and replaced by personal computers. We used to use Lotus 123, Fortran IV, and other databases. We were learning about spreadsheets and how we could use formulas and calculations on the spreadsheets. It was a powerful tool for making reports, analysis, and problem solving. I also worked with statistical programs. Statistical analysis was given a lot of importance in my work. I have been always interested in learning computers. Even when the stuff first came out, I used to go to stores to learn the computer by playing around at the display units. I hooked up a unit to the TV, as was done several years ago, and the modem made some extra-terrestrial noises before the connection was established. This was the pre-Internet era. I took courses at the university on Fortran IV and graphics. In those courses, we learned how to develop flow charts before we wrote the program. Also, we learned the programming language.

While in Rothschild, Wisconsin, I applied for jobs at other Weyerhaeuser mills. I attended quite a few trade shows and expos to learn more about the trade. Notable among the trade shows were the plant engineering shows and expos at McCormick Place in Chicago. There was a lot to see and learn, and we could take home ideas to apply in our own mill. As far as the other quests in my career, I made trips to Everett, Washington; Longview, Washington; Oklahoma; Georgia; Boston, Massachusetts; Virginia Beach; and more. I was fortunate to be able to travel to all these places at the company's expense. I expanded my horizons by looking at operations at the other mills. I liked the state of Washington for its scenic beauty. I drove by miles and miles of trees lying down like toothpicks after the eruption of

Mount St. Helens, which I believe happened in 1980. I was awestruck to imagine and feel the power of nature. I visited the museum dedicated to the volcano and was impressed. I saw the film about this volcanic eruption of Mount St. Helens several times.

Now let's have a break to ponder some questions *Jeopardy* style. Are you ready to play?

- The Summer Olympics were held in this city in the mid-seventies. The estimated cost was $310 million to stage the games. However, security concerns and other issues raised the cost to $1.5 billion.
- The games were stolen by this teenage Romanian gymnast. She scored seven perfect tens on her way to winning three gold medals.
- This country's airborne commandos attacked Uganda's Entebbe Airport and freed 103 hostages held by pro-Palestinian hijackers on an Air France plane.
- A little member of our family started schooling at Evergreen Elementary in Kronenwetter, a suburb of Wausau. Needless to say, we were all excited.

I will give you the answers in the next few pages.

Wausau was named a Great American City in those days. I do not know what criteria the city was judged on or who made the decision. I do not recall which other cities in Wisconsin were named this way. If I am not mistaken, Madison was also named a Great American City. A member of our family migrated from India to America while we were in Wausau. He'd always wanted to come to America to make a good life for his family, especially the three kids he had at the time. I am talking about my younger brother Asif. Asif and I have been close all our lives. I missed him a lot while I was in this country for thirteen years. Needless to say, I was thrilled to see him here in the United States. He had a good job at the university in Bangalore, India. He could have come to this country a lot earlier, but he waited because he wanted to come as an immigrant, not as a student. This makes life easier, obviously. My brother's wife, Nasreen, came to this country after about a year or so. Like everybody else, Asif had to try different jobs in the beginning and finally took a state government job at the University of Wisconsin. Along with his many jobs, he worked at Weyerhaeuser in Rothschild, where I used to work, before he moved to Madison, Wisconsin, to take the job with the University of Wisconsin. I was glad that everything worked out well for him after that.

Asif's and my kids are about the same age. They all went to DC Everest High School in Weston, Wisconsin. We were blessed to experience a good life in Wausau. Both of my children were athletically inclined. Our son, Shakeeb, excelled in track and other sports. He was good in field events. One year, he was a Frisbee champion. He also excelled in his academic achievements. In connection with a big event for the school, one of the local restaurants on the main street of Wausau encouraged Shakeeb by displaying his name on a big banner in view of the main road traffic. DC Everest High School was a famous school in the area. These claims to fame led Shakeeb to become a star player on the football team for the school. He started in several games. Shakeera and I encouraged him every step of the way in his sports. Of course, we agreed that only if he did well in his academia could he do the sports and athletics. We had no doubt he was doing excellent in school. Shakeeb also played soccer and baseball. In football, he played wide receiver and running back. In soccer, he played the center forward mostly and other positions too. We took him to all the games and events outside of Wausau, to towns as far as Eau Clair, I believe. Like they say, "All work and no play makes Jack a dull boy." We were fortunate and blessed by God that both of our kids are hardworking even today at the time of the writing of this book. My daughter also was an exceptional athlete in high school. We attended all their games and events and encouraged them to excel. May God bless both of them and reward them for the hard work they do.

At this point in time, let's refer back to the questions I posed a little while ago.

- What is Montreal, Canada?
- Who was Nadia Comaneci?
- What was Israel?
- Who is our daughter (Beati) Farah Deeba Rahman?

I had several challenging projects at Weyerhaeuser Company. I completed them successfully, on time, and within budget, and my work was appreciated. I got promoted to a higher step in project engineering. I was always on the lookout for bigger and better opportunities. I used to visit other mills to study similar projects they had running. One time, Jim Hampton, my boss, and I visited a paper mill in Park Falls, Wisconsin, called Flambeau Paper Mill. At that time, I did not know that in a few years, I would be the head of the utilities department at that mill.

While in Wausau, Shakeera and I became interested in owning some rental property to supplement our regular income. Shakeera, from time to time, did childcare at home. We purchased a duplex on Alderson Street in Rothschild or Wausau. My first renters were my bother Asif and Dillu, my brother-in-law. The house in Alderson had lots of problems. It had a flat roof, oil furnace, and septic system. The fumes from the oil furnace were bad for the tenants. The flat roof was a problem in a northern location like Wausau. Snow, as it accumulates on the roof, can seep through the ceiling into the rooms as it melts. It has no way to flow away, as there is no slope to the roof. Also, I think one time, the septic system backed up through the floor drains in the house. This was a big mess, as you can imagine. Therefore, we decided to sell the house back to the seller, who was a real estate agent in Wausau. After some discussion back and forth, he agreed to buy the house back. After this venture, we bought a duplex in Weston, on Camp Philips Road. I wanted to live on one side and make enough money off of it to pay for the mortgage. However, there was disagreement between Shakeera and me, and we rented the place. Asif's family rented half of the duplex from us.

People at work who knew about this asked me, "Do you charge money from your brother for rent?"

I said, "Of course, guys. I have to pay the mortgage. I am not my brother's keeper anyway."

Well, at this point, let's examine what happened in the world around that year. Consider this trivia.

1. Snow fell in a city in the southern United States for the first and only time. What city was that?
2. What gentleman from the South succeeded Gerald Ford as the president of United States?
3. Fiber optics was first used to carry live what traffic?
4. General Muhammad Zia-ul-Haq overthrew the first elected prime minister of Pakistan. What was his name?
5. A family member from India immigrated to the United States. Who was that?
6. An English-born comedian passed away. What was his name?
7. A horrific and gruesome thing took place in Guyana. Do you remember what happened?

I will let you think about this and give answers after a while as you read through my story.

We made several good friends in Wausau. Several were the parents of my kids' friends. There was a family from Hyderabad, Dr. Akhtar Hussain and Malik Taj. Then there were Ajit Chowdry and Swapna, V. J. Narahari and Nalini, Deepak Gandhi, Hugh and Diana Jones, Barbara and Leo Todd, and Rashid and Saadqa. At work, I was friends with Jim Hampton and Ken Geogh. Also, Ajit Kumar from Green Bay used to come to the Wausau mill for some projects. In Stevens Point were our friends Chandar and Jyoti. In Appleton, we had friends like Majid and Nasreen, to name a few. We used to get together quite a bit. We used to play cards, watch wrestling and other sports, arrange picnics, and go swimming. We used to sing Bollywood songs and tell jokes. We all had good times and got along well.

While at Rothschild or Wausau, I was offered a job at a Longview, Washington, paper plant. There was a good raise included, and they were going to buy my house in Wausau and finance my move in every way. This was a good deal. I consulted with my brothers, close relatives, and friends. Dick Paliki, my manager at the Rothschild plant told me, "If you decide to go there, you will start with a clean slate. You will have a chance to excel and prove yourself."

Jim Hampton said, "It will be warmer over there than in Wisconsin." Some people said it would be gloomy and rainy most of the time in the state of Washington.

At that time, Shakeeb was new at a college in Michigan. He was in the field, which he liked. I tried to get him to co-op in other companies out west. Farah was doing okay at her schoolwork in Wausau, and she had made some close friends in Wisconsin. While considering moving, I took Farah, who was a teenager at that time, to the Pacific Northwest and showed her around. Shakeera and Farah did not encourage me either way. They left it up to me to make the decision. It was a career move. However, it meant moving the family more than halfway across the country. My first thought was *I like the job, the place, and the people, so why not accept the job?* And I did. At that time, I did not know what to do. I could not think straight. I was not happy with the decision, but at the same time, I was excited. Due to the "What if?" questions in my mind, I could not sleep properly. I told Shakeera, "I am the only one who wants to go. I should not go and take the family over there. If the other people in the family are not excited, what good is it for me to move in this direction?"

I thought about the whole thing deeply, and within three or four days, what I did will surprise you. Asif was in Madison at that time. I visited Madison and had a meeting with Dillu, my brother-in-law, who was also visiting there, and my brother Asif. Nobody would say what I should do. I had to make my own decision. I had accepted the job already at Weyerhaeuser's Longview mill. For years, I'd wanted to move to a warmer climate, which I thought was available there. I studied the pros and cons of the move. I felt moving the family that far would isolate me. I was not open-minded about it all. In life, it is best to make decisions by taking time to study all the possible consequences. Once one has made a decision, one has to stick to it no matter what happens. This is true in most situations.

CHAPTER 5

The Northwoods of Wisconsin

I became the victim of indecision. This was one situation in which I could not think straight at all, and there were no elders or wise guys who would lead me to make this hard decision. I'd stayed in Rothschild with the same paper mill where I was for about eleven years. During those days in my career, I had trusted certain people to give me a good reference. One of them was Jim McGinnity. He always trusted me to be a good engineer. Jim called me one day and said, "Hey, Mohammad, how about coming to Park Falls, where we can offer you a managerial position at the mill? We have an opening for the job of manager of utilities. Think about it, and let me know."

Jim and I met at a bar in Tomahawk, which was halfway between Wausau and Park Falls. We had a detailed discussion about the job offer. I asked several questions. At the end of our meeting, I was confident about the job.

Needless to say, I was delighted at his offer. He sent me a letter stating the position's responsibilities and salary. It looked good to me. He also offered a substantial signing bonus. All this seemed nice and attractive to me. I trusted Jim as a buddy of mine since he was at Rothschild. I debated in my mind what I should do. At that particular time, I was working in a process engineer position at Rothschild. I was learning a lot. I was pursuing new avenues in the process-engineering field. I was getting good experience in the utilities field and also in water chemistry. My performance evaluations noted that my next logical move would be to become a manager of engineering of some sort. I'd always longed to be a manager. I knew it was not much use to discuss the decision with Shakeera. As always, she would say, "It is all up to you. I will support you in whatever decision you make."

In the meantime, my position at the Rothschild mill was shaken up a little bit, as I was fickle-minded about my Longview move. I was still regretting not taking the position at the Longview, Washington, mill. Was it the right decision for wrong reasons, the wrong decision for wrong reasons, the wrong decision for right reasons, or what?

I knew that Park Falls was a small town. Also, it was in the northern part of Wisconsin, where the winters could get much harsher, and the snow piles could get much higher compared to central Wisconsin, where I was. After much thought, I ended up accepting the position at Park Falls. I trusted Jim McGinnity. Jim was a good friend of Ajit Kumar, who was also a friend of mine. Ajit was working for Jim at the Park Falls mill and seemed to be happy there. He had a house on Butternut Lake. Unlike Schnur's Lake, Butternut Lake was not a private lake. There were quite a few public landings into the lake. I called Ibrahim Syed, a friend and relative of mine in Louisville, Kentucky. He told me over the phone, "Hey, guy, you are moving in the wrong direction. People from India should be moving south, not north."

I realized later on that Ibrahim was right. Park Falls can be counted as one of the winter wonderlands of Wisconsin, or it can be called a frozen tundra.

It is time for me now to answer the questions I laid out toward the end of chapter 4.

1. Miami, Florida
2. Jimmy Carter
3. Telephone traffic
4. Zulfikar Ali Bhutto

5. Asif, who came to the United States in 1977, first to Detroit to Anwar, my younger brother
6. Charlie Chaplin
7. Reverend Jim Jones influenced a group of people to go with him to make a new home in the South American nation of Guyana. He had good control over his people. He asked them to build new homes in the jungle for themselves. It was hot in the area, and they worked long hours. He held these people against their will. Word started spread, and the media started to criticize what he was doing. A US congressman named Leo Ryan wanted to see for himself what was happening there. He, after investigating what was happening, wanted to take some people out of the compound to freedom. But he was shot and killed. Jim Jones knew that some people had left the compound. He told people in the temple, "Now that the congressman has been killed, the US government will react aggressively against us. They will kill our innocent babies." He had a chemical liquid prepared—enough to serve one thousand people—made with grape juice, cyanide, and valium, and he served everybody and told them not to drink yet. He had installed a loudspeaker to address his followers. He summoned everybody to come close to where his mike was. More than nine hundred men, women, and children gathered. He gave them a lecture about how and why they should be ready to leave this world. He asked them to drink from the cups they all had been served. As soon as they drank the quick-acting poison, they fell on their faces, dead. There were altogether 918 victims, and of them, 276 were children. Jim Jones himself did not drink the poison. He was found dead with a single shot to his head, killed either by himself or some of his men. This breaking news shook up the whole world, and no one could digest it for a while.

At the Park Falls mill, I had tremendous responsibility on my shoulders. The utility department was one of the most crucial departments of the mill. I was to oversee the operation of four hydroelectric dams that provided power to the mill. The mill had a wood-burning boiler and four natural gas–burning boilers. The entire budget of the department was under my control. Every week, I needed to make a presentation about the state of the department to the executives of the mill. This was a highly visible position and was a big challenge for me. Goals were set, and if everything ran according to the plan, I was okay. Sometimes you are bound to fall short of a plan. Things break down unexpectedly, and you need to allocate some funds to repair the situation. I was responsible for providing utilities to the mill in the most economical way. Everything was looked upon in a measurable context. The budgets were tight. The production department was unforgiving. On top of all this, I was responsible for maintaining the environmental standards. Park Falls was a town of about three thousand people. Most everybody in the town was watching the mill's stack. We were responsible for what we emitted out of the stack of the boilers. There was a local DNR (Department of Natural Resources) office in Park Falls. Somebody in that office used to watch our boiler stack all the time. If black smoke came out of the stack once in a while, they used to call us and ask us to check and correct it. Most of the time, the scrubber, a device that washes the flue gases before they are emitted, was not working properly. Sometimes there was trouble in the fuel ratio. The mill was close to residential areas, and some of the homeowners complained that our stack gases colored the siding of their houses. It seemed we were always under the microscope. It was a big challenge, and all the fingers pointed toward us. Eventually, the buck stopped with me. The operations supervisor, Dave Wagner, was on top of things most of the time. There were several decisions to be made on a given day. The boiler operators were efficient and good. However, they were not paid to make decisions.

The state government required that we perform stack emission tests on the boiler stack and comply with only a certain amount of pollutants emitted into the atmosphere. We hired certain companies who would do the test and make a report. Other considerations were sulfur dioxide in the coal and associated acid rain problems. I just wanted to give you the flavor of the environmental regulations we needed to comply with in that job.

Also, I was responsible for production and distribution of electric power to the mill. There were four hydroelectric dams within the jurisdiction of the mill. The equipment in the dams was old and outdated. These were small power plants. The height of the water in the reservoir ahead of the dam and after the dam determines the head of water, which makes a difference in the amount of electricity made. We normally used to keep a record of the water level in the flowage upstream of the upper dam. People liked to fish in the reservoir. The floodgates of the dam had to be adjusted to keep the level in the reservoir in control. Our department was also in charge of the transmission lines for transmission of power from the generators to the final use points in the mill.

Another important aspect of hydroelectric dams is the safety of the structure and operations of the dam itself. For example, when the floodgates have to be opened again after being fully or partially closed for maintenance or some issue downstream, the public has to be notified. A federal government department inspected the four dams we had on a regular basis. An inspector from the Federal Energy Regulatory Commission used to visit and inspect the dams once a year. An inspection report was generated, and we kept track of the repairs or whatever was flagged in the report. The public uses the dam facility and the associated land, river, and reservoir for recreational purposes, such as canoeing, fishing, and hiking. I was not aware of this, but the hydroelectric dams were supposed to be operated under license from the federal government. This license was supposed to be renewed every thirty to fifty years. Our four dams were up for license renewal during my tenure as the manager of utilities there. We hired a company called Mead and Hunt from Madison, Wisconsin, to get our license renewed. Mead and Hunt assigned Ashok Rajpal for this task. Ashok and I went to work to tackle the enormous task of applying for the license renewal of the four dams. At that time, our paper company was called Flambeau Paper Mill. The license-renewal project was a time consuming and extensive project that involved lots of surveys, data collection, meetings with the city, and meetings with several public organizations and tribal leaders. A hydroelectric dam effects all the people who live nearby. The distance from Park Falls to Madison was about four hours, but Ashok and his team used to fly from Madison to Park Falls in a small company plane. Normally, I picked them up from the airport and drove them wherever they needed to come to Park Falls. Jokingly, I used to call my help Park Falls Limousine Service. We asked the dam tenders to record the activities where and how people used the dam facilities. Also, we counted the bald eagles that visited the trees in the vicinity of the dam. This might sound boring, but somebody had to do it. It was all part of the deal. Hydropower facilities are some of the most regulated facilities by both the federal and state governments. Usually, if the owners comply with the federal regulations, they will automatically comply with the state. We used the media to notify the public about the water flows and environmental issues. It was a visible process. It usually takes a couple of years to complete all the studies. It was an interesting project. I enjoyed it. However, I still had the responsibilities of running the utility department of the mill. They also brought Ed Kruel to the department to carry a certain load. At that point, there was a power struggle in the department. I am not going to talk about the details here, but some people were aggressive. They would walk all over other people, and with a little bit of support from the management, you know what happens.

As I said, my family did not like it in Park Falls, and I was overwhelmed in the job. There was tension building up. Bob Byrne, my boss, had a tendency to yield to the politics within the departments. Also, I must say that Park Falls was an all-American town. Some people in the mill told me that if a nonwhite person came to town, he would be forced somehow to leave town within forty-eight hours. There was an incident I would like to share with you here. I had a new Bronco car in those days. One day I saw that a large vehicle had hit the front end of my car, and I don't think it was an ordinary car. It could have been a front-end loader or a bulldozer. I wanted to investigate further. I called a meeting, but some union people said, "Are you accusing us of purposely hitting your van?" Anyway, I read the writing on the wall and slowly started to plan to leave Park Falls. This was a big decision. I was going full gear with my job. I'd fulfilled a dream for myself and the family by purchasing a late-model Cadillac. We all liked it. It was loaded with optional equipment. We had a house on a private lake. My children and friends liked this house. Shakeera and I took extra pain in furnishing and decorating it. My brother Altaf and his wife, Sabiha, from India visited this place and liked it. We purchased a small boat and went sailing in the boat often. We used paddles to propel the boat. We had a pier, which was installed in the water right in front of the house. It had to be taken out every winter and installed again during the onset of warmer weather. During one fall, our friends Rashid Ahmad, Sadqa, Ilyas, and Azra came over and enjoyed the place. We had great times there. However, Shakeera and I were thinking that this place, as great as it was, was not for us. I started thinking hard. I definitely wanted to move out of there. That was the best for the family. But before I tell you what happened, let me take a break from the story, and we will examine what happened in the world while all this was happening in my life. I would like to cover these facts in a fast-forward manner, as so much happened during that time. I do not want to go into details but will just mention the highlights here. Just a note that most of the following historic events took place between 1979 and about 2001 I believe.

1. Mother Teresa of India was awarded the Noble Peace Prize.
2. Iran's Ayatollah Khomeini declared the United States "the great Satan of the world."
3. An Islamic revolutionary group in Iran overthrew Mohammad Reza Shah Pahelvi's government.
4. Shah died in 1980.
5. An eight-year war between Iraq and Iran began.
6. Ronald Reagan was elected president of the United States.
7. Bangladesh president Ziaur Rahman was assassinated in Chittagong.
8. Hosni Mubarak was elected president of Egypt one week after Anwar Sadat was assassinated.
9. A major nuclear accident occurred at Chernobyl, near Ukraine.
10. George Bush was inaugurated as president of the United States.
11. Iraq invaded and seized Kuwait, creating a major international crisis.
12. The Department of Energy announced plans to increase oil production and decrease consumption to counter Iraqi-Kuwaiti oil losses.
13. President Bush declared the end of the Cold War as the Soviet Union collapsed.
14. Michael Jackson's *Thriller* sold twenty million copies to become the largest-selling album ever.

15. Sally Ride became the first American woman in space. (We used to say, "Sally Ride—what a ride.")
16. Indira Gandhi, prime minister of India, was assassinated.
17. The space shuttle *Challenger* exploded.
18. The stock market dropped 22 percent. The Dow Jones Industrial Average fell 508 points.
19. I was offered a job at the Longview, Washington, mill of the Weyerhaeuser Company.
20. The Soviets left Afghanistan.
21. Benazir Bhutto was the first woman to head the Islamic nation of Pakistan.
22. Salman Rushdie was wanted dead by Iranian leader Khomeini. (Rushdie is the author of the book *The Satanic Verses*.)
23. Burma changed its name to Myanmar.
24. The Iran Contra affair took place. Ronald Reagan was the president of the United States at the time.

All of the above historical events affected our lives in one way or another. While we were in Park Falls, we heard the news of the death of an extended family member in India. He was a good friend of mine. He had a good sense of humor, and we criticized each other in a positive way. We liked to be in each other's company quite a bit and grew up together during our formative years. He was a modern, smart, and sportive guy. He represented the university in soccer and was a star player. Later on, he turned very religious, grew a beard, and came to this country for Islamic conferences. I am talking here with much grief about my favorite cousin, Mumtaz. When I first came to the University of Wisconsin, I looked for ways to get him into the university. I think, if I am not mistaken, there was no curriculum for veterinary science in those days at the University of Wisconsin. I was surprised to see that. Later on in his life, he was against his own brothers going abroad, especially to the USA. His philosophy about this country was not great. However, after a long while, he might have changed his thoughts about this country, as he himself came here about two times. His brother Parveez has been in Virginia Beach, where he visited. Parveez arranged for me and Mumtaz to be able to talk on the phone while he was ill. We had a sad and emotional talk. That was the last time I talked to Mumtaz. May Allah (SWT) rest his soul in peace and place him in Janna. We all miss him very much.

One day during those days, I stopped at the US Forest Service office in Park Falls. A young guy helped me look up some jobs available at the Forest Service offices throughout the nation. Not being familiar with government jobs, I was not sure what was available and how to assess them. The guy explained everything. He was helpful. This effort changed my life from that point on. I was intense in my search for a federal government job. With my kind of experience, I thought I should be able to land a job quickly, but it was not easy. I also applied to state jobs. One time, I went to Hayward in northeastern Wisconsin, where I applied for a State of Wisconsin job in the department of natural resources. I was intense in my efforts to make a switch. The young guy at the Park Falls office also informed me that there would be a big meeting of executives at the Park Falls office of the Forest Service, and a large number of bigwigs would be coming to town. He said, "This will be a big opportunity for you to introduce yourself and talk to them and state what you are seeking."

I met two executives: one from San Dimas, California, and another one from Missoula, Montana. Both men explained the nature of the job and the geography of the place to me in detail. Both places had their own merits and demerits. However, after much thought, in my mind, I chose California. I explored the place a little bit more. At that point in time, I did not explore any further about the job in Montana. I was more or less attracted to the weather in California. However, also, the job seemed to be interesting. I kept in touch with the gentleman from San Dimas, California. One day, while I was seeking to complete my application for the California job, I received a call from the executive.

"Would you be interested in staying in Wisconsin and applying for a job in Madison, Wisconsin?"

All these events were happening at a fast pace. Moving to Madison seemed less stressful to me. I told the gentleman from the Forest Service, "Yes, I will be happy to pursue this further."

I did apply for that job. I thanked the two gentlemen for taking time from their busy schedules to talk to me. Applying for federal government jobs was not easy in those days. I had to collect all my certificates, documents of qualifications, and references. I completed the application. As with anything, a complete application will serve a better purpose. It was a time-consuming process. I was determined, though. In some private companies, they hire a headhunter or a staffing company to hire engineers, but I found out that in the government, department executives do all the work of checking references, etc. In my case, my future boss who interviewed me told me I had good references. I finally got the job, and it was at a higher scale than I'd expected. The Forest Service took care of all my incidental expenses for our move from Park Falls to Madison. Actually, I had two houses to be moved from. We still had our house in Wausau and our house in Park Falls. I sold the house in Park Falls on my own. The only expense I had to pay was hiring a real estate guy to do the paperwork for the sale. At one point, I thought of keeping the house in Park Falls. It was a full-year house but also qualified as a cottage since it was on a lake with nice, peaceful surroundings. Shakeera and I thought it was not practical to keep the place. As a second thought, it occurred to me at that time that I would have easily kept the place as a vacation home. We would have enjoyed it.

Shakeera was busy in Wausau, getting rid of a few things we did not want to move to Madison. She sold quite a few items in Park Falls too. Shakeera likes to throw away stuff. One of the neighbors told us, "I want to be around when Shakeera moves, as she throws away a lot of things. Her junk could become my treasure."

My thoughts are different in this context. We collect items over the years and enjoy them, and it is hard to get rid of them just like that. You develop a certain sentimental attachment to these things. A few items will also have an antique value too. Anyway, Shakeera either sold or junked several household items both in Wausau and in Park Falls. We rented a U-Haul van to move stuff from Park Falls to Madison. Shakeeb helped me move the stuff from the Park Falls house. Asif also came over to help. We stayed in an apartment in Middleton for a while. Middleton is a small city next door to Madison. When Asif first came to Madison, he used to stay in an apartment near Lake Mendota of Madison. At that time, Shakeeb was pursuing his studies at the General Motors Technical and Management Institute in Michigan. I think Farah moved to Madison with us.

The job at Forest Products Laboratory was good and challenging. I felt secure with the federal government job. At that point, we needed to sell our house in Wausau. The real estate values in Wausau had not gone up much. Like they say, there is a buyer for every house. The buyer who purchased our house in Wausau wanted to have a ten-year mechanical and structural warranty from us. The house was in good shape, with only a few problems, including an ice dam formation on the roof in winter. Shakeeb and I used to go up to the roof to try to break the ice dam. The ice dam usually occurred at the edge of the roof. It was not an easy job. Sometimes we got up on the roof and cleared the snow accumulation. If it was not for Beta Shakeeb, I could not have done it. It was a risky job. A guy could slip and fall about twenty feet or so. It would not be a pleasant experience. There were lots of pine trees around the house. The sunlight did not reach the roof adequately to cause the snow to melt. At one time, we took a little snow blower on top of the roof to blow out the snow. This should not be done ever, as it could damage the roof shingles. Also, I learned that a good layer of snow on the roof would act as insulation for the house. My idea in those days was to do things myself. We probably could have had somebody's services for the various jobs we did around the house. We were young and took pride in working around the house on various projects and saving money. In our Green Bay house as well as our Wausau house, one of the projects was to finish the basement. Lots of homeowners did it on their own at that time and bragged that they'd finished their basement on their own. It was a big show-off item for quite a few of the men who owned their homes. In doing so, I learned carpentry, electrical work, insulation work, and more.

Another problem we had with the house in Wausau was the septic tank. It was a big several-gallon concrete tank buried in the backyard. All the sewage from the house was directed to it by pipes. It needed to be emptied out once a year at least. All of the houses in the area were equipped with septic tanks and drain fields. The window air conditioners were common in those days. I fitted one in our bedroom. Soon after that, we found out that the whole house could be cooled by a central air-conditioning system. As you can tell, I have backtracked a little bit here to explain the problems in the house in Wausau. In my estimate, no house I owned had as many problems as that house in Kronenwetter.

Several times, I climbed into the attic space and checked if the insulation was okay. We had to be careful in the attic, as there was only a crawl space in some parts. I learned that a house has to breathe properly. There should be proper airflow in and out of the house. Some people suggested attic fans for this purpose. I just wanted to share with you the number of problems we had in this house. This house was built from the ground up from scratch. The basement was a block basement rather than a poured basement. We finished the basement by hiring a fellow who worked on the house when it was built. I was handy—or played handy—in those days. We wallpapered the bathrooms, the master bedroom, and some other rooms in the house. We installed a wood-burning fireplace in the basement to supplement the regular forced-air furnace. The wood needed to be stored close to the furnace. The biggest problem was bringing the wood into the basement. We did not have an access door to the basement, as some houses had. We did not even think about it when we built the house. I think they call it a walk-out or daylight basement. Therefore, the easiest way of bringing wood from outside into the basement was through one of the basement windows. We used the window closest to the furnace. This way, several cords of wood were stored in the basement near the wood-burning fireplace. There were centipedes and other insects in the house, especially in the basement due to the stack of wood stored there.

The drain field was also an issue. The drain field refers to a bunch of pipes that extend into the yard from the concrete septic tank, thus discharging the water portion of the septic system into the soil. There was a vent installed on this system, which smelled like human sewage sometimes. We were supposed to put some chemicals into the toilet bowls to avoid some of the trouble. Based on that house, I learned never to buy a house with all these problems, especially a septic tank. At the time of this writing, though, several expensive houses are built on the outskirts of the city, where no city sewer and water are available, and the only way is to have a septic tank. Maybe the technique has improved a lot. Since there was no city water main available, each house in that rural area had to have its own submerged well system. The well had to be on the opposite side of the house from the septic tank and drainage field, for obvious reasons. I am describing these things to make the reader aware of potential problems. However, a septic tank, if properly maintained, can last for four or five decades. The water from the well should be tested to make sure it is free from any contaminants. Prior to building a septic tank system, a percolation test is recommended to verify how porous the soil is.

I liked the slogan some septic tank pumpers displayed on their vehicles: "Your shit is my bread and butter." I am not discouraging anybody from buying a house in a place where the only choice is a septic system and a submerged well. This kind of a system has undergone enormous improvement since a system I saw a long time back, which was a big well in the ground and a plank or two for people to go empty themselves. As far as I remember, there might not have been any bridge or handrail either. I would say that type needed a vast improvement. Luckily, in my whole life, I have seen only one of those. I did not mean to spoil your dinner. Let's move on.

I was glad to have accepted that federal government job in Madison. I had heard about the good benefits and job security with government jobs. Asif and Nasreen both had been in state government jobs for some time in Madison already. I was thankful to Allah (SWT) for giving me the opportunity to land a job like that. I took a little cut in salary to move to that job. However, I was still satisfied to get out of the zoo in Park Falls and the situation I was facing there. I promised myself I would work hard and give them the best performance ever. Our house in Wausau was almost paid for at that time. Eventually, the house was sold, and so were lots of my prize possessions. I had put in so much work on that house. I became emotional when it was sold. A house that was supposed to be my dream house was sold. There were lots of memories connected with that house. I learned how to cut and fell trees. Ken Geogh, a guy I worked with, and Hugh Jones, our neighbor at that time, helped me get rid of some of the trees. In the village of Rothschild, where I worked for Weyerhaeuser Company for about twelve years, we were subjected to some racial tensions. My children were called names at times. But at the same time, it was considered one of the best towns to raise children in, as it was for the most part drug and crime free. My kids have lots of memories of that town, and they made lots of friends.

My job in Madison had a one-year probation. My boss and I had mutual respect for each other. Larry Andersen wanted an experienced engineer, and he concluded that I was a good fit for his department. I worked on in-house projects that had to do with indoor air quality, ventilation, dust collectors, air handlers, paint booth exhaust, steam generators, oven rooms, conditioning rooms, installation of a stainless-steel storage tank in the wood preservation department, expansion of the wood-burning laboratory facilities, parking lot resurfacing and paving throughout the facility, exhaust fans, and booths in the composites lab. Besides these, there were several contract administration projects. On farmed-out contract projects, one has to thoroughly study the drawings prepared by the outside engineers and examine them to make sure everything has been done right and as we wanted. Usually, the contract engineers complete the requirements per the specifications we have given them. Based on the engineering design and plans, a contractor is hired to implement and construct the project. It is the owner engineer's responsibility to supervise the construction and make sure everything is done right and as per the design and plan. Also, it is the responsibility of the engineer to make sure the contractor is paying the workers on time and in the right amount per the agreement. In our case, a daily diary needed to be maintained by the engineer. A contracting officer was responsible for the various nonengineering aspects of the project. The engineer who ran the contract project was known as the COR, or contracting officer's representative. I had several contract projects, but the most significant of them was the herbarium project. The herbarium project was about building a conditioned room wherein samples of various woods were stored. A small building was built attached to the main building of the forest products lab. It was a poured-concrete building. The ceiling had concrete-reinforced beams. A drain tile was put in around the building. At about the roof level of the building was the drive surface for vehicles to go to other parts of the lab. This drive surface was blended or with the same level with the roof of the herbarium building. Cars were allowed to be parked above the roof of the herbarium, which was really a paved surface extension from another elevated level, as described. This building became so strong based on its construction that some people called it a tornado shelter. Also, we installed high-density compact shelving in the building, meaning the shelves were mounted on carriages and moved on tracks built into the floor. The shelves could move either left or right. The advantage of compact shelving is the elimination of unnecessary aisle space. You might have seen these kind of shelves in some libraries. When a person pushes the particular button and the aisle opens up he or she can walk into the aisle. A safety feature is that if stuff is left on the floor, it will stop until you clear it. When a person is in the aisle, the shelves in that aisle cannot move and the person is safe that way. This is a low-maintenance system and works well. The herbarium officials were more than happy with the entire project

Another aspect of my job was to prepare drawings on AutoCAD for the projects I worked on. There was no T square or drawing board like in the older days. Everything was created on the computer and sent to the printer, which automatically printed it. It was a neat thing to see the pen move on the paper at a high speed. The software I first used was called Ashlar-Vellum, which was popular at that time. The mouse was a spherical ball, which we rolled into its holder instead of moving it on a flat surface, as we do at the time of this writing. I have seen various progressions of CAD drawings, each more powerful than the last. There is a big advantage to CAD drawings: they can be edited easily. Unlike with manual drawings, we do not need to erase the whole thing and redo it. It is right there on the computer screen and can be edited and sent to other people electronically for review. I used to do manual drawings on a drafting board with a T square, straight edges, and other tools and then make copies of the final drawings on a blueprint machine. Sometimes I worked on 3-D models and wire frames, even though I did not master those. A wire frame of an object can be produced with CAD and rotated on the screen to see different views of the object, and it can be printed as required. For various details of an object, software called Solid Works was also available. In this field, rapid learning ability is key. Programs keep changing, and new versions keep coming. In my career, I worked with AutoCAD R13, AutoCAD R14, and more. The *R* stands for *release*. We also had some Apple computers. I think I mainly worked with Apple computers for my CAD drawings. My colleague Paul Wright, senior engineer, always did his drawings on a drafting board the old-fashioned way. He did all the details, 3-D views, schematics, bill of materials, etc., on the drafting board. He was good at it. Paul and Larry Andersen, my boss, never worked on CAD. However, Larry encouraged me to work with the CAD, which had become the industry standard during that period.

I mentioned oven rooms. There were several of those built on the campus in various buildings. There had been a big fire due to overheating of an oven being used by an employee for an experiment. Since that time, they assigned me the project of fireproof oven rooms with fire-rated doors, walls, and ceilings.

One of the lab buildings was being hit by lightning often. It had some cracked walls and other damage due to this. I looked into installing some lightning rods on the building for its safety. I worked on various oven rooms for treating wood. I worked on several projects with Bob White, who was a scientist at the wood preservation lab at the Forest Products Laboratory.

At this point, let us take a break to test ourselves on our past history.

1. What was the name of the company that agreed to pay $470 million to the Indian government for the damages it caused in the deadly Bhopal disaster?
2. What company spilled 240,000 barrels of oil into the ocean in Alaska?
3. What was the name of the hurricane that devastated the Caribbean and the southeastern United States, causing seventy-one deaths and $8 billion in damage?
4. The fall of what wall occurred during that time?
5. A court in Milwaukee sentenced a serial killer to life imprisonment. What was the name of the serial killer?

6. In Albuquerque, New Mexico, a seventy-nine-year-old woman was burned by a cup of hot coffee at what fast food restaurant?
7. Who sold two houses in northern and central Wisconsin, respectively, to buy one house in southern Wisconsin? Name the three cities involved.

Try to answer all the questions correctly, and I will give the answers in the next chapter.

Now, to continue with my story, I wanted to keep my house in Wausau, as it was almost paid for, but various options, such as renting it out, did not seem practical or proper. Even though I had a few challenges with that house, I liked the house and the area. Like I have mentioned, there were lots of memories connected with the house. When we came to Madison, we started looking for a house. I told Shakeera that we needed to look for a unique house. My wish was that the house should be on a dead-end street or a cul-de-sac and in a hilly place or on the lake. In Madison, the houses on the lake were very expensive. There are four lakes in the Madison area: Mendota, Monona, Waubesa, and Kegonsa. There is a fifth smaller lake called Lake Wingra. The first four are big lakes with enormous recreation facilities.

I mentioned the challenges I had with my job at the federal government facility. I felt secure in that job. The benefits were good. In the beginning, when we came to Madison, Shakeera could not get started right away on her childcare services. She wanted to have certification as a childcare operator. She took the required exam and passed it. As a result, she established a day-care center in the house. She worked as a volunteer for a short while at the Forest Products Lab, where my job was. Before we purchased the house in Madison proper, I looked for houses outside of the city. I looked for houses on the lakes in Mazomanie, which is a little town outside of Madison, and other areas. It was a time-consuming task. The person who spends most of the time in the house should be happy in it. Therefore, I trusted Shakeera to pick a house of her choice. First, she decided we should live within the city proper, as it would not be convenient to be away from the city. The decision also had to do with her childcare business. Most of the working people stayed in the city, and if we bought a house far away from the city, it would be hard for us to commute, and potential childcare customers would shy away from traveling far to have their kids taken care of. I agreed with the location selection that Shakeera made; it made sense from every point of view.

We bought a house about six miles from my work. I got along well with Larry Andersen, my boss. At times, when he was gone, the staff took turns in filling his job. It was a big responsibility to run the department for a week or even a couple of days. I enjoyed filling in for my boss. I had the authority to approve the staff's paychecks for that week and such. Unlike in the mill situation, everybody in the department was a salaried worker. There was no distinction for engineers and mechanics, etc. There was a worker's union, and there were some dues we needed to pay to belong to the union. The union had some good officers, and they had an open-door policy. The union took care of the employees' issues well. The Forest Products Lab had many well-known scientists. Quite a few high-level research projects took place while I was at the lab, including ones involving wood use, new roofing material, and the fire resistance of various woods. All of the important research was published in a journal.

Also, there was a mentor program offered by some scientists to whomever wished to participate in it. I had a mentor relationship with a senior scientist, John Klungness. He had some special, interesting projects for me. One of the projects had to do with the drying of paper. Paper drying is an energy-intensive process. John had some research ideas that he shared with me, and I designed the equipment to facilitate his research. This mentor thing was outside the realm of my regular duties as an engineer at the lab. My boss, Larry Andersen, approved this kind of activity as long as it was reasonable in time consumption. Various research experiments have been applied to the paper-drying process on the paper machines. While I was in the industry, a large twelve- to fifteen-foot-diameter Yankee dryer was filled with steam on some paper machines. On other machines, there were a series of smaller dryers, maybe four to six feet in diameter, which were also filled with steam. In the drying process, the paper passes over these dryers at the dry end of the machine and gets wound over a large reel as an end product. All this is done at a certain high speed. Obviously, the higher the speed, the more production of paper. The entire process has to be optimized, of course.

I worked for about eleven years at Forest Products Lab. When I announced that I was going to retire, some office people were surprised that I was retiring that early. But from all points of view, it looked right for me to retire at that time. A fellow employee from another department, Gary, asked me, "Why don't you stay for one more year?"

I told Gary, "No. The decision has already been made. I have decided to leave."

Again, however, I found myself to be a victim of indecision. I had mixed thoughts about retirement. I was only in my late sixties. I knew some people well into their seventies who were still working. There was an inner urge in me that said I could do other things when I retired, such as traveling and spending more time with family.

A joke comes to mind in this context. When David Letterman, host of a nightly show, announced his retirement, his ten-year-old son said, "Dad, you have been busy with this show of yours for more than thirty-some years. How are you going to spend time after retirement?"

Letterman replied, "Son, I will be spending more time with my family."

The son replied, "Sure, Dad. You have plenty of those to go around. Don't you?"

David Letterman was known to be a womanizer. In my case, I am still married to my first wife, Shakeera, by the grace of God, and I love her dearly. She is the mother of my children, and that means a lot to me. It goes without saying that children are a gift of God.

CHAPTER 6

Government Work Is God's Work

The above words are carved prominently on the state building offices in Bangalore, India, at the main entrance near the rotunda. The architect of the building was Hon. K. Hunumanthiah, the chief minister of Mysore State, as it was called in those days. Mysore State, at the time of this writing, is called Karnataka State. Bangalore is the capital of Karnataka State, and the state office building is called Vidhana Soudha. It is a significant landmark of Bangalore, or Bengaluru, as it is called at the time of this writing.

Now for the answers to the quiz from the last chapter. Are you ready?

1. A gas leak at the Union Carbide pesticide plant killed twenty-five thousand people, and about five hundred thousand people were exposed. The leak of the deadly methyl isocyanate was considered one of the worst industrial disasters in history. It occurred in Bhopal, India, on December 2, 1984.
2. It was Exxon Oil Company that spilled 240,000 barrels of oil into the ocean in Alaska.
3. The name given to the hurricane was Hugo. It caused horrific damage in the southeastern United States and Puerto Rico.

4. For thirty years, the Berlin Wall stood as a manifestation of the Iron Curtain preventing citizens in communist East Germany from fleeing to democratic West Berlin. In 1989, East German authorities suddenly opened the border crossing. Thousands of jubilant Germans celebrated by dancing on top of the wall and chipping away at it with hammers and chisels.

5. President Bush and Russian premier Yeltsin declared the end of the Cold War.

6. Jeffery Dahmer, also known as the Milwaukee Cannibal, was a serial killer and sex offender. He was convicted of rape, murder, and dismemberment of seventeen men and boys during the years 1978–91. In some cases, the murder involved cannibalism.

7. The scalding coffee case took place at a McDonald's. The woman's name was Stella Liebeck. The story goes that she was in the passenger seat of her grandson's car, when she was severely burned by McDonald's coffee served in a Styrofoam cup at the drive-through window. It seems that Liebeck placed the cup between her knees and attempted to remove the plastic lid from the cup. In the process, the entire contents of the cup spilled into her lap. She suffered third-degree burns over her body, including her inner thighs and groin area. She sought to settle for $20,000. The coffee was 180 to 190 degrees. Coffee at other restaurants is normally cooler, at about 155 degrees. The jury awarded Liebeck $200,000, and then the amount was reduced to $160,000 based on the fact that she was partly at fault. The jury also awarded her $2.7 million in punitive damages, which was reduced to $480,000. It is said that the temperature of the coffee at McDonald's restaurants was dropped to 158 degrees. However, the case was closed by a secret settlement that was never revealed to the general public.

8. Yours truly sold two houses, one in Wausau, Wisconsin, and one in Butternut (Park Falls), Wisconsin, to buy a house in Madison, Wisconsin.

Shakeera and I had lots of memories in both of these houses. We had made several good friends in both Wausau and Park Falls and the surrounding areas.

In any job, the first thing you need to do is earn the trust of the people you work for. Your immediate customer is your boss. Quality in what you think, say, and do is of prime importance. Your immediate supervisor and the people you work for or with explore you in the beginning. They put out feeler gauges to see what you can do and how well you can do it. The subordinates also feel you out to determine how little they can work and still get your tolerance, etc. Of course, different people have different ethical standards. In my job, we had employee performance evaluations twice a year. Accuracy in design, proper selection of the material and equipment, and final results were important. When you are a project engineer, your hands are in other people's pockets. In other words, some department head is sponsoring you. You do not have much leeway to experiment. You need to do it right the first time; otherwise, it will result in wastage of time, money, and energy. It is not the quantity but the quality that matters. People remember the bad things you have done and seldom remember the good things you have accomplished. People usually never get a second chance to give a good first impression.

With all of the above philosophy in my mind, I worked hard in my job. Some people who were close to me used to tell me, "You do not have to work that hard. You are working for the government now."

I felt secure in that job. I took a little bit of time to work on my other passions, such as Urdu poetry. I made some contacts in Chicago and started attending poetic symposiums (mushairas) there. When I was in Wausau and, especially, in Park Falls, I used to hear about the mushairas in Chicago, but it was a heck of a long way to Chicago. From Wausau, it was five hours, and from Park Falls, it was about seven hours. Therefore, at least in the beginning, after coming to Madison, Wisconsin, I took advantage of going to Chicago often. We used to go to Bollywood celebrities' shows in Chicago also. We have been to Lata Mangeshkar and Kishore Kumar shows and enjoyed them a lot. We went to a show featuring Juhi Chawala, Akshay Kumar, and Sharukh Khan. There was hardly a well-known celebrity show that Shakeera and I missed. We were enthusiastic and excited about those shows. Things are different at the time of this writing. We hardly find time and enthusiasm to go to those shows anymore.

I would like to bring up a little bit of nostalgia here about the Indian Bollywood movies. For several years after we came to this country in 1964 and 1966, respectively, we craved Indian movies. We could not watch any, as they were not available at all. We found out in the seventies that we could rent Betamax tapes with prerecorded movies on them. Shakeera and I went to Chicago from Wausau and bought a Betamax machine. It was a beautiful machine but expensive. The TV had to be set to channel 3 or 4 to watch a cassette. It was such a big deal that we invited Dillu (Haji Masood Javeed), Shakeera's younger brother, and Asif to watch it with us. We enjoyed it. It was a big excitement for all of us. We obtained Betamax movie cassettes from Moeen, a friend of ours from Bangalore, who used to be in Dallas, Texas. We ordered four or so cassettes each time from him and watched them excitedly. Of course, Shakeera was more excited about these movies, and she kept a log of all the movies we saw. I think within about five to seven years, Betamax became less attractive to consumers. Then came Video Home System (VHS). There was a big competition between the two companies. Betamax had a smaller cassette, and VHS was a little bit bigger cassette. Anyway, even though Betamax cassettes were of better quality, it lost its market and slowly faded out. My Betamax machine became obsolete. We started getting the movies on VHS and needed a machine to play the VHS cassettes. Shakeera did not care about the format. She wanted to get the Indian movies and watch them. We started building a library of VHS cassettes. She got rid of several of those, but we still have some we can watch. Besides movies, lots of other programs got recorded on VHS. Weddings, special events, mushairas, and more were recorded in this format.

Another problem we confronted in those days was that there were two different systems for playing DVDs in the United States and in Europe and other countries. The US system was called NTSC, which stands for National Television System Committee. The corresponding system in Europe and other countries was called PAL, which stands for Phase Alternating Line. It had to do with the fact that in the United States, electrical power was generated at 60 hertz, and in other countries, including India, electrical power was generated at 50 hertz. If we tried to play a tape from India in the United States, the picture was scrambled, and the voice quality was terrible. However, there were conversion kits available, and there were professionals who would convert the tape for a fee. I heard it was a time-consuming process. I had to have a couple converted in Chicago. Obviously, there were no problems watching DVDs produced in the United States in the United States. Recently, I have not heard of any problems of this nature. During my book release and other events, we recorded some DVDs in India and were able to play them well in the United States. Also, my nephew Tanseer's wedding videos worked out well. They might have resolved the problem.

I had a good and challenging time with the federal government job. There were good fringe benefits. I kind of regretted that I retired so early. Along with my day job, I had a part-time job too. It had nothing to do with having enough money to support the family. Somehow, I was compelled to supplement my income. Since the Forest Products Lab was affiliated with the University of Wisconsin, I was able to become a member of the gyms that are part of the university. I used the facilities from time to time while at the Forest Products Lab. The Natatorium was built in 1961, and the Southeastern Recreation Facility (SERF) was built in 1982. Both are excellent facilities. There is another facility at the university, called the Shell. The Shell is a large facility, and I think some sports events take place there. Some exercise machines are also there. At one time, we were paid or given time to go exercise for about one half hour during the day on the government's time. Some years, we faced a budget approval crisis in Washington and were given furloughs. Also, we were encouraged to take our vacation during that time. If Congress fails to appropriate the necessary funds for the federal government, the government is forced to shut down and cannot operate without any funds. Between 1976 and 2013, the government was forced to shut down eighteen times. The fiscal year of the government runs from October 1 to September 30 of the following year. If the appropriations bill fails to get approved, a continuing resolution can be passed up to a certain date to keep things rolling. The majority of these fights lasted one to two days, with a few exceptions lasting more than a week. It is a big crisis, as many essential operations can get stalled, and employees face nonpayment of their salaries. It is in everybody's interest to avoid this crisis as much as possible. In my service, I think I got caught in this kind of a situation only once or twice.

Mike Kaspaszak was my new boss. His designation was head of facilities engineering. I got tempted to throw my hat in the ring for the job, but I did not go forward. There were some people who would not have been happy or would not have tolerated it if I were in that position. They brought in Mark Kaneabe from another department, and he had some experience in engineering. Paul Wright, our senior engineer, had retired by then. I was doing well in my job as an engineer. More responsibility means more stress, which can affect the health. I weighed all those factors and did not throw my hat in the ring for the position of group leader. I kicked myself for not taking that step, but time passed on, and it was not taxing. The nineties were a busy time for the Rahman family.

At this time, let's take a few minutes to jog our memories of the early nineties and see how much we remember the past history. We will continue with our story from where we left off later.

1. The Dow Jones Industrial Average hit a record of which of the following?

    a) 5,400   b) 3,803   c) 15,000   d) 4,500

2. Which former US president passed away?

    a) Gerald   b) Abraham   c) Richard   d) Lyndon
    Ford   Lincoln   Nixon   Johnson

3. Who was the model in India who earned the title of Miss Universe when she was eighteen years old?

    a) Sushmita   b) Lara Dutta   c) Madhuri   d) Kajol
    Sen   Dixit

4. One hundred sixty-eight people, including eight federal marshals, were killed in the bombing of a federal building in a southern city in the United States. Where did this tragedy take place?

    a) Atlanta   b) Dallas   c) Memphis   d) Oklahoma City

5.   Scientists in Scotland cloned a mammal for the first time. What was the mammal?

    a) dog   b) cat   c) pig   d) sheep

6.   A wedding took place in the immediate Rahman family in the nineties by God's grace. Name the couple.

    a) Naazneen and Shakeeb   b) Tina and Arthur   c) Farru and Rahmat   d) Raja and Rani

Good luck with your multiple-choice history test. I will give the answers after a few pages.

I continued with my challenges at the job, which I decided would be my last career job. My retirement was vested. I had good benefits. I had a double whammy for a while: I got paid my salary, and my social security funds were coming in also. A few years earlier, you could not earn full social security if you worked, even after you reached a certain age. A certain amount was withheld from social security for every thousand dollars or so you made.

President Clinton made the change that full social security would be given to employees who claimed it, even if they worked full-time. I felt lucky in that regard.

While I was enthusiastic about the job and making good progress in Madison, Wisconsin, I always had an eye on moving to a warmer place with the government. I applied here and there a little bit. Nothing serious came through. I applied as temporary engineering help at the Santa Barbara, California, office. This office was for the Los Padres National Forest on Hollister Avenue in Goleta, California, near Santa Barbara, a beautiful and expensive place. I was selected to be at that office for about four months. I jumped at the opportunity and packed up to go there. I seldom missed an opportunity to visit California. I like the weather, beaches, and landscape beauty. The one drawback is the possibility of earthquakes. Anyway, I got permission from my department head, Mike Kaspszac.

He said, "If you want to go there, you can. We want their performance evaluation of you while you work there."

I said, "There should be no problems." I was close to retirement at Forest Products Laboratory. Not knowing much about California, after quick research, I reserved a room at Meadowlark Inn in Solvang, California. I had plans to stay for a few months in California; therefore, I rented a place where I could cook. The Meadowlark Inn had a little kitchen. It was pleasant in California in May. It was the year 2002. Gasoline was cheap at that time. I rented a car and drove to work in Goleta every day. I also drove to different project sights in Santa Barbara County. Soon I realized that the hotel I was staying in was too far from work, so I moved to another hotel in Santa Barbara, which saved a lot of travel time. I was only a few minutes from the office.

Some of the projects I was assigned were as follows:

- upgrade of the barrack facilities
- construction of a septic tank system at a fire station
- replacement of the Ozena Fire Station water storage tank
- construction of restroom facilities at various National Forest parks

Unlike at the Forest Products Lab, where the work was mainly confined to the twenty-six buildings on the campus, at the forest, the projects could be anywhere within the forest. There was quite a bit of travel involved, at least within the adjacent counties. I liked driving around the various project sites with a new state, new job, and new people. I took the challenge and tried to live up to it. The boss was a decent young Chinese woman. For some reason, she did not get along well with me right from day one. Maybe I did not completely fulfill her selection expectations. She hurried through the selection process and got me, and I was not 100 percent what she wanted. Anyway, I started my job in the office with full zest. Some of the engineers and technicians, including the department head, were good to me. I had to learn a new CAD program and the new ways of operation of the new office.

I felt I was too far away from home all by myself. I missed Shakeera and the rest of the family. However, I took the job seriously and worked on my projects hard. I was on the expense account of the forest, so all my expenses were charged to the project I was working on. Knowing the budget process for the projects, I knew exactly how this worked. I had to sell and justify every hour that I worked on a certain project. I, being a conscientious person, felt responsible about it and wanted to be as efficient as possible.

There was a casino near Santa Barbara, and I went there a couple of times. I used to go to the beach to take walks. I developed a severe pain in my left knee while I was there. It was becoming nearly impossible for me to walk. I fought it out and stayed on top of my projects. The pain was unbearable, and I applied lots of ointments to my knee. In a certain store in Santa Barbara, I met a young woman from India, and we exchanged our thoughts and stories about the place. She introduced me to her father, who was a doctor. I asked the good doctor his opinion of my knee pain.

He told me that he was not an orthopedic specialist. He was a heart specialist. Anyway, after looking at my knee, he said the cartilage between the two bones might have been worn out to the point that there was bone-to-bone contact. I was starting to have second thoughts about this assignment in California. I liked to drive around to my projects. At times, I had to drive to elevations seven thousand to eight thousand feet above sea level. The storage tank for the Ozena Fire Station was at an elevation of about eight thousand feet above sea level. The area was scenic.

One guy at the fire station told me there were rattlesnakes in the area. The firefighters were supposed to keep fit. Hence, they took walks around their station almost daily. One firefighter told me, "If you ever see a rattlesnake close to you in the bushes, do not panic and try to move swiftly. Rather, you should remain silent and freeze at first and then slowly move away." I did not confront any rattlesnakes in my paths, luckily. I was always on the lookout, though, and took precautions.

I talked to Shakeera on the phone almost every day. She kept telling me to come back home. By taking this job, I was expanding my horizons. Working in a forest outdoors was much different from my facilities engineering work. That year, Shakeera was planning to visit India by herself. At first, I was not going to go because of my job. However, after considering the entire situation, I changed my mind. I decided to go to India with her. I resigned the job at Santa Barbara and received permission from the department to go back to Madison, Wisconsin. Nobody had any objection, though they were surprised somewhat that I was leaving so early. I also gave them a letter from the Indian doctor friend about my knee situation. As much as I regretted that I could not complete my assigned duties at that job, I was glad to return to Madison and to home. My boss at Forest Products Lab was surprised to see me back.

In June and part of July of that year, we visited Bangalore, India. We had a good time. In 2002, the international airport in Bangalore was still in the planning stage, and we had to go to Bombay and then fly to Bangalore HAL airport using Indian Airline routes. It was time consuming and inconvenient. All this was a thing of the past in 2008, when the modern international airport opened in Bangalore. Since then, many international flights, such as Lufthansa and KLM, can fly directly to Bangalore. I read somewhere that it is one of the busiest airports in India. I am glad to see that my hometown, which was hardly even counted among the big cities in India in my day, is now called the Atlanta of India. Also, it is called the Silicon Valley of India. At least thirty Fortune 500 global companies have their offices in Bangalore. When I came from India, I passed the certification exam for construction inspector given by the United States Forest Service. I felt proud of myself for having passed the exam. However, my mind-set was to retire from service soon. I took some hydrotherapy for my knee. Mike Kaspszak asked me to convert all Ashlar-Vellum drawings into AutoCAD format. This was a boring assignment. I announced that I would be retiring from service next March.

Mike announced in the next monthly meeting that I would be retiring soon. "Fellows, be nice to Mohammad. He is retiring soon," he said.

I went about my business of completing assignments as usual. I returned all the books I had borrowed from the laboratory library. I brought all my personal belongings home. Finally, March 8, 2003 came fast, and they gave me a farewell party. Some of my friends and well-wishers came to the party. There was a big spread. Tom Jacobson made a speech thanking me for my contributions. Tom was acting in place of Mike Kaspszak that week. I was honored to see that the director of the lab also stopped by. People were always nice to me anyway. My degree of penetration with the workers was, if I may say so, excellent. The workers did not work for me directly; they really worked for Gary Lichtenberg, who was the maintenance supervisor. I knew he'd worked at the lab for several years. I heard he was a welder before and worked his way up to the supervisory staff. He was kind of a know-it-all type of person. Because of his long service, people relied on him. He got along well with the managerial staff as well as the scientists.

While I was visiting Farah and Mubeen in Mesa, Arizona, I heard the tragic news about the passing of my dad in India. I had not seen him for a while. He was sick and bedridden for a while. Afroz, Almas, and the other siblings took care of him at home. Afroz kept us updated about his health. One time, Dad was walking down the road, and a bicyclist hit him, which resulted in a fall and lots of bleeding. Since then, Dad was cautious about going out, especially walking on the sides of the streets. At that time, in some Bangalore suburbs, there were no sidewalks as such. As a result of this accident, Dad quit going out completely. Dad was a health-conscious person. He used to wash his hands and face whenever he came into the house from outside. On the day of his departure, he was quiet and a little uneasy, it seems. Afroz asked a doctor to come home and examine him. Local doctors make house calls in India even now, it seems. Anyway, the doctor, after examining him, had nothing much to say but left with a grim face.

That night, my dad left this world to meet his Creator. When you lose your dad, it feels as if you lost a part of yourself. May Allah give his soul a place in Janna. We all felt and still feel a big void without him. My dad taught us important matters of life, such as how to be frugal with respect to your money, how to value and respect time, how to respect people and earn respect from others, how to get along with each other, and how to be a responsible and nice person overall. The values my dad taught me are still with me, and I am sure they are helping me. Another characteristic of Dad was to fight for justice. He hated people who tried to take undue advantage of him. He opposed unjust people until they returned to the right path. He was particular about our education. He believed that a good education was important for his kids. When I failed an intermediate college exam, he became concerned and talked to some tutors to assess my ability and wanted to improve me and help me pass the exam. One tutor told him, "He should work long hours in a day in order to prepare himself for passing the intermediate exam." Intermediate in those days was equivalent to the PUC we have now. He made sure I went to private tutorial institutes in order to catch up and prepare myself to pass the given exam. He directed me to move to Mysore to the house of Phuppijan (my cousin Dilshad's mom) to go to a tutorial college called CTC (City Tutorial College). I stayed there with my aunt and cousins for a while to study. That incident shows how important my education was for him. Today I owe a great debt of gratitude to my dad for taking care of me in that manner. Whatever I am today, I have no doubt it is due to his genuine effort and concern in instilling the values of education in me.

I have lots of memories of my federal government job, and I enjoyed every moment of it. They recognized me as a good performer. I supervised several significant projects and contracts. I learned about boilerplate, which is standard phrasing universal for every writeup regardless of the nature of the contract. For example, a clause about a contractor having an insurance certificate has to be repeated for all contracts. I learned how to be systematic in the administration of contracts for the government and keep notes and document everything, including phone conversations. The notes should include whom you talked to and a brief summary of the subject and the time of the conversation or telecon.

Now, I know you are curious to find out the answers to the quiz you took earlier. Please go to the next chapter.

CHAPTER 7

Retirement from Career Service and Beyond

Right at the start of this chapter, let's go into the trivia. Are you ready? Here we go!

1. The Dow Jones Industrial Average hit a record of 4,500 in 1995 and 5,400 in 1996, as compared to greater than 16,000 at the time of this writing.
2. The question was which former US president passed away in the early 1990s. The answer is Richard Nixon.
3. The Indian model who earned the Miss Universe title when she was only eighteen was Shusmita Sen.
4. The city was Oklahoma City.
5. The cloned mammal was a sheep.
6. My son, Shakeeb, married Naazneen.

Planning to retire was exciting. I was about sixty-eight years old when I retired and had about thirty-six years under my belt in various jobs as an engineer. They say that retirement is stressful for some people. A person works most of his or her life and retires with no job and nothing to do per se. To many, retirement means no job, no stress, no boss, and no alarm. I'll tell you something: retirement is not all about relaxation. There are things in life you cannot do while you are a full-time employee, and you'll want to catch up with your work at home, I suppose. There are some passions in life that you want to be a part of.

There are hobbies to catch up with. I, for one, did not have any significant hobby. I temporarily pick a hobby here and there and stick with it for a while, and that's it, such as working around the house, gardening, and small building projects. During different stages of my life, I had different hobbies or vocational activities. When I was about ten or eleven years old, I got interested in building huts. With the help of our servants, my brothers and I used sticks to build walls, doors, and roofs for these little huts. There was one for myself, one for Asif, and one for Altaf. We all took pride in what we were doing. For the roof, we used a palm tree's small branches. For the flooring, we used cow-dung paste, which we mixed with water for proper consistency. At first, these hut-like buildings were not connected; they were independent. After a while, there was a suggestion that we should have entry doors from one hut to another. Anyway, we used to spend quite a bit of time building them and staying in them. We enjoyed them as if we owned real estate. We used to, with the help of the servants, make our own kites and fly them. That was a lot of fun. Also, some of the servants used to tell us stories of Hindu mythology about Ramayana and Mahabharata. At that age, those stories were fascinating to us. We spent hours listening to those stories. A friend of mine when we were growing up—his name was, I think, Iqbal—used to make toy cars out of cigarette carton boxes. He was a talented guy. He had a brother named Fiaz. Both were highly trained artists. To us, they were known as the drill master's kids, as their dad was a teacher (probably of physical education).

Some guys choose not to retire when they become eligible, as they do not have any hobbies. In this country, retirement is celebrated. People think you earned your retirement. You successfully completed your working period. In my home country, even today, *retirement* is a bad word. They are not proud of it. When some folks are young, they desire to retire, but when the time comes to retire, it is a different feeling sometimes. They want to keep going, or they don't know how to spend the time on their hands.

Anyway, for me, the time came, and I retired on March 8, 2003, after almost thirty-seven years as an engineer. I enjoyed the challenges and the successes. The path was not smooth in any way. There were promotions and step increases. I experienced pride of accomplishments, good comments, and some bad comments about the work. I worked throughout my service. I did lots of liaisons between different departments. I had to satisfy the department head or the sponsor who funded the project. As you can imagine, every department is responsible for their budget. They have to justify every penny of their budget. When you are spending other people's money, you do not have much time to experiment. You had better do your homework right. Your slogan should be "Do it right the first time." You carry a lot of responsibility on your shoulders. You'd better put your heart and soul into every aspect of your work.

My daughter, Farah, and Mubeen (my ex-son-in-law) threw a retirement party for me. There were some close friends and family. It was a joyous atmosphere. Whoever made speeches and gave me gifts wished me well. At the end, I gave a little talk. Some of the greeting cards were funny. I read all the cards. One card said, "With retirement, I am done." However, I know there are lots of opportunities for me yet. I did not intend to work full-time after retirement. I wanted to do something different.

I worked for the City of Madison for a while. I was in the engineering department, doing a sidewalk repair program. There was quite a bit of busy work in that program, which was at least a ten-year program in which the city identified sidewalks that needed repair, replacement, or an upgrade. My knees were kind of getting bad. The right knee was really bad. However, I kept on doing the job. It was a seasonal job anyway. My partner on the job was a guy from one of the South American countries. In that job, I happened to learn a lot. In a given block of houses, all the odd numbers for the addresses will be on one side, and the even numbers are on the other side. This is helpful when you are searching for a house in a certain block of the city. When reading the city charters, I found out that minority contractors were encouraged to bid on city projects. Also, a certain small percentage of projects were reserved for minorities.

I applied to the state for opening up an engineering business. After they approved my business plan and checked up on a few important things, I got approved for doing business in Wisconsin. I was thrilled. I frequently visited the city engineering office to find out what contracts were open for bidding. I picked up the drawings and specifications from the city, went to the project site in question, and studied the project thoroughly. I had to have the equipment in order to do the contract. Since I did not have the equipment, I went to the appropriate contractor companies and negotiated with them so they could partner with me to bid on a particular project. I did this on several projects, but I was not the lowest bidder on any one of them. If you are the lowest bidder, you are likely to be picked up for an award. After all that hard work and planning and working on the project, you get nothing out of it if you're not selected. This frustrated me.

Since I was prepared to do most any kind of job, I picked up odd jobs. One of the jobs I signed up for was as a crossing guard. I saw quite a few seniors work that kind of job. Like they say, "I am ashamed to be here and not ashamed enough to leave." I had the proper attire and florescent vest, braved bad weather and slippery road conditions, and performed this job for a while. I realized how hard it is to make a buck. The boss was a good person. Even today, she invites the retired or ex-crossing guards to summer picnics.

I just want to take you through my thought process in my quest for a job after retirement. I wanted to do something and, at the same time, make a buck. In the crossing guard job, the pay was not too bad, and we were appreciated by the community and the city. While I was at the intersections, I met a guy who used to drive a school van, and his name was Mohammad. He was from Somalia, Sudan, or some other African country. I asked this guy, "Hey, Mohammad, what is it like to drive a school bus? How is the company Laidlaw Transit?"

He said, "It was not bad. You are better off getting a commercial driver license."

Hence, I made it a point to try for a commercial driver's license. I took books from the Transportation Department, studied them, and passed the written exam. I had been driving a long time on the roads in this country. At the department, before you take the road test, they ask you, "What kind of vehicle will you be driving?" The road test will involve a yellow school bus with seventy-eight passengers (students), a van, or whatever. For the school bus, they call the qualification an S endorsement. Another endorsement is the P endorsement. There are strict rules for the school bus and passenger bus license. The *S* stands for "school bus endorsement," and *P* stands for "passenger endorsement." Both of these tests involve written exams.

You are carrying in the bus the most precious commodity: the young students. You've got to follow the rules to the exact clauses that are spelled out. Being a crossing guard helped me out to some extent regarding the safety aspects of the young students. Some companies give their own training to potential employees about school bus driving. It is their name that is on the bus. There is a contract between the company and the school district. I worked for a company called First Student from Verona, Wisconsin. I enjoyed driving the school bus. Sometimes an attendant helps the driver keep order. Without the attendant, the students can get unruly at times. It is next to impossible to maintain order on the bus as well as concentrate on driving.

I am not ashamed to work as a school bus driver. With the Indian kind of mentality, driving a bus could be considered a lower-grade job, but I am proud I was able to work as a yellow school bus driver. I performed my job safely, reacted to emergencies in a reasonable manner, and made sound decisions on the road.

Anyway, as a school bus driver, I worked for Badger Bus Lines of Madison; Durham School Bus Services; Laidlaw Transit; and First Student. Some companies hired drivers to transport special needs students. Different companies had different rules for the drivers. Most of the companies had pre-trip and post-trip forms to be filled out by the drivers. The main thing was to transport and deliver the students safely to the school and bring them home safely and on time. The pre-trip report involved all the equipment on the bus and if it was working properly. When backing up in a company parking lot, you need to get assistance from the attendant to guide you in proper backing. It is usually recommended that the attendant gets out of the vehicle and guides you and also helps you check the directional signals, brake lights, stoplights, etc. The roof hatch needs to be checked for proper operation. Proper adjustment of the side-view and rearview mirrors is important. Some companies had better training than others. For some reason, the high-top vans of the Laidlaw Company burned a lot of oil. We needed to top the engine oil almost every day.

If there is an attendant, bus driving is okay. If not, the driver, besides driving, has to keep an eye on these special needs students. It becomes a challenge then. Another aspect of this job with special students is working with a hydraulic lift for people who are not ambulatory. You have to be extra careful in those cases. You have to brace them properly within the bus and also while they are on the hydraulic lift. The hydraulic lift is wonderful equipment to have, but it needs to be operated properly. There are insurance underwriters sometimes who ride with you to inspect the operation. It is all for the safety of the person being served and for the overall safety of the equipment. Also, the school buses have to be inspected every year by the state. During such time, all the buses and related equipment are examined, and a certificate is issued. It is the responsibility of the management to have all buses go through this examination. This way, the buses are in good running condition. It is also important that the CDL driver do the pre-trip and post-trip test on the bus. He or she has to file a report before taking the bus on the road. I just want you to get a feel for how important this job is. While I was in this job, I was careful with driving my own car, as you cannot afford to get a ticket for any moving violation. Parking violations are not bad, however.

Another job I took was as a van driver at an assisted living facility. The job entailed hauling residents of the facility to churches, clinics, and weekend outings. For the weekend outings, I took them to nearby farms and specialty shopping places. Most of the passengers were senior citizens who were residents at the place. The vans were equipped with hydraulic lifts. As with any commercial vehicle, I needed to check the vehicle before every trip. Some of the residents used walkers. I needed to help them board and disembark the bus. It was fun driving the residents to the outskirts of Madison, Wisconsin, where the facility was located.

While I was doing all that, I also worked as a cashier in various parking facilities. I was a cashier at city lots in Madison. It was a fast-paced job. At times, there were thousands of cars in and out of the lots due to special events. Madison is a state capital and a big-ten university town, so there is a lot of activity, especially during the weekends. It was fun to work in these facilities, as there is a lot of hustle and bustle around you. While I was at the university hospital parking lot, I made some good friends, such as Efram and Gazai. As those jobs were not my career jobs, I had no stress. They were mostly just fun jobs. While I was at the university and city lots, I accumulated an employee trust fund, which came in handy. The employee trust fund is the amount the state contributes to employees during their tenure with the state. I think a certain percentage of their salary needs to be contributed, and the state matches accordingly. This is a good benefit that state employees have.

A friend of mine was telling me that one of his dreams was to be able to drive a large bus like the school bus. When I was young, I used to sit in the front seat next to the driver and watch the driver's hands and feet to see how he drove. I thought it must be fascinating to be a bus driver. My dad was a gazetted officer, and it was a privilege to sit in the front passenger seat next to the driver in those days. This gave me a chance to watch the driver closely and learn his actions. For those of you who do not know, a gazetted officer has a certain rank in the hierarchy of the government officers in the state government. These officers get benefits, such as having servants at the house almost around the clock, including a cook. As we were Muslim, my dad always requested a Muslim cook, as he would be familiar with our kind of dishes. My uncle Mohammad Ahmad, being in a higher post, had more servants, including a cook and a driver for his car. These benefits and privileges are unheard of in this day and age, unless I have been away from such officers long enough to lose touch.

I have mentioned before that I trained on the job to be a cashier. The most important thing in a job to understand is that you are working with other people's money. Therefore, you have to be extra careful; you have to balance the books every day at the end of the shift. The balance sheet should show the starting money and the profit in an orderly fashion. The gate operation should also be correct. As a person who has experience as a money handler, you could be a cashier most anyplace, such as in a store or bank. It is good job for a student or a senior. It is not physical.

Some friends of mine said, "How come you are doing such an ordinary job? Can you not find something more dignified?"

My answer to them was that dignity of labor has to be respected. Sitting around and doing nothing was worse than this. Most of the engineering jobs I looked into were full-time jobs. The magnitude of the job called for full-time attention. I thought, *What is the use of retiring if you do a full job anyway?* I did not need money. I am fortunate to have a good pension, social security, and earned incomes. My need is to get out of the house on a regular basis and be able to contribute to society. In other words, I want to give something back to society. Also, I learned from my parents and grandparents that being active is wonderful. Sitting around on your duff and twiddling your thumbs, as long as you are healthy, is not recommended for anybody. As you age and retire, this is even more important. My dad, grandma, and grandpa were active till the end of their mature lives in their own way. When you are able, you're better off doing something. What else are you going to do with your life? If you get up in the morning and have to think about what you are going to do that particular day, to me, that is boring. I hope I'm never bored in that manner. I pray to God to always keep me engaged in something and never make me bored. In fact, I read or heard somewhere that whomever God wants to punish, he will first make him or her bored. I believe this. I never want to run out of projects or things to do. I understand that health is the most important thing in life. Let's all pray to God to give us good health.

A well-known Urdu poet, Mirza Ghalib, eloquently said,

Tung Dasti Agar na ho Ghalib
Tandurusti Hazaar Nemat Hai

The translation of the verse is as follows: "If you have enough means to live in this world, there is nothing as worthy as health itself."

Nothing could be as true as this statement from Mirza Ghalib. In my view, he was one of the greatest Urdu and Farsi poets of our times.

One of the purposes of my book is to share some knowledge with you. I would like to talk about the Smith System of driving. The Smith System of driving has five keys to good driving habits. They are as follows:

1. Aim high in steering. This applies as much to car driving as bus or van driving. What this means is to look higher into the roadway or the space in which you are driving. Get a good view of the surroundings. Do not just look at the vehicle in front of you. Look fifteen seconds into the future.

2. Get the big picture. You need to look beyond what you see immediately. For example, is there a cross-traffic possibility? Is there an uncontrolled intersection? Who has the right of way? Is there a traffic light coming up? What color is the light at the moment? Also, check the counter to see whether the light is going to change to the next color and when. Are there cars parked on both sides of the street or on one side? Look at the lane markings, and obey as required. These are all commonsense practices and become second nature to most drivers, but these are part of the teaching points for commercial drivers. I cannot stress these rules enough for your regular driving as well as commercial driving. Look for hazards, such as two-wheelers, bicyclists, pedestrians, and vehicle door openings.

3. Keep your eyes moving. Every eight seconds, you need to be watching the left-view mirror, right-view mirror, and rearview mirror. The traffic picture keeps changing every few seconds. The driver needs to be in complete view of what is happening. You need to be scanning the road ahead of you as well as keeping track of what is developing on the right and left sides of the vehicle. Long ago, there was only one side-view mirror on the vehicle. I think it was the left side-view mirror. The instructors at that time used to stress that when you made a lane change to the right, you needed

to carefully turn around and look over your right shoulder for the oncoming traffic to your right. Even with the mirrors, there will be some blind spots that you cannot quite see in the mirror. You have to be careful. Besides the mirrors mentioned above, there are crossover mirrors that present a view of both sides of the bus from the front to the back. Also, another important thing you need to do when lining up the buses at the school curb at the end of the school day is to park your bus close to the bus in front of you so that no student can pass between the two buses. This distance can be seen in the cross view mirrors. This is an important requirement. Many accidents can be avoided if this rule is followed. Train yourselves in proper scanning techniques. Don't just stare into a limited area. Use peripheral vision.

4. Leave yourself an out. This is an important rule also. Do not be surrounded by other vehicles in the immediate lanes for a long time. In case the vehicles stop suddenly, you should have a place to steer to without crashing into the vehicle in front of you. In other words, you should have some open space, such as a shoulder, in case you are surrounded by traffic. How many times have you been faced with this kind of situation? I once had to swerve to the left and jump onto the median when my vehicle started skidding during winter. I would say I lucked out at the time. Therefore, pay attention to the rule: leave yourself an out.

5. Make sure they see you. This is an important rule. Have you seen the statement on trucks and vans "If you cannot see my mirrors, that means I cannot see you either"? Especially for large trucks with trailers, this is important. Light travels in a straight line. The side-view mirror on a truck is an important device for the driver to see what is behind him. Some drivers get down out of the vehicle to see what is in the back before backing up the vehicle. Therefore, pay attention to this. Also, pedestrians and bicyclists should make eye contact with the driver around corners before they cross the streets. In most states, we are supposed to stop the vehicle for pedestrians and bicyclists. These rules make a lot of sense for all drivers and are there to prevent collisions.

I also worked at a place where we wrote and submitted applications for grants to do scientific research work. The federal government has in its budget funds for researchers who work on different topics. Government agencies—such as Homeland Security, the National Health Institute, the Environmental Protection Agency, and the departments of commerce, transportation, defense, energy, and education—set aside funds for research in different areas. The grant forms need to be filled out properly and submitted electronically to the agency in question. Each question has to be answered properly for consideration. I obtained some on-the-job training in writing grants and being able to submit. I found out that minority researchers are given consideration. There are courses you can take for writing grants that sell. I think one of the important items is the plan of the research paper itself. This is usually written by the actual researcher. It is the central idea of the whole project, and the success of obtaining funds depends on it. There were only three or four employees at that company. The lawyer who was the CEO of Excite Optics was a slick person. His name was R. J. Twilegar. He employed a chemistry PhD, some researchers, and me. The lawyer told us up front that he could not pay us our wages until we successfully got the funds. When I first came on board, they were successful in getting a grant. They worked with a minority doctoral candidate. During my tenure with them, we submitted several grant applications, but we were not successful. At least he was able to keep the PhD guy with him for a while. I do not know how this slick owner did it; he did not even have money to pay the rent regularly. The owner of the business was from Boise, Idaho, and registered his business in Rhode Island for some tax reason. I do not know any more details about this business. I was freshly retired, and I wanted to have something to do. It was an interesting job in the sense that we worked with researcher Kela Fleming and got to know the aspects of grant writing, buying scientific equipment on eBay, and more. We sometimes also employed the services of an editor once the write-up of the grant application was complete. People have different ways of making money. The editor, Lori, charged quite a bit for taking a look at the writeup and correcting it. I hardly got paid at that job, but I wanted to learn stuff. This was in Oregon, which is about a twenty-minute drive once you are on the belt way. I used to have a small Ford pickup in those days, and gas was cheap. I learned the whole process of getting funds from the federal government by submitting grants. The details can be found at www.SBIR.gov. I think that in Madison, Wisconsin, there are plenty of opportunities for that kind of activity, which is called small business innovative research.

I worked part-time for another company called Avescend, a hospitality company. Customer service was the number-one requirement of employees at that company. My assignment was to drive a sixteen-passenger wide van to bring the employees from the parking lots to the hospitals. The parking ramps at the hospitals were expensive. The employees chose to park their cars at remote lots for free and took the bus to and from the lots. The transportation companies had contracts with the hospital. The van transportation was free for the employees. The employees from Dean Clinic and St. Mary's Hospital took advantage of this arrangement. Another hospital in Madison also had a similar arrangement with a company called Right-Way Leasing. This idea of remote parking is good, as parking outside the city and taking a bus to the city will solve lots of problems, such as congestion, pollution, road rage, and stress. This model of parking is being tried in different cities around the globe. I know that in Madison, Wisconsin, this system has been in place for years. Every city should be following this example. In my city of birth, Bangalore, India, they should do the same. The traffic situation is horrible. The city roads in most places are like a parking lot; the traffic hardly moves. People can go faster on two-wheelers, as they can maneuver them easily. Sometimes they even go onto the sidewalks and get around the crawling cars. When I was growing up in Bangalore, a bicycle was a common mode of transportation. I went to engineering college on a bicycle for about four years. Cha Cha (Abdul Basith) went to his work for years on his Raleigh bicycle. Nowadays, you hardly see any bicycles on the road. In fact, bicycling on the streets along with the fast-moving vehicles is not recommended.

I currently volunteer at Meriter Hospital in Madison as an escort as well as a gofer. They use me wherever they can, usually in customer service chores. At the time of this writing, I still enjoy doing this. I work early in the morning for only a few short hours every week. The people are friendly.

I first volunteered to teach students who were preparing for the GED (high school equivalency) at Omega School. The principal of the school told me the school got a subsidy from United Way. I asked him to give me a full-time job at the school, but it has not materialized so far. The principal, Oscar Mirales, helped me a lot.

I worked as a maintenance person in a company that managed several buildings in Madison. They were all commercial buildings, either private or governmental. One of the buildings they managed was the Department of Corrections and Wisconsin State building. There were many aspects of maintaining the building. The jobs included the replacement of light fixtures and snow removal from the parking lots and driveways during winter. The guy who hired me expected a lot of hands-on work from everybody. We were given extensive training on the various systems, including the low-pressure heating boilers in the building. In a way, I was familiar with that kind of a job. However, it was not my bag to be able to work with my hands. I like planning the jobs on paper and getting them done in the field by others. I carried a tool pouch, as I was supposed to. Some of the repair jobs required me to bend, stoop, and rest on my knees, which I had a hard time doing. The company thought that a Degreed Engineer would be able to do all that. Engineers design things and make everything work, but not all of them can work with their hands. We use our brains and put together projects that need to be implemented. Needless to say, I did not last long with that company. I think the year was 2006, and we were planning to go to Hajj (pilgrimage in Mecca). I asked for some time off for going to Hajj. My boss instead asked me to come to his office to talk. I kind of sensed what was coming. He told me they would have to let me go and asked me to return all the keys and other belongings of the company. I did not regret it at all. I did not like the job anyway. I thought, *I will go to Hajj without any kind of burden on my shoulders.* That's exactly what I did. Asif's and Afsar's in-laws, Shakeera, and I all headed to Saudi Arabia for Hajj. Losing the job was like a burden off of my back.

One more job I did was working as an AVID tutor. Advancement Via Individual Determination is a nonprofit organization that provides professional learning for educators to improve college readiness for all students, especially those who are traditionally underrepresented in college readiness success in a global society. I, along with three other tutors, worked in a middle school, observing and helping teachers and students in AVID classes. There is a specific methodology in the students learning organization techniques, independent thinking, presentation skills, group dynamics, and leadership. Like they say, a job is more than just a paycheck. It is dignity; it is a means of earning respect for oneself, contributing to society, and achieving self-fulfillment.

I want readers to take away from this discussion that nobody is hurt by working, so it is best to keep working as long as you are able to. In retirement, you should be able to do some kind of a part-time job, consulting, or light business. I believe in being active if you can most of your life. Never run out of projects.

CHAPTER 8

A Little Bit of This and That

At the start of this chapter, I would like to jog and challenge your memory a little bit pertaining to the 1990s. Good luck.

1. Some European countries agreed to forbid cloning of what?

   a) sheep
   b) humans
   c) rabbits
   d) dogs

2. The Dow Jones closed at more than _____ for the first time.

   a) 8,000
   b) 9,000
   c) 10,000
   d) 12,000

3. Mother Teresa received honorary citizenship of what country?

   a) Pakistan
   b) Canada
   c) England
   d) USA

4. What leader wrote a declaration of jihad on Americans occupying sacred places and made a call for the removal of American military forces from Saudi Arabia?

   a) Osama Bin Laden
   b) King Fahd
   c) King Abdul Aziz
   d) King Faisal

5. An alleged affair with a woman led to the possible impeachment of a president of the United States. Name the president and the woman.

   a) Kennedy and Marilyn Monroe
   b) Clinton and Monica Lewinsky
   c) Roosevelt and Lucy Mercer
   d) Jefferson and Sally Hemmings

While you are pondering these questions, let me proceed with my story.

Several things in my life have happened by coincidence. I never thought I would ever visit one country in particular. Of all the places in this world, there is one I would have never thought of visiting. Somehow, I stumbled into it. A Chinese woman named Yan Hong Li was arranging for some people to go to China to teach English. She already had some people lined up and was still looking for one or two more. I signed up. She said, "Yes, we would like you to join the rest of the people and get ready with the visa." I was thrilled to learn about this opportunity. At that time, I was busy with some part-time jobs and was not sure whether I should go or not. The China opportunity was voluntary.

They would provide the room and board. We had to pay for our own airline tickets. Transportation inside China was paid for. At that time, I was newly retired and had lined up a part-time job. I was in a dilemma regarding whether I should go or not. I consulted with the family, and they said, "You should take this opportunity. It is the opportunity of a lifetime." I listened to them, and I completed all the formalities and planned to go to China. I asked Shakeera whether she would like to accompany me. At about the same period, we had been invited to go to a reception in San Francisco. We decided she should go to the reception, and I would go to China. Needless to say, I was excited.

In the following pages, I would like to give you an account of my visit to China.

On July 6, 2006, I flew from Madison to Detroit and then to Tokyo en route to Shanghai. It took almost seventeen hours to reach my destination. I was excited to be in China, as it was my first visit to this beautiful and historical country. I and other participants in the program were received in the Shanghai airport by our coordinator, and we were transported in a taxi to a five-star hotel. It was late at night, so we retired as soon as we were in our rooms.

The next morning, we were transported by bus to a city called Nanjing, which is about a six-hour trip from Shanghai. Nanjing is northwest of Shanghai and is the capital of Jiangsu Province. On the way, we enjoyed taking a look at the countryside. We saw plenty of rice fields. The rice fields were sectionalized and had been irrigated well. We had to learn the conversion of money, and then we purchased some food with the help of our interpreter. Along the highway, we met with lots of traffic. As it was the month of July, it was warm. I saw a few truck drivers who wore no shirt.

When we reached Nanjing, we were received warmly and treated like VIPs. There was a big banner that said, "Welcome, Foreign English Teachers," on the entrance to the building where meetings were to be held in the morning for welcome briefing, information, and discussion of expectations. In the afternoon, they took us through a bus tour of Nanjing. I was surprised to see the hustling, bustling city full of vigor. There were modern buses, two-wheelers, cars, rickshaws, and bicycles. Our guide took us to some points of interest. One landmark of interest was the Yangtze River Bridge. The bridge is four miles long, with four lanes of vehicle traffic on the upper deck and two railroad tracks on the lower deck. The Chinese are proud of this engineering marvel of their country. From the top of the bridge, we enjoyed a panoramic view of ships, barges, smaller boats, and parks next to the river. I must say, it is one of the most beautiful rivers in the world. Then we visited a freshwater pearl cultivation farm, where a farm employee explained to us the whole pearl cultivation process. Then the employee, without knowing the outcome, demonstrated splitting an oyster shell, and surprisingly, there were fourteen pearls in it. Everybody said, "Wow." That was amazing. Needless to say, we were all impressed. When we got back to our hotel rooms after the tour, we mingled a little bit more with each other and then took off to the streets to explore a little bit. We'd been told to bring certain necessary items on the trip, but still, we had forgotten some of them. Therefore, we went shopping for stuff, such as mosquito repellant.

The next morning, we were on our way to the city of Xuzhou, about three hundred kilometers (about 187 miles) northwest of Nanjing, where we were supposed to teach English to middle schoolers. We, the teachers, were treated well throughout our stay. We were accommodated in a nice hotel, and our boarding, lodging, and transportation were all covered by the school district. For lunch, we were served rice, curry, and fruit. I felt at home. Among the foreign teachers, there were about fifty to sixty people from various English-speaking countries, such as Australia, the United States, the United Kingdom, Canada, and New Zealand. Our group of eight people were all from the United States. Julia Fuller and I were the only ones from Madison, Wisconsin.

Xuzhou, pronounced suzho is an interesting historical city of about eight million people, with beautiful parks, shopping centers, museums, lakes, ancient tombs, and other historical monuments. We were excited to teach English to the kids. The kids were well behaved. They respected us all the time, and they even got attached to us. We exchanged our thoughts on different matters with the teachers from the Chinese middle school as well as with the students. Most of the English teachers had an English first name. Also, some of the students had an English first name. That made it easy for us to communicate with them. I asked them to sit in the same place every day of the class; that way, I could identify them by the chart I made with their names for my own information. It was challenging. Not all students obeyed my orders, and they sometimes switched seats.

I want to give a little bit of the history here. The Qin Dynasty ruled China from 221 BC to 207 BC, the Han Dynasty ruled from 207 BC to AD 220, and the Zhou Dynasty ruled from 771 BC to 256 BC. In the tomb, we saw jade-glazed preserved bodies of ancient emperors lying in glass coffins. It was amazing to look at. The ancient Chinese believed that jade had magical properties of preserving the dead. The tombs of the emperors were decorated with jade and bronze ornaments. It was believed that the afterlife is a continuation of life on Earth. With this in mind, the ancient Chinese buried the servants and attendants close to the tombs of the masters and kings so they could continue to serve them in the afterlife.

On display at the museum were jade and brass, ornaments, plates, plates, cups, and knives, which were unearthed by archeologists. Some of the artifacts are believed to be two thousand years old. In these old relics of the buildings, there were treasure storage rooms that looked like dungeons or caves. The openings to the interior rooms were covered by sliced-up stones that served as doors.

Another spectacular exhibit we saw was a replica of the Qin Dynasty Terra-Cotta horses and soldiers inside special glass-covered trenches. Near the beautiful Yunlong Lake is Lakeside Park, a swimming area with a shelter and pagodas. The building is shaped like a diving whale. Fish of various sizes and shapes, including sharks, are raised there. One can get a panoramic view of the whole area from a cableway 1,200 meters long that runs along Yunlong Hill and the lake. While riding along, we saw some open roadside restaurants; shade-tree barbers; small one-stall shops; and plenty of bicyclists, scooter and moped riders, and shoe repair men. The far right and far left sides of the street, maybe about ten to twelve feet wide, are reserved for the scooters, bicycles, two-wheelers, and other slow-moving traffic. The big buses, vans, and cars use the center portion of the road. It is orderly and safe. Bicycles in China are a means of transportation, and people often carry light loads. There are no beggars, as begging is prohibited.

A huge breakfast buffet was common in the hotel where we stayed. There were plenty of soups, dumplings, rice, fruits, and more. The orange juice was served warm. I do not know why, but that's the way it was. I noticed that tea was more common than coffee there. You must all have tasted Chinese tea at one time or another. We saw McDonald's, Pizza Hut, and KFC all over. The dollar goes a long way. Their unit of money is called a yuan, and at the time we were there, the exchange rate was eight yuans to a dollar. There were supermarkets, malls, electronics stores, and reasonable taxis available. People there are interested in Soccer, Ping-Pong, and Basketball. In general, people are good natured and helpful.

China has a population of, at the present time, 1.35 billion—roughly 20 percent of the world's population—and it is the third-largest country in land mass after Russia and Canada. The Chinese government had a rule that a family could have only one child, and the goal was to reduce the population of the country to seven hundred million. At the time of this writing (October 2015), however, they have changed the rule to two kids per family. The rule was relaxed based on the health of women who had to have abortions to keep up with the rule. It was taxing on women's health.

We learned a lot about the people, culture, and history of China. I perfected (not really) the use of chopsticks for eating food. I always asked for a spoon and fork just in case. In the school, teaching conversational English was not that difficult, as the students were enthusiastic and cooperative. Sometimes the school staff came to the class and watched our performance. For fun and entertainment, we watched some Walt Disney and other movies. From the cards that the students made for us, we could tell how much the kids enjoyed our teaching. Needless to say, we all had a wonderful time in China. The parting was sad. Some kids shed tears as they were saying good-bye to us. I was moved to see such a deep emotional attachment developed in such a short time.

I thanked all the people in my group and the Chinese teachers and their company for making my stay in China wonderful and pleasant. I made some good friends in China and have lots of fond memories. I thank Mr. Li, our coordinator, and Mrs. Yan Li of Madison for her efforts in making this wonderful trip possible for us. I would also like to thank the Jiangsu Provincial Government for sponsoring and undertaking such an enormous project and succeeding in it. I have been trying to go there again to see other parts of China, especially Beijing and the Great Wall of China.

China is a great place to visit for sightseeing as well as exploring. China is also the second-biggest economy in the world.

On the way back from China, I stopped in Tokyo, Japan. I found out that Tokyo is an expensive and fast-paced city. I stopped at a fast food place near the big railway station and talked to some people there. English was a little bit more common in Japan than in China, I thought. You will be dealing with big numbers in money when you are in Japan. I was in an ordinary hotel, where I think I paid ten thousand Japanese yen for one night. The conversion was about 121 yen to a dollar. The weather in Tokyo was much cooler on my route to the United States. The largest airport is called Narita International Airport, which is about seventy-two kilometers from Tokyo. Something new that I noticed was a dedicated space for temporarily storing umbrellas at the entrance of public places. It is self-managed in the sense that you put your umbrella in a slot, take a token, and take your umbrella back when you are done with your business. Of course, you pay for this self-service. I always wondered why we did not have those in the United States or other countries. An attendant does not have to be present all the time, and it is a quick way of making some money too. My hotel room happened to be not far from the railroad station, and the street was a hustling, bustling street. I also saw quite a number of people walking on the sidewalks on both sides of the street. My son, Shakeeb, has visited Japan a number of times. Since I was in Japan only for a short time, I did not bother to take any tours. I was anxious to reach home also. In Tokyo, I saw several American fast food restaurants, such as McDonald's. I did not want to miss my flight to the United States, so I went to the hotel to rest up and catch the next shuttle to the airport. All in all, it was a fun trip, and I had a great time.

Image 1: Author with his granddaughter, Laila Maryam Khan.

I have not arranged the pictures in the book in any order. In this picture, you see my little princess, Laila Maryam Khan. She is my favorite granddaughter. In fact, God has blessed us with only one granddaughter. By the grace of God, Shakeeb has two sons, Amaan and Jibraan, and later on, Farah had a son, Zayd. In the picture, Lailu is holding a pretty crown she used to wear quite a bit while being a princess. She enjoyed, as a little girl of three or four, being called a princess, and we enjoyed playing along. When she was little, she used to get excited whenever we visited. She used to run from her room to the living room, bringing her new toys to show to Shakeera and me. Her excitement knew no bounds. She used to make little projects with adhesive, paper, cardboard, glue, glitter, crystals, etc. Her dad, Mubeen, used to keep her busy with these little projects, and she enjoyed them. At the time of this writing, Laila has just turned eleven, and she is busy with her schoolwork at Stoner Prairie Elementary School, which is a good school. Little Zayd is also going to the same school. The school is in Verona School District. Both Laila and Zayd take the yellow school bus not far from our house in Madison. Farah has an arrangement to take the kids to and pick them up from the bus. Sometimes she asked me to pick up the kids from the school bus at the end of the school day. I loved this opportunity to pick up the kids. I consider it quality time when I spend time with the grandkids.

There is a saying in the Urdu language that the profit is dearer to people than the original sum of money invested. All children are a gift of God, but grandchildren are a special gift of God. You can spoil them, but you do not have to raise them. Rather, you are not directly responsible for raising them. At the same time, you cannot cast a blind eye to the issues of their upbringing and education.

At this time, I would like you to take a moment to read and enjoy these quotes:

> What a bargain grandchildren are! I give them my loose change,
>   and they give me a million dollars' worth of pleasure.
> —Gene Perret

> A grandfather is someone with silver in his hair and gold in his heart.
> —Unknown

> If becoming a grandmother was only a matter of choice, I should advise every one of you to become one. There is no fun for old people like it.
> —Hannah Whitehall Smith

> Grandma always made you feel she had been waiting to
>   see just you all day and now the day was complete.
> —Marcy DeMaree

An Urdu poet has beautifully put it:

> *Sham ko khali haath jab ghar jata hu'n mai'n*
> *Muskura deate hai'n bach-che aur mar jata hu'n mai'n*

This translates as follows: "Whenever I go home empty-handed in the evening, the kids become happy, and this makes my day." *Empty-handed* here suggests poverty.

Amaanu, as we call him with love, was born prematurely. However, by the grace of God, he grew up pretty normally without any problems. When he was a baby, he used to have a pretty smile, which he still has. When we visited Detroit, where Shakeeb and Naazneen live, we spent quite a bit of time with Amaanu and Jibbu (Jibraan). We love to do that. Shakeeb and I attended the sporting events of both kids. I watched Amaan play soccer. I think he used to be a star player. Amaan had a competitive edge and always wanted to excel in any sport or any project he undertook. By the grace of God, he has done that and has a good attitude. Amaan is a gifted student. While in Detroit, I once took him to a company called Sullivan for writing a competitive exam. I think he had good results. We are proud of that boy and wish him well in his high ambitions. May Allah provide all the necessary facilities and means so that Amaan can excel in his studies and pursue his dreams.

Jibraan is a sweet boy. He is about five years younger than his older brother, Amaan. They get along well. Hopefully, Amaan finds time to help his baby brother in his studies and other valuable aspects of life. Once, I took Jibbu to a sporting event of his brother and also to an ice cream social at his school. Little Jibbu was excited and requested I take him to different places in the school. He must have been about eight years old at the time. I noticed that Jibbu did not want to be in pictures. One time, he covered his face with his hat when the picture was being taken. Once, I went to a baseball game in which Jibbu took part. Jibbu, wearing his gear and carrying a little bat, was cute. The coaches were close to these little boys. One time, at the request of Shakeeb and Naazneen, I took Jibbu for a picnic at his classmate's house in one of the suburbs not far from Shakeeb's house. The house was beautiful and had a swimming pool, a terrace, slides, and other play facilities for the kids. The kids were mostly wearing their swimming trunks. The lady of the house put out a big food spread, which everybody enjoyed.

Another time, we took the kids to a University of Wisconsin event in Madison. There were lots of fun things to do while the kids were learning stuff. There were lots of opportunities to learn and have fun at the same time. There were inflated slides, basketball throws, and more, which the kids enjoyed immensely. Even Naazneen and Shakeeb enjoyed it. I am sure there will be more in this book about my grandkids from time to time. Like I said, children are a reward of life, and grandkids are even more so. I think grandchildren should cherish and always appreciate the quality time they can spend with their grandparents. My kids, Shakeeb and Farah, did not see much of their grandparents. When they were growing up, my dad was in India, and Mom had passed away. Also, Shakeera's parents were in India, and in those days, it was considered difficult to visit the United States. At the time of this writing, though, the parents of nonresident Indians visit easily enough. They even have visitors' insurance nowadays. All these facilities were unheard of when we were new in the United States. The world has become a small place now. It is good that even though we miss India, our country, a lot, there is more room for adjustment.

In our early days in America, there were no phones in our houses in India. We called the house of a neighbor who had a phone, and the neighbor would go to our house to tell our family there was a call for them. We had to wait almost three days to get a connection through the telephone company. It was a big hassle to talk to relatives in India. No wonder I missed India so much in the beginning after our arrival in this country. The only other way to communicate was to send a good old letter, which took about ten days to reach India. Travel within the United States for students was hard too. We always picked the bus for travel. Airplane travel was not as common as it is today.

Image 2: From the left: Sister Rehana, Sister-in-law Sabiha, and Shakeera

In this picture, my wife is holding my second Urdu poetry book, which was published in Bangalore in August 2015. Sitting with my wife are Sabiha, my brother Altaf's wife, and her sister Rehana.

I do not want you to wait any longer to find out the answers to the questions I enumerated at the beginning of the chapter. Here are the answers.

1. Cloning of sheep was banned. However, cloning of humans for experimental purposes was not banned.
2. In 1999, the Dow Jones closed at more than 10,000 points for the first time.
3. Mother Teresa, in 1996, received honorary citizenship of the United States.
4. Osama Bin Laden wrote the declaration of jihad and wanted American forces to leave the holy lands of Saudi Arabia.
5. President Bill Clinton denied a relationship between himself and Monica Lewinsky for about a year and then finally admitted it was true.

How did you do on your quiz? Great. We will have more as we go further in the book.

Like I was saying, I kind of felt a void that my kids could not readily see their grandparents. The grandparents felt bad about this as well. We all were sensitive about this matter. We decided to take the kids to India so the grandparents could see them and vice versa. We tried our best in that regard. The concept of quality time was not as prevalent with younger people as with the older people. Sometimes I thought about taking my kids to nursing homes to spend time with the senior residents there. The residents would be glad to see the young children, and also, they would have some good time with the children. I don't know if this ever happened, but I knew it was a good thought. During my fiftieth wedding anniversary in March 2014, during his presentation, my brother's son-in-law talked to the kids from the stage regarding how important the grandparents are in their lives. He said, "I did not have my grandparents when I was growing up, and I missed them very much." He said the kids should enjoy time with their grandparents, cherish the moments with them, and deserve their blessings. Parents and grandparents always want and pray for the best for their children and grandchildren.

I will include much more about my grandkids from time to time in this book, but first, let me bring up some trivia about some important events that happened in the world that might have affected our lives in one way or another during the turn of the century.

1. The chairman of a large US company stepped aside from the position of CEO and took up a different position in the company. What was the name of the company?

   A) US Steel
   B) General Motors
   C) Microsoft
   D) Apple

2. The Taliban destroyed some giant statues of a famous person in Afghanistan. Who was the person?

   A) Stalin
   B) Buddha
   C) Saddam Hussain
   D) Alexander the Great

3. What country is considered the first to allow legal same-sex marriage?

   A) United States
   B) Netherlands
   C) France
   D) Germany

4. A US retail giant announced it was going out of business after 128 years. Name it.

   A) S. S. Kresge
   B) Service Merchandise
   C) Montgomery Ward
   D) Sears, Roebuck, and Co.

5. A white American man was executed for his role in a federal government building bombing in a city in the United States. Name the city and the person.

   A) Chicago, Joseph Franklin
   B) Dallas, Joseph Duncan
   C) Seattle, Ted Bundy
   D) Oklahoma City, Tim McVeigh

Let's try hard to get the right answers. No peeking, please.

At this point, I would like to talk about something of general interest: a famous car that was different from other cars of that era. The automobile I am talking about featured gull-wing doors, a fiberglass chassis, and a brushed stainless-steel body. The idea to build this car emerged in the midseventies. The weight of the car was 2,712 pounds. About nine thousand cars were manufactured. The car I am talking about is the DeLorean DMC-12. Some of the celebrities who ordered and owned the car were the famous talk show host Johnny Carson and the singer and actor Sammy Davis Jr. Models were constructed for other countries, such as the United Kingdom. John DeLorean required millions of dollars to develop and keep going with the company. He faced tremendous budget overruns and eventually went bankrupt in 1982. Production halted in 1983. John DeLorean was arrested in October of 1982 for drug trafficking and was ultimately found not guilty—but it was too late.

It seems the dies for stamping were dumped off into the ocean, and some of them have been used as anchors for nets at a fish farm in Ireland. The original price of $12,000 was the equivalent of $65,000 in terms of 2014 money. DeLorean was six feet four inches tall and designed the car to fit someone of his stature. There were some twenty-four-karat-gold-plated cars manufactured, priced at $85,000 each. The last news about those cars was that they were going to manufacture an all-electric model for $90,000. These cars are now on display in various museums. I happened to see one in Las Vegas in those days. No doubt it is a beautiful car.

Now I would like to mention the most-talked-about murder case of the midnineties, involving famous football star O. J. Simpson. O. J. Simpson was born in 1947 and nicknamed Juice. He is a retired football player and broadcaster and a convicted felon currently incarcerated. Simpson played college football at the University of Southern California, where he won the Heisman Trophy in 1968. Subsequently, he played professionally for the NFL with the Buffalo Bills from 1969 to 1977 and the San Francisco 49rs from 1978 to 1979.

Simpson was the first NFL player to rush more than two thousand yards in a fourteen-game season. At a later date, the season was changed to sixteen games, which is what we have now. O. J. was inducted into college football's Hall of Fame in 1983 and professional football's Hall of Fame in 1985. After retirement, he started a career as a football broadcaster and actor. He was in a commercial in which he ran through airports to get someplace. Simpson was married when he met Nicole Brown in 1997 while she was working as a waitress at a nightclub. Simpson started dating her, even though he was a married man. Brown and Simpson got married in 1985. The marriage was not going well. Brown filed for divorce in 1992 based on irreconcilable differences. There was breaking news in 1994 that Nicole Brown Simpson and her friend Ron Goldman had been murdered. Simpson was found liable for the wrongful stabbing deaths of

Ron Goldman and Nicole Brown. As per the news, Brown and Goldman were found stabbed to death outside Brown's condo in LA. Simpson was found to be the person of interest in their murders. He failed to turn himself in, and what followed was watched by millions on the television screen. On the freeways of California was a slow-speed chase in which police pursued O. J.'s white Ford Bronco for about two hours. It was a live chase on TV. I remember watching it. All eyes were glued to the TV. Everybody knew that the murder suspect was in the SUV. Nobody knew what was going through the mind of the suspect. Some people thought he might kill himself as the chase was in progress. I do not recall if there was a communication attempt between the Bronco and the police cars. The police cars could have sped up and caught the suspect and arrested him easily. O. J. could have killed himself if the police had done that. We were wondering what strategy the police were adopting. What was going through the minds of the authorities? The police cars could have gone past the Bronco and surrounded him. Anyway, a number of things could have happened. Everything was unfolding right in front of our eyes on the TV. We were all on the edge of our seats and could not blink our eyes, for fear of missing part of this horrific drama. This chase interrupted coverage of an important final NBA game.

The pursuit, arrest, and trial were among the most widely publicized and watched events in the history of American television. "We will find Mr. Simpson and bring him to justice," the police said.

Simpson's friend Kardashian read a letter from O. J. in a news conference, which read as follows: "Don't feel sorry for me. I have had a great life, great friends. Please think of the real O. J. and not this lost person. Thanks for making my life special. I hope I helped yours. Peace and love, O. J."

Finally, Simpson arrived at his Brentwood home, and negotiations for surrender began. Police issued an all-clear bulletin, and O. J. was in custody. The trial of the century, as it is called, took place. People watched it tirelessly. I watched it closely too. The defense team consisted of late Johnnie Cochran, Robert Kardashian, Robert Shapiro, and F. Lee Baily, and on the prosecution was Marcia Clark. O. J. hired the most-powerful lawyers he could find. They were all powerhouses in the field of criminal law in those days. All of the lawyers had proven backgrounds and brilliant track records.

One of the most important witnesses in the O. J. Simpson case was Mark Fuhrman, the retired Los Angeles detective. Fuhrman is known to have planted a blood-stained glove at Simpson's Brentwood estate in a racially motivated effort to frame Simpson in the double-murder case. Defense Attorney Baily asked Fuhrman if he had used the word *nigger* lately.

Fuhrman replied that he had not used the word in ten years. However, the defense produced four witnesses who proved he had used the word much more recently. The time I am talking about here is based on the time during the trial period in the midnineties. The detective faced a perjury conviction and was ordered three years' probation and a fine. In an interview, he said, "Yeah, we worked with the niggers and gangs. You can take one of these niggers, drag them into the alley, and beat the shit out of them and kick them". "It relieves my tension" Furhman said. "We had them begging that they will never join a gang again." He said he used to tell them, "You do what you're told. understand, nigger?" He was asked if he planted false evidence, and he invoked the Fifth Amendment. Fuhrman, being a convicted felon, is prohibited from serving as a police officer in most states since then.

Even today, once in a while, we ask ourselves, "Where were you when the O. J. verdict was read?" On October 3, 1995, Simpson was found not guilty. President Bill Clinton was briefed ahead of time on security measures in case rioting occurred due to the verdict. An estimated one hundred million people worldwide stopped whatever they were doing to watch and listen to the announcement of the verdict. Long-distance telephone activity declined by 58 percent. The trading volume at the New York Stock Exchange was reduced by 41 percent. Water usage decreased, as people avoided using bathrooms for the duration. Government officials postponed their meetings. All this lack of activity resulted in $480 million worth of lost productivity for the nation as a whole. (Dorshwitz 2004)

I have not forgotten that I need to give you the answers to the quiz given earlier. I am sure you are curious to find out.

1. Microsoft
2. Buddha
3. Netherlands
4. Montgomery Ward
5. Oklahoma City, Tim McVeigh

CHAPTER 9

Story Behind the Pictures

Please refer to the pictures as they are labeled. I've given captions wherever possible.

Image 2. In this picture, you see my wife, Shakeera, holding my second published book of Urdu poetry. This book was published in Bangalore in 2015. Our time in Bangalore was short. We were in Bangalore from about July 15, 2015, to about September 3, 2015. In the beginning, I had no plans of getting this book published. I had taken my handwritten material just in case. When I went to Hassan, I talked to people and to my friend Gaffar about the possibility of publication. He gave me some names of individuals to contact. I did contact some of the people. The result was not to my satisfaction. The material needed to be composed in Urdu, the page layout had to be done, and the book had to be sent for publication. One important step was proofreading. I contacted several people, but nothing materialized to my satisfaction. Some people told me to go to Hyderabad and said it could be published easily there. Mr. Gaffar gave me a contact or two, but they did not come to terms with me or did not have time to take on the project.

I knew that the Urdu Academy would publish Urdu books for considerably less cost. I contacted a fellow called Afsar, and he gave me some names. I knew Afsar from 2010, when I went to Bangalore as a delegate for the World Urdu Conference. I was fortunate and honored to be selected as a delegate from the United States to participate and contribute to this conference. I was asked to address the conference on the topic of Urdu in America. I was glad to prepare a talk on that topic. In cities like Chicago, LA, New York, and Dallas, people have kept the Urdu language alive by arranging and holding poetic symposiums (mushairas) and other Urdu literary activities.

My first Urdu poetry publication was named *Meri Shayeri Meri Zindagi*. In a way, the title reflects my commitment to Urdu literature and Urdu poetry. I was thrilled to publish it. I was blessed by famous poets, such as Riyazyddin Atash Saheb of Chicago, Niaz Gubargavi Saheb of Chicago, and Fiaz-Uddin Sayeb Saheb from Arizona. Janab Haneef Akhgar Saheb was my main inspiration and mentor. I owe all of them a great debt of gratitude, particularly Hanif Akhgar Saheb. He taught me a lot of the ropes of the Urdu *shayari*, and those directions helped me a lot in my work. He not only gave me valuable suggestions on every word of my book but also directed me on the design of the book. Hanif Akhgar Saheb used to work for the United Nations in New York. He had a high post. When he retired, he moved to Houston, Texas, with one of his sons. He has been called the Jigar Moradabadi of modern times. Jigar Moradabadi was an outstanding poet of all times. Several organizations have given Hanif Akhgar Saheb awards for his work. I am fortunate and blessed by Allah (SWT) for the opportunity to meet him and become his disciple. When Ustad-e-Mohtarim Hannef Akhgar became ill, he turned me over to Tariq Hashmi, who was a good friend of Hanif Akhgar Saheb. I do not have enough words to praise Tariq Hashmi from Pakistan, who tirelessly gave his valuable time for my book. I used to call him at home and at work. Hanif Akhgar always used to say, "Always do something that will enhance your honor and dignity."

Image 3: HRHA English School

Image 3 was taken during a school function. The school's name is Haji Rasool Haji Aziz English Medium School. Haji Rasool Saheb was the name of my wife's grandfather. When her grandfather was working, he served in the military during the Second World War. My father-in-law was a big proponent of education. Not having much education himself, he appreciated people who had education and liked to pursue education, so he established this school and was successful in getting accreditation. He ran it successfully during his period, and now my brother-in-law Fiaz Hussain is running it. This is a great legacy that my father-in-law has left. In our religion, Islam, building or establishing a school to promote education, building or contributing in some way on a mosque project, or writing or publishing a book is considered to bring eternal blessings from God.

My father-in-law, Haji A. R. Abdul Aziz, was a great man, and I always pray to Allah to place him at the highest level in Janna. He worked hard to get my passport and visa to enable me to travel to the United States for higher studies in mechanical engineering. Those were times when I felt proud of myself. I felt as if I were on cloud nine. Like they say, success breeds success. I passed the BE degree exam from Mysore University. Engineers were considered the cream of the crop in society. Parents with young eligible girls kept an eye on the young engineering grads so they could have a chance to arrange marriages. In my days, there were seldom any girls in engineering. Kids from rich families came to BMS Engineering College in Bangalore to pursue engineering education. Several of them gave big donations to get admitted. I was lucky to have the recommendation of my uncle. My brother Akhil also tried to get accepted by the college but was not successful. I feel fortunate and blessed. A seat in engineering was at my doorstep, which I tried at the government engineering college after I passed intermediate college several years ago. I shared with you the story of why I did not get into engineering college at that time. It was one of the worst disappointments of my life. I think I could have been in engineering by 1954 and could have earned the degree by 1958. Life would have taken a different turn if that would have happened. Well, who can fight with fate? Whatever was written had to happen. That changed my life. I lost several years of my life.

Let's talk about the picture a little bit. From the left, you see Kareem Saab, a distant cousin of my father-in-law. He helped my father-in-law with the school affairs. Next is my father-in-law, Haji A. R. Abdul Aziz Saheb. Next is Haji Javed Hussain (Dillu), my brother-in-law. The little guy next to him is my youngest brother-in-law, Dildar Hussain. Next to him is Shakeera, who also briefly was a teacher at the school. The rest of the people in the picture are either teachers or administrative staff at the school. My father-in-law was fond of conducting functions at the school and invited political and other important people to the school. He also challenged Shakeera, Zaheer Saheb, Fatima Ahmad, me, and most any young person to give a speech. At that time, we did not realize it, but it was a great thing to overcome the stage fright that we all have. In India, at least when I was growing up, there were hardly any classes in which the student had to go up front and face the class to give a speech. I think that at times, we were asked to stand before the class to recite a poem or something. It was a great thing. I remember memorizing a portion of Shakespeare's play *Julius Caesar*. I recited in front of the class, "Friends, Romans, countrymen, lend me your ears; I come to bury Caesar, not to praise him." The excerpt was about twenty-five or so lines long. It was a challenge to memorize all of that. When I was younger, I was asked to memorize *soras* from the Quran. My English teacher made Shakespeare's plays so interesting to the students that everybody listened when he recited the poems, almost like an actor on the stage. My friends from the class and I had a great time in the class. This was at the intermediate college in Hassan. Everybody was interested in going to the English drama class. "Whichever class I will miss, I will never miss the drama class," most of my friends used to say.

Image 4: My wife putting a garland on my dad.

It is customary in India to show respect to elderly people by putting a shawl on their shoulders and back or putting a flower garland on them. My father was invited to a party at my father-in-law's house, and in this picture, you can see my wife putting a garland on him. He appreciated it very much. I appreciated Shakeera for doing this too. In our custom, a father-in-law should be respected as a father.

Image 5: My wife, Shakeera, and me

Image 6: Shakeera and me

Image 7: My daughter, Farah Deeba

This is my daughter, Farah Deeba. I think she is wearing all yellow just before her wedding. It was going to be her *haldi rasam*. There is a tradition that the groom as well as the bride get smeared with haldi paste on the face and hands. This is supposed to enhance the beauty of the girl before the wedding. I don't know what the significance of the boy's turmeric, or haldi, treatment is. Anyway, we have seen this in all Muslim weddings. Usually, this function is done within the private family. Not many outside guest are involved. You can take videos and photos for records.

Image 8: My son, Shakeeb, and grandson Amaanu Rahman

Image 9: Music maestro Naushad Ali, Shakeera, superstar
Dilip Kumar, and my brother-in-law Fiaz Hussain

Image 10: Mrs. Naushad Ali, music maestro Naushad Ali, Shakeera with Farah, Dilip Kumar with Shakeeb, and my brothers-in-law Dildar Hussain and Fiaz Hussain

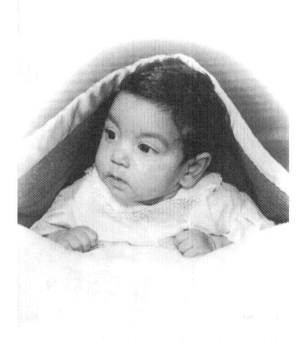

Image 11: My daughter, Farah Deeba, as a baby

Image 12: My wife, Shakeera, and me

Image 13: The author reciting poems from his
book during the book-launching ceremony

There was a book-launching ceremony in Bangalore for my first Urdu poetry book. We considered the Shadi Mahal as one of the places where we could do it. The Shadi Mahal is a hall originally owned by Shakeera's grandfather and dad, and it is conveniently located in Munireddy Palyam, where Shakeera grew up. However, Shakeera's dad decided to donate the facilities to a nonprofit organization so it could be rented out for community activities, such as weddings. Later on, even for our functions, we had to fill out an application to rent it. Still, it was a convenient place for our family functions and get-togethers.

One time, when we were visiting India, we wanted to hold a function there. A friend of ours wanted to do some singing as part of our function. The owners would not allow us to set up speakers there. However much we pleaded, they would not permit loudspeakers for the function. I, in my heart, regretted the day my father-in-law and others decided to donate the facilities to another organization.

Image 14: Program and Invitation card of the 2010
World Urdu Conference in Bangalore

Image 15: Shakeera and me

In this picture, Shakeera and I are posing in front of the Taj Mahal. When we flew to India that year, we flew to New Delhi directly. Normally, if we went to Bangalore, we got stuck there and didn't get the opportunity to see the other places.

As we were planning to visit India, Shakeera and I discussed our options. "Maybe we should plan to go to Delhi or something, and then after seeing other places, we can go to Bangalore," I said.

Shakeera agreed. We were young and took risks. We went to Delhi, Bombay, and, lastly, Bangalore. We enjoyed taking tours around the cities we visited. We had a blast.

Image 16: My son, Shakeeb, and grandbaby Amaan

I came to the United States on August 19, 1964, via Trans World Airlines. I do not know if they were able to fill enough fuel in the airplane for the entire flight in those days or not. The plane stopped at various places, such as Dhahran, Greece, Paris, and London, on the way to the United States. Upon our arrival in the States, they flew us from New York to Minneapolis en route to Madison, Wisconsin.

As I arrived in New York, my eyes were dazzled by the bright lights and the people. I was excited to be in the United States. That was my dream fulfilled. I had landed in America, the land of opportunity.

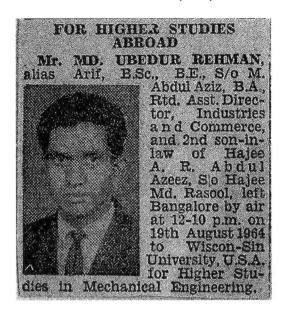

Image 17

Image 18: Authors Mother Amina Begum d/o Qazi
Mohammad Hussain. D.O.B not known. D.O.D 1946

In Image 18, you can see my mom holding my cousin Ather Ali's hand, I believe. My cousin Ather Ali, who worked as a professor at a university in Canada, lives in Montreal, Canada. In our travels, Shakeera and I have visited Montreal. However, we could not meet Babai (Dr. Ather Ali). Montreal is a beautiful city. While I was in Park Falls, I applied for a job in New York State. When I was called in for an interview, I took Shakeera along. We flew to Canada and then drove in Canada quite a bit. The speed limit signs were all in kilometers. Driving was the easy way to reach the place where I had the Job Interview. It was a paper mill in Potsdam, New York.

I had an all-day interview with various people in the plant. They gave me a tour of the place, and it looked interesting. I had heard that the taxes are high in New York. One of the officials also gave us a tour of the city. He took me to the mill power plant and introduced me to the people in charge there. Everything looked familiar to me. The interview went so well that the human resources guy and I thought they would offer me the job. But it did not happen. Needless to say, I was disappointed.

I worked at the Forest Products Laboratory, a division of the US Forest Service, which is a division of the United States Department of Agriculture. I joined this job on January 12, 1992. I was lucky to get this job. At the time when I was trying to change jobs, I was in Park Falls, Wisconsin, a small town in the northern part of Wisconsin. When I first told some friends at the paper mill that I was going to join the federal government, some of them asked me, "Are you going to be an FBI agent or something?"

"No, I will be an engineer at the Forest Products Lab, which performs research on paper products," I explained. I myself did not know much about the job at that juncture. It was an interesting place to work. They conducted all kinds of research on wood, paper, and other related products. Scientists from all over the world came there to work. The lab was also affiliated with the University of Wisconsin. The doctoral candidates from the university came to the lab to do their research. They used the lab's research facilities to do their projects. I recall scientists from Nigeria, India, Switzerland, Indonesia, Iran, and more working there. The scientific research papers published were available to the industry at no cost. There was a special library for the publications alone. At the time I was at the lab, a friend named Masood Akhtar had an office in the lab. Also, another scientist from India, Umesh Agrawal, worked in the lab. I think that at the time of this writing, he is still working at the lab. He worked on the brightness aspect of fine paper or white paper. He used, as I was told, Raman spectrography in his research. Sir C. V. Raman was a prominent scientist from South India. Raman was born in 1888 and died in 1970. He discovered the phenomenon of the scattering of light, which is known as the Raman effect. Dr. C. V. Raman won the Noble Prize for his discoveries in physics. He was also awarded the Bharat Ratna, one of the prestigious awards from the government of India. It is surprising to find out that he only had to spend two hundred rupees to make this discovery. Today it costs millions of rupees to work with his experiments and research.

Top picture; Dr. Gopi Chand Narang from India is being honoured
at the International Urdu Conference in Bangalore 2010
Middle picture: Dr. Taqi Abidi is being honoured at the same conference.
Bottom picture: Author is being honoured by the Governerner of
Karnataka State, Hans Raj Bhardwaj and Minister Dharam Singh.

Image 20: Group picture taken during the book launch
ceremony of the first poetry book of the author. (2010)
From left: Author, Mohammad Jaffer, cousin of author, Altaf,
brother of author, Professor Turab and Aziz Belgaumi

STATE OF WISCONSIN
EXAMINING BOARD OF ARCHITECTS,
PROFESSIONAL ENGINEERS, DESIGNERS
AND LAND SURVEYORS

CERTIFIES THAT IT HAS REGISTERED
AND AUTHORIZED TO PRACTICE IN
THE STATE OF WISCONSIN

MOHAMMAD O. RAHMAN

AS

PROFESSIONAL ENGINEER

IN TESTIMONY WHEREOF THIS CERTIFICATE HAS
BEEN ISSUED BY THE AUTHORITY OF THE BOARD
CERTIFICATE № E-17181 ISSUED NOVEMBER 22, 1977.

STATE OF WISCONSIN EXAMINING BOARD OF
ARCHITECTS, PROFESSIONAL ENGINEERS,
DESIGNERS AND LAND SURVEYORS

CHAIRMAN

SECRETARY

Image 21: Registered Professional Engineer License awarded to author

Mohammad O. Rahman, energy and utilities manager at **Flambeau Paper Corp.**, Park Falls, recently attended the sixth international power systems conference in Bombay, India.

Delegates from various countries, including the **Mohammad Rahman** United States, Soviet Union, Canada, Australia, China and India, participate in the conference, which provides general debate on innovative methods of energy sources, quality upgradation of power systems, evaluation of new technologies and economic as well as policy issues.

Image 22: Author selected as a delegate to the International Power conference held in Bombay India in 1990.

I was selected as a delegate for an energy conservation conference that took place in Bombay, India. At that time, I was working as an engineer and manager at Flambeau Paper Mill in Park Falls, Wisconsin. The mill partially shared the cost for me to attend the conference. It was nice of them to do that. The conference was in a building close to Film City in Bombay. I am curious about the places I visit. Altaf, my brother, used to work at the Reserve Bank in Bombay at that time. His quarters were near S. V. Road in Santa Cruz, Bombay. When Shakeera and I visited Bombay, it was warm and muggy there. Altaf's quarters were nice, but the airport was close to his house.

"Every time the airplanes take off, it wakes me up," I told Altaf the next morning after the first night.

"As time goes, you'll get used to it," said Altaf.

It was so warm that I preferred to take cold showers while I was there. I think we stayed about four days or so. We had a blast. We visited Haji Ali Dargah, Nariman Point, Chowpatty Beach, the Gateway of India, the Taj Mahal Palace Hotel, and Juhu Beach. It was nice of Altaf to take us to all those places.

At that time, TV was not common in India. A serial called *Sher-e-Mysore-Tipu- Sultan* was running. I saw that people were interested in that show very much.

We took a boat ride by the Gateway of India. Altaf, Sabiha, Shakeera, the kids, and I were there. When Altaf was there in Bombay, quite a few of the relatives from the United States visited him when they traveled to India.

A unique thing about the route to Haji Ali Dargah was that the small road leading to the *dargah* building got submerged under the sea water at certain times of the night. It emerged again during the day. We were awestruck when we heard about it. We talked about it a little bit when we visited the dargah.

We all believed it to be *karamat* (some kind of a holy power) of the famous wali (saint). Only God knows, but it could be due to the tides of the ocean.

It has been awhile since I have given you a quiz about past world events. Hold on for a while. I will get to it soon.

Image 23: Author's wife Shakeera Rahman

Image 24: Author's wedding March 8, 1964. All
his close family, extended family, relatives, friends,
nephews and nieces can be seen in the picture.

Image 25: Author's youngest grandkid, Zayd Skare

Image 26: This is a single passenger electric car being
experimented at the University of Wisconsin, Madison

Image 27: My grand children. Laila Khan and Zayd Skare

Afroz (author's youngest brother), author, Ghouse Peer

Anwar, author, Asif

Asgar and his second baby

Asif, Afsar, author during Hajj

Author was manager of this power plant, 1988-92

Author with his daughter, Farah

Author, Shakeera, Azimathulla, Munira, Nasreen, Zahir, Asif

Author, Zahir, unknown, Azhar (cousin), Kishwar
(cousin), unknown, Sageer, Asif, Altaf

From left: Cousin Fiaz, Nisar, Author's Dad, sister-in-law
Nasreen, Imtiaz, Author(groom), Dillu, Didar(Brother-in-
laws), Father-in-law A.R.Abdul Aziz, Cousin Mumtaz,

Ayjaz, Altaf, author, Nadeem, Akhil, Fiaz (cousin)

Dildar (b.i.l.), Azeeza

Sajida Shariff (author's sister-in-law)

Yasmin, Zahir, Altaf, Nasim

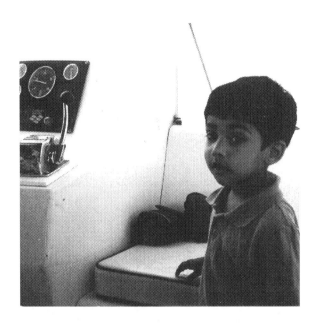

Jibboo

Jibboo and Leah

Farah and Naazneen

Dr. Ismail Shariff, Shakeera, and Author

Ismail Shariff and Sajida at the wedding of their first son Mansoor

Shakeeb and Naazneen

From Left- Shakeera, Farah, Naazneen,
Shabana, Shabana's Mom Nasreen

CHAPTER 10

More Reminiscences

Are you ready for another fun quiz about the events that happened in past history?

1. What airline was hijacked in 1986 with 360 people aboard, including a brave, selfless air hostess who saved the passengers without caring for her own life? What was the name of the stewardess?
2. In the early eighties, an Indian religious guru moved to the northwestern United States, established an ashram there, and attracted several Westerners to join his cult. What was his name?
3. The author landed a prestigious managerial job at what company and in what year and what town?
4. For more than a billion Muslims around the world, a certain month every year is marked as the month of blessing, prayers, fasting, and charity. What is that month known as?

With a bigger job comes bigger responsibility. I enjoyed the government job. The first year was a probation period. I easily passed that. I wanted to take it easy a little bit, as this was a government job, but I knew I could not take the job lightly, whether it was a private or government job. I liked the proximity to Chicago from Madison. I used to hear about mushairas (poetic symposiums) in Chicago when I was in Wausau and Park Falls.

Going to Chicago was within reach for me now, and I made a number of trips to Chicago.

Even though Shakeera did not like the mushairas much, she accompanied me quite a few times. A couple of young friends accompanied us sometimes. One was Rafeeq Rakhangi, and another was going to Edgewood College (I forgot his name). The kid from Edgewood used to publish selected *shers* from renowned poets on the Internet. Once, he published my couplet on the Internet. It went like this:

Mujh ko yeh kehke yaad kar lena, ek diya tha so bujh gaya aakhir

The translation is as follows: "You can remember me by saying there was a candle that has extinguished finally."

We used to drop Rafeeq at an Indian movie and pick him up on the way back to Madison. It was lots of fun for all of us. The mushairas in Chicago started at about nine or ten o'clock at night and ended at about two or three in the morning. When a person is young, he or she takes a lot more risks in life. I used to come back alone after the mushaira in the early morning. I used to do the same in Bangalore. Those days were something else. Even if I wanted to do that now, I could not possibly do it. However, quite a few times, I have stayed in a motel in Chicago after the event and come back to Madison the next day.

I have already given an account of the project work I did at Forest Products Lab. It was an interesting place to work. I made quite a few friends there. A friend of mine in the office told me, "Slow down a bit. You are not working for the private industry anymore; you are working for the government. Relax."

I'd heard similar comments, and my conscience told me to take it easy a little bit. I worked hard on my job, and at the same time, I listened to my heart a little bit. I got involved in my passions.

In Madison, I met Dr. Farhat Abbas and Dr. Hashim Waris, who were poets themselves. We exchanged our poetry among each other. Also, we used to have get-togethers at which we recited poetry. We all had good taste. Dr. Arif Ahmad arranged quite a few such get-togethers. There was a guy named Seemab who also wrote poetry and added a little humorous touch to it. It was a lot of fun. Seemab owned a restaurant on Reagent Street in Madison. Eventually, he moved to Toronto, Canada.

Everybody wanted to let the good times roll in Madison. We were all together, and there was a friendly atmosphere. Dr. Akbar moved to Madison from the Beloit area. He was also a poet in the Urdu language. From time to time, he recited his poetry at community get-togethers. He and his wife were singers also and occasionally invited people to their house for a little singing and poetry party. We all had a good time.

One time, the Pakistan Students Association arranged a function at which they talked to Dr. Sir Mohammad Iqbal, the famous and renowned poet. They invited me onstage to say something. Since the notice was short, I had not prepared a speech or anything. I recited Iqbal's well-known poem:

Sare jehan se accha hindoosta'n hamaara, hum bulbuleai'n hain iski yeh gulsitaa'n hamara

The translation is as follows: "Our beloved country, India, is the best in the world. We are the nightingales who live in it, and this is our garden." Sir Mohammad Iqbal was one of the greatest poets of our time. He wrote mainly about reformation, religion, people, and community. He was widely known as Allama Iqbal. He was a poet, philosopher, and politician. He inspired the Pakistan movement. He published many books. One of his famous quotes is the following: "Nations are born in the hearts of poets; they prosper and die in the hands of the politician." I keep reading his works, but I had the opportunity to read all his works when I was a youth. Dr. Iqbal was born in 1877 and passed away in 1938.

Another great poet was Mirza Asadullah Khan, born in Agra in December 1797. Both his father and uncle were of Turkish ancestry. Ghalib received no formal education and only learned from tutors at home.

He claimed he was a Persian poet, listing Urdu poetry as just a side effort. However, the fame of Ghalib evolved from his Urdu contributions.

In 1810, he got married and moved to Delhi. Apparently, he seldom cared for his wife. He had love affairs outside of his marriage. He talked about a love affair with a professional singer and dancer whom he had heard singing his ghazels. Even though he could live comfortably, he always had trouble maintaining his lavish lifestyle. He admired several women in his lifetime.

Ghalib began writing poetry in Urdu at age ten. He used Asad as his pen name in the beginning and then used Ghalib as his pen name. He switched to Persian poetry for a long period. His poetry was complex. His love of drinking booze and his lavish lifestyle kept him on the brink of poverty. Ghalib was never employed by the Mogul courts until his rival, Ibrahim Zauq, passed away. Ibrahim Zauq enjoyed the prestigious status of being the court poet, and he was the tutor of the last Mogul emperor, Bahadur Shah Zafar. Ghalib felt jealous of Zauq. Ghalib was disgusted with the British rule over India in those days.

The story goes that Ghalib was owed a pension from the British government. He tried to get it but was not successful. He eventually needed to go to Calcutta to get a lump sum or something, so he took off from Delhi to go to Calcutta, and it took him three months to eventually get the money. When he came back, he had barrels and barrels of booze on the backs of donkeys, which he bought as a reserve stock for his use.

People said to him, "Ghalib, sir, you had such difficulty in obtaining the money, and now after you got it, you spend it all in booze. What is the matter?"

"God has promised us that as long as we live, he will make all the arrangements for food, but he never promised us about drinks, did he? That's why I have to make all the arrangements for drinks myself," Ghalib replied.

There was once a poetic symposium (mushaira) in Delhi during his era. Ghalib and another poet from Lukhnow, Uttar Pradesh, were going back to their rooms at about two o'clock in the morning after the conclusion of the mushaira. On their way, they saw some donkeys eating mango shells. The outsider poet wanted to taunt Ghalib and said, "Sir, what is this? Do you have jackasses too in Delhi?"

Ghalib was a quick, smart, and witty thinker and replied "No, but sometimes they come here from outside."

This certificate is
presented to

Mohammad O. Rahman

upon your retirement from the
Government of the
United States of America
following ___11___ Years
of loyal service

March 8, 2003

Chris Risbrudt
Director

Image 28: Certificate awarded to the author at
his retirement on March 8, 2003.

This picture was taken on the occasion of the release of my first Urdu poetry book, *Meri Shayeri Meri Zindagi*. From the left, you can see the author with a red tie on, holding his book proudly. Next to me is my cousin Akhil, followed by Altaf, Professor Turab, and Azeez Belguami.

The book launch ceremony in Bangalore was a huge success. The book was launched in Madison, Wisconsin, on August 1, 2010, and in Bangalore in 2011. I am glad and thankful to God for providing me the opportunity to publish and launch this book. The book has been received well by Urdu-knowing people, and needless to say, I am proud of this contribution to Urdu Literature.

Ghalib was good at writing prose also. His "Ghalib ke Khutoot," or *Ghalib's Letters*, is respected as a good piece of Urdu literature.

Ghalib's poetry was unique, controversial, and complex. At one time, someone asked him to recite some of his poetry. Instead, he said, "Prior to that, let me tell you something. I will exchange all of my poetry for this one verse of Momin: *'Tum mere pass hote ho goya jab koi doosra nahin hota.'*" Momin was a famous poet of the same era, and the verse translates as follows: "You are as if with me when nobody else is around." In a way, it addresses the beloved or also God.

I could talk about many aspects of Ghalib's life and poetry, which are beyond the scope of this book. Ghalib is the most-talked-about Urdu poet, and his books are selling well even today. A number of movies and dramas have been made about him. Ghalib is one of my favorite poets, and I have read most of his collections. Naseeruddin Shah acted in a serial called *Mirza Ghalib*, and I watched it with great interest. It is a great production. There are other dramas also based on Ghalib's life and work. Ghalib died in 1869 at the age of seventy-two.

Now, without further delay, let's go to the quiz I gave in the beginning of this chapter. Do you recall any of these events?

The name of the Pan Am flight stewardess was Neerja Bhanot. The flight number was 73, and it was scheduled to take off from Mumbai, India, and fly to Karachi, Pakistan, through Frankfurt, West Germany, to reach New York's JFK Airport. In Karachi, when the plane was in preparation, four armed Palestinian men entered the plane forcefully. The pilots left the airplane by opening the roof hatch in the cabin. They sensed that there was some kind of a hijack trouble. They took a high risk and left the plane. There were 360 passengers on the plane, who were forced to stay on the plane by the terrorists, who were believed to be from the Abu Nidal Organization. Abu Nidal, or Sabri Khalil Al-Banna, was the founder of Fatah, a revolutionary council and militant Palestinian group commonly known as Abu Nidal Organization. He was born in 1937 in Palestine and died in 2002 in Baghdad, Iraq.

Neerja, the chief stewardess, opened the emergency slide, whereby the passengers slid off the plane safely. She could have escaped first, but she selflessly saved the 360 passengers on the plane. She gave her life for her passengers. All in all, twenty passengers were killed in the ordeal. She will be remembered for her heroic act forever.

The answer to the second question is Bhagwan Shri Rajnesh. Rajnesh, the Indian mystic guru, was born in 1931. He was a professor of philosophy and traveled throughout India as a public speaker. He criticized Mahatma Gandhi and socialism and became controversial. Some people thought he stood for open sexuality, and he has been called a sex guru. He reinterpreted the teachings and writings of various religious leaders, mystics, and philosophers. He settled in Bombay in 1970 and then opened up an ashram in Pune, India, in 1974. His ashram attracted several Westerners. There were mounting tensions between him and the Indian government. In the early Eighties, he moved to the United States to the State of Oregon. He established a community called Rajneshpuram. He had conflicts with the authorities as well as local residents over land use and other issues. Both sides exhibited hostility. His followers donated material items, including Rolls-Royce cars, to him. At one time, he had about ninety-three Rolls-Royces in his possession and had about two thousand followers. In 1985, he was accused of some bio terror (food poisoning) attacks. It has been brought up that he poisoned seven hundred people. He was arrested for immigration violations and was deported from the United States. Twenty-one countries in the world denied his reentry. He returned to Pune and died in 1990.

My career took a turn in 1988, when I was offered a job as a Manager of utilities at Flambeau Paper Mill in Park Falls, Wisconsin. I was using McGinnity as a reference for seeking managerial or other advancements in my job. I have talked several times before about this job. I was at the highest rung on my job ladder. I knew that supervising people was the most difficult part of a person's job. Under me were Dave Wagner, the operations supervisor; Dennis Morgan, the maintenance supervisor; and a planning supervisor whose name I forgot. Every week or twice a month, I gave them a list of things to complete. This list was regularly reviewed the next Monday to see what they had accomplished. This was a lot of work, but I did not know any other way of controlling and being on top of the goals of the department. I was accountable to management about the accomplishments.

Every Monday, there used to be a meeting of all managers in the conference room. I was supposed to address the group as to the state of the department during the past week. This was a big challenge. At the end of my presentation, there was a question-and-answer session. Besides these, there were emergency meetings regarding how to plan paper production during the outage of a boiler or other issue. The utilities department is critical for production. If there was not an adequate supply of steam, they started looking at the utilities manager. The boilers in the power plant did not run smoothly all the time. The boiler tubes leaked or broke. The associated equipment for the boiler could have a malfunction. There were many things that could break down. That's why preventive maintenance is important. We used to have big planned outages for the utilities department. There were contractors from all over, and our mill looked like a city with all the hustle and bustle. We budgeted for these outages. Everything had to be crystal-balled properly. Our hands were full during these outages. It was an opportunity for us to fix things in our department. We were always on the lookout for what needed to be done during these downtimes. Even after all our careful planning and preventive maintenance, mechanical things tended to break down. It was a big challenge. I kept working well into the evening hours sometimes. It was not unusual to go to work on weekends sometimes.

In addition, there were environmental constraints we needed to comply with. There was a Department of Natural Resources office in Park Falls, not far from the mill. We were responsible for all the rules and limits, and once a year or so, we needed to prepare a report of compliance. In order to satisfy this requirement, we used an outside company to do the stack test. The outside company gave us guidelines to do this project properly. The company we hired had all the tools necessary to carry out this test properly. The boiler fuel and different parameters were changed, and we directed all that with the boiler operator. These tests took several days and needed to go to different heights in the stack.

Even though we had a beautiful house on the lake in Park Falls, we still owned the house in Kronenwetter (Wausau). Park Falls was a beautiful small town, and traffic-wise, there was no rush hour. In fact, while I was there at the end of the eighties and in the early nineties, there wasn't a single traffic light in town. It was not needed, I suppose.

The next answer is the holy month of Ramadan. Ramadan, or Ramazan, is the ninth month of the Islamic calendar. It is the month when the revelation of the Quran occurred first. The month lasts about twenty-nine or thirty days. It is supposed to be observed by all adults, except those who are sick or traveling or women who are undergoing their monthly period. The people fasting are supposed to refrain from eating, drinking, smoking, and sexual activity. In many mosques, they complete the Quran recital in that month. There are *hafiz-e-Quran* (people who memorize the whole Quran). Extra prayers are held during that month.

The author's name is Salman Rushdie. The book he wrote was called *The Satanic Verses*. Ayatollah Khomeni of Iran was of the opinion that the book was offensive and insulted Prophet Mohammad, the last prophet of Islam. The ayatollah sentenced him to death. The book was banned in several countries. I went to the local mall bookstore and saw that the book was available. I kept myself from buying and reading it, but I was surprised we were able to get the book easily.

Salman Rushdie is a British Indian novelist born in Bombay, India, in 1947. Because of the fatwa in Iran and possible threat to his life, the British government put him under police protection. In 2012, he published a memoir, and he also has written some explanations about his controversial book. However, the fatwa still stands.

CHAPTER 11

Love of Bollywood Films, Dramas, and TV

I was about eleven or twelve years old when I had the experience of watching a movie in a regular theater. It was in Bangalore. Our uncle Cha Cha took Asif and me to the movies. We used to wear caps at that time. It was customary for Muslims to wear caps in that era. Altaf must have been too young for Cha Cha to take him along. I think the name of the movie was *Chandni Raat*. Naseem Banu was the heroine in it. Naseem Banu was the mother of Dilip Kumar's wife, Saira Banu. We saw old films in theaters such as Prabhat Talkies and States. The street called Kempegowda Road was full of cinemas in those days, including Prabhat, States, Alankar, Sagar, and Kempegowda Talkies, and on the side streets, there were theaters as well. Down the street was the Majestic. In South Parade (Cantonment), on M. G. Road, there were a bunch of cinemas, including Liberty Talkies, Plaza, Empire, and Rex. Also, I remember Himalaya Talkies, Elgin Talkies, Movieland Talkies, and Santosh. In the city market, there was Paramount Talkies, where, as youngsters, Akhil and I used to watch Nadia's *Spy Smasher* and other films. We liked the excitement of fight scenes in pictures. Joh Kawass was another guy we watched.

We watched several Kannada films in those days. In the small Karnataka towns where my dad was posted, there was no demand for Hindi films, or nobody understood them. The movies were shown in reasonably large tents. I think either they connected to the city utility or they had a generator of their own. I was too young to bother thinking about that.

In a town called Madhugiri, near Koratagere, where I attended middle school studies, Saleem, my cousin, and I had a deal with the local police inspector. The deal was that if we brought some water from the public tap to the inspector's house, he would let us go into the tent to watch movies. Police inspectors, in those days, especially in India, had a lot of clout. They got free bus rides, free entrance to the theaters, and all kinds of privileges. So whenever we decided to go to the movies in the only tent theater in town, we asked Inspector Saheb if he needed any water at his house. I am talking about 1945 and 1946; there was no running water in most of India in those days. So we completed our wish that way. We also learned how to stealthily get into the tent sometimes. We did not even have to carry water to the inspector's house. Of course, this was done carefully without the knowledge of the inspector.

When I was about eleven years old, I developed an interest in plays. I used to watch live dramas and movies about Mahabharata and Ramayana in small towns, such as Hiriyur. We were in Hiriyur when India became independent from British rule. Also, Dada Saab passed away in Bangalore that year. Bavajan was newly married to my second mother.

I used to make headgear like the kind Ramayana and Mahabharata used to wear. I also tried to tinker with a lens and a cardboard box to project an image. I even directed and performed in a play at home, and we asked my dad and my aunt to watch our play. It was all home-rigged with a lot of enthusiasm and energy behind it. The stage actors were Asif, Altaf, and perhaps Akhil. I do not know how much my audience enjoyed the play. We watched Kannada plays called *Aliya Devaru* (*Son-in-Law, the God*) and *The Maqmal Topi* (*The Velvet Cap*). Usually, there was lots of down-to-earth comedy in them. We watched quite a few plays. There were also some tent movies. In these small towns, there was no building for a theater. The cinema was kind of cheap entertainment in those days. Everyone enjoyed two to three hours of entertainment. People forgot their worries for that duration, and the cost was not much. The farther you sat from the screen, the more expensive the ticket. I noticed that in America, there was no classification as such. Some people wanted to sit closer to the screen, and some wanted to be farther away from the screen. I have heard that if you sit close to the big screen, it is bad for your eyes. It's the same way with the television. I have always advised my kids to stay away from the screen when watching TV. However, they more often than not lie down close to the TV to watch.

There was an actor from Mysore who was good with animals, especially elephants. It was as if they listened to him. He tamed them well. Mysore is a beautiful city about eighty miles from Bangalore. I have roots in Mysore, as my father grew up in Mysore. Also, I passed high school at St. Philomena's High School in Mysore. Even though I played at some mischief, I liked the studies. I missed passing in first class by eleven marks. That was a big disappoint for me.

The name of the actor from Mysore was Sabu. He became famous in those days. All of the Mysoreans were proud of Sabu. He went to Holly wood and Britain to act in movies. Sabu was born in 1924, and his religion was Islam. He was the son of an elephant rider. He acted in films called *Elephant Boy, Thief of Baghdad, Arabian Nights, White Savage,* and *Cobra Woman.* He became an American citizen in 1944 and married a little-known actress named Marilyn Cooper. He had two kids with her. His career started to decline after World War II, as Hollywood was not able to offer him great roles like the ones he used to have in the British film industry. He met with sudden death in 1963 due to a heart attack. His wife used to say that two days before his death, during a routine medical checkup, his doctor told him, "If all patients were as healthy as you are, I would be out of a job."

I used to see movie advertisements posted on the compound walls of public buildings. My uncle used to talk about them. There was a middle school (red building) not far from where we lived. I used to see all kinds of billboards about movies on its compound wall. One I remember was *Kunwara Baap* (*Bachelor Father*). There were several others too. Most compound and other walls displayed ads for movies. Close to our Malleswaram house, there were two theaters that I recall. One was Central Talkies, and the other one, a little ways up the road, was Swastik Talkies. My cousin Akhil's mom used to go to the movies there. We used to walk past Swastik Talkies to go to our middle school in Sheshadripuram. The race course was close by. The Bangalore race course attracted many Bollywood celebrities. It was a big gambling event. Some people climbed tall trees to watch the horse races without having to pay any entrance fee. I was generally interested in the races but was never so desperate. However, we used to play cards a lot and gambled a little bit. Mr. Zaheer Uddin, Sabiha's father, joined us in these sessions. Asif, my brother, was considered the principal of this cards school, as he was the one who arranged these sessions. It was a friendly atmosphere.

One time, I decide to collect pictures of film celebrities. I made a book, and with the help of gum, I attached pictures in the book. I stuck in there all the pictures I could get my hands on. The pictures were neatly clipped from papers and magazines and became part of a register that I browsed quite a bit. As soon as my aunt saw that, she tore it into pieces and was angry at me for acquiring such a bad habit instead of paying attention to schoolwork. I was disappointed but helpless. All my hard work and collection were washed away at the snap of a finger. Part of my desire was to know the names of the artists and little bit about their background. Whether they were heroes, heroines, comedians, or character artists, I felt comfortable in knowing their names. Even today, even with small screen artists, I feel comfortable if I know their names. Asif is the same way.

I want to mention here the names of some old actors whose pictures I have seen. Here we go: Mubarak, Pritima Devi, Yakub, Gope, Shobana Samrath, Ulhas, Shanta Apte, Surendra, Kishore Sahu, Karan Dewan, Jeevan, Jayant, Noor Mohammd Charlie, Prem Adib, Agha, Sapru, Trilok Kappoe, Nirupa Roy, Durga Khote, Bhagwan, Moti Lal, Meena Shori, and Geeta Bali. Each one made his or her place in the industry. There are a lot more I recall, but I cannot list them all. At that time, the word *Bollywood* had not been coined yet. Most of the films were shot in those days inside the studio. The photography was not that sharp. Films were only black and white. Color technology was not there yet. They colored some black-and-white films, but the effect was not great. Since the pictures were shot within the confines of the studio, the effect was poor. After several years, they took the cameras outdoors, which worked well. The photography was much clearer and sharper. The film industry had to learn a lot.

Then they started making pictures in color. The technology was in place and used to the maximum effect. Today Bollywood makes more pictures per year than Hollywood. However, there is a lot to be desired from the Bollywood movies. The directors and producers want to make movies only for entertainment value. They seldom make movies that have a goal of reformation or a lesson or are based on a famous novel. Sometimes they make biographies of famous heroes, such as Neerja Bhanot, Bhagat Singh, and Mahatma Gandhi.

In Hindi cinema, with the main concept being entertainment, people look for a number of dances and songs as well. Most of the time, the songs go along with a dance number. In my time, there was a famous dancer named Cuckoo, who was an Anglo Indian. For those of you who do not know, Anglo Indians are English citizens who sometimes were crossed with the Indian community. Quite a few Anglo Indians, after the independence, went back to England, and quite a few stayed in India. In Bangalore, they stayed in communities like Benson Town and Frazer Town, and of course, they spoke English and little Hindi or Urdu. I mentioned before that I worked as a bill collector and sales promotor for a leading newspaper in Bangalore called *Indian Express*. In that job, I traveled all over Bangalore on my bicycle to make customer contacts. This was a summer job or interim job in between my studies break. It was a hard door-to-door kind of job. Sometimes there were housewives alone in their houses. I also tried to sell magazine subscriptions along with the newspapers.

Let's go back to the dancers in the movies. Helen became popular in dancing. There was hardly any movie without a dance from Helen. The song numbers and dances she did became popular. Helen also took a major role in some movies. Some original South Indian actresses were good at dancing also. Vaijayanti Mala and Sri Devi come to mind. As per some surveys, a list of some top dancing stars was made. I am not giving the actual standings, and you can be the judge on your own or have your own list. My own personal list includes Katrina Kaif, Priyanka Chopra, Aishwarya Rai Bachan, Jaya Prada, the item girl (Helen), Urmila Matondkar, Shri Devi, Vaijayanti Mala, Meenakshi Sheshadri (the youngest woman to be crowned Miss India in 1981), Madhuri Dixit, Karina Kapoor, and Karishma Kapoor. They were all formally trained to be dancers along with being actresses.

Of course, the male actors don't have to be staying behind as dancers either. There are Hrithik Roshan, Shah Rukh Khan, Salman Khan, Ranveer Singh, Akshay Kumar, and Ranbir Kapoor. In this era, if you are not a good dancer in Bollywood, you will normally be classified as not a good actor either. In other words, you need to possess good dancing talent in order to be successful. There are other kinds of professional dancers also in the industry. Some other dances in India and in Bollywood are bhangra, bharata natyam, dandiya, kolatam, manipuri, garba, kathak, and kathakali. In one way or another, they might have been presented in Bollywood movies.

Songs were the highlights of the Hindi pictures. Some of the old songs I remember are "Diya Jalao," "Mere Liye Jahan Mein, Chain Na Kharar Hai," "Chal Chal Re Nau Jawan," and "Jawa'n Hai Mohabbat." Some of the actors were singers also. There was no playback singing or lip syncing in those days. I know that Ashok Kumar, Suraiya, Sehgal, Surendra, and Shyam sang their own songs. There might be others I am not aware of. While I am at it, let me share a tragic event in Shyam's life. Shyam was born in Sialkot (now Pakistan) in 1928. He became a successful actor at a young age and acted with famous female superstars of his time, such as Munawar Sultana and Suraiya. He acted in many famous movies, such as *Dilligi* and *Bazaar*. One time, while he was shooting a horse-riding scene for *Shabistan*, the reins slipped from his hands, and he suffered a nasty fall that caused injuries to his head. He was rushed to the hospital, but he succumbed to the wounds he received. He was only thirty at the time. The film industry suffered a big loss at the time.

The Villains played an important role in the film industry. Usually, the stories in Hindi films were about a boy meeting a girl, and then there was trouble between them due to a guy who also wanted the girl and did everything to break up the two lovers. There were lots of fights and chases, and finally, the villain was defeated, and the original couple was able to get back together. This type of story in Hindi movies was common. The villians I grew up with were Pran, Dilawar, Jeewan, Gulshan Grover, Prem Chopra, Amjad Khan, Ranjeet, Ajit, Sadashiv Amrapurk, and Amrish Puri. Some of these villians, even though they posed as bad men in the movies, were good, gentle men in real life.

Who does not want to have a good laugh, even if it has to be at the expense of others? Comedy plays an important role in Hindi cinema. It's an important ingredient of movies. People want to have a good time when they go to the movies. I grew up with comedians like Gope, Yakoob, Mehmood, Johnny Walker, Asrani, Johnny Lever, Paresh Rawal, Mohan Choti, Jagdeep, Kader Khan, Rajendra Nath, and Devendra Verma. Stand-up comedy was not common in the Hindi film industry. At the time of this writing, stand-up has become more common. Kapil Sharma and Shekar Suman have become famous in this area. Like they say, it is a big challenge on the part of the comedian to make people laugh. The films today are a far cry from what we used to have. Shooting used to take place in Ooty and other outside locations. However, nowadays, they travel to Europe, America, and different other locations. First, they were confined to the studio; then they came out of the studio and stayed mostly within India; and now, most of the time, we find the industry shooting films outside of India.

The poets and songwriters that I grew up with were Shakeel Badayuni, Sahir Ludhianvi, Jan Nisar Akhtar, Qamar JalalAbadi, Kaifi Azmi, Khateel Shifai, Gulzar, Majrooh Sultanpuri, Rajender Krishan, Jawed Akhtar, Hasrat Jaipuri, and Shailendra. These were all great literary poets. For films, sometimes they needed to write stuff that was light and easily understandable by the general audience. Sometimes the songs were released before the movie itself was launched. I mentioned to you earlier that we all used to listen to Radio Ceylon and Binaca Geetmala every other week.

They rated the songs as per their quality. Singing along and repeating Hindi songs was a big hobby for us as youngsters. Basheer, Mohammad Jan, Akhil, and I used to go to isolated or secluded building porches to practice Hindi songs. I became fond of Mohammad Rafi, Mukesh, and Talat Mahmood songs. Sometimes I used to sing female songs too. Our relatives sometimes asked me to sing a song from the latest movie we all watched. I am not joking that I was able to repeat the song exactly as it was after hearing it only once in the movie. In the early days, I did not pay much attention to the lyrics of the song. The only thing that was important to me was the tune. We were always wondering how the music director made tunes given a set of lyrics. We figured out that in the newer films, they do not have to create a tune; it is the opposite. In other words, the music director gives the tune to the lyricist, and he or she will find words for the given tune. Makes sense, doesn't it? I seldom watched any English or Hollywood movie, unless it became very famous. In those days, I watched *Come September*, *The Ten Commandments*, and *Samson and Delilah*. To tell you the truth, I could not follow the movie dialogue well. Culturally, it was all Western or American culture, which was not easily understood by Indians who had never traveled overseas.

I won't be completing my talk about Bollywood unless I talk about the film directors. I think the biggest burden for the success of the movie rides on the shoulders of the director. Some of the directors I grew up with are Satyajit Ray (Pather Panchali), Guru Dutt, Bimal Roy, Mehboob Khan, A. R. Kardar, K. Asif, Raj Kapoor, and V. Shanta Ram. All these directors made unforgettable contributions to the film industry and brought several great films to the industry. I also cannot complete my discussion without mentioning the names of veteran actors Sohrab Modi, Pratima Devi, Ashok Kumar, Nazir Hussain, K. N. Singh, Sajan, Prathivi Raj Kapoor, and Dilip Kumar. They all made big contributions to the film industry. Besides these, there were some child actors in those days who might be in their sixties or so at this time. I can recall Daisy Irani, Baby Tabassum, and Baby Naaz. Before I end this chapter, I would like to see how much Bollywood knowledge you have.

1. Name some of the extramarital affairs in the past years between the actors and their heroines.
2. A member of our family watched the film *Nagin* fourteen times. Who was it?
3. Name three actors who have committed suicide.
4. Which famous actor was a fan of Suraiya in his youth and walked miles to watch *Dilligi* forty times?
5. A member of our family was so fond of Suraiya that he named one of his daughters Suraiya.

I would also like to say a few words about TV. At first, Shakeera liked soap operas a lot. Of course, these were all American. We watched comedy shows a lot. All we had when we first came to this country was a black-and-white TV. When Shakeera and I started making our first home, I rented a TV, believe it or not. That was the quick way of getting her something to watch. We did not have kids at the time. Also, we bought a sewing machine, and we financed it. With my meager income as a student, we could not make ends meet. Shakeera did not have any idea how to make money. She became a caretaker for a single woman and watched her kids in her apartment for a while. I used to take her over there. I think sometimes she took the bus. I was busy with my studies for the master's of engineering degree. We used to watch shows including some westerns, *MASH, Good Times, Sanford and Son, Gilligan's Island, The Beverly Hillbillies, Green Acres, My Favorite Martian, Get Smart, Mission Impossible, Hogan's Heroes, The Munsters, I Love Lucy, I Dream of Jeannie, My Three Sons,* and *Happy Days.* Some of them with good comedy became my favorites. Late at night, we used to watch Johnny Carson regularly.

In the early days, we usually had only three major channels broadcasted: CBS, NBC, and CBS. The educational channel and some others ended at about midnight. There was no reception at all. Only some colored vertical lines appeared on the screen. Many homes, including ours, saw the luxury of color TV with better reception. The consoles were retired in 1978. Per a survey, there are more TVs in a house than there are people, or there are TVs in every room of the house. *TV Guide* became the most popular magazine in homes. It was in high demand in our house. Cable TV brought several channels to the home TV. The dish revolutionized the TV industry further. We, in our house, have both cable and a dish. The dish is mainly for Indian channels. Accessories, such as the Betamax and VCR, allowed us to record the shows we liked and watch them whenever we wanted. For me, it was never a straightforward process to record anything on the TV using the VCR or Betamax. The cassette sizes were different from Betamax to VCR. We ended up buying a VCR machine, and we already had Betamax. Betamax lost its charm fast. The Indian movies were only available on VCR. We used to buy prerecorded VCR movies form Moinuddin of Dallas. Moinuddin is a friend from Bangalore. He used to live near Chicago once, in Elk Grove Village. People used to be fond of meeting each other once. I do not know what happened, but they do not care for each other much anymore. Moin's brother Noor was also a friend of ours, and we have lost touch with him for quite a while. He had a telephone refurbishing business for a while, which he closed up in a hurry. Both Moin and Noor turned out to be business-oriented people. Noor put to work everyone in the family in his telephone refurbishing company. Kishwar also knew Noor well at one time.

At the time of this writing, people are enjoying their dish service for Indian and other movies and cable for most of the regular channels. There are many accessories now, such as Apple TV, which is sort of Internet connected to the TV. Also, by using proper cables, we can project the computer screen onto the large TV screen. We can connect flash drives to the TV with Dynex TV. We can watch pictures from memory cards on the big TV screen. We can watch videos on the TV. Pictures from smartphones can be watched on the TV screen also. There is a revolution, I would say, in the possibilities with various accessories and the right gadgets that we can buy. If I need to connect our computer to the television screen, there are connections called VGA and HDMI. I have covered some other related stuff elsewhere in the book.

CHAPTER 12

More Ramblings

In retirement, lots of people reflect on their previous work lives. Lots of nostalgic thoughts come to mind. There are some failures, and there are some successes, hopefully. Not all of our wishes come true. Like they say, man proposes, but God disposes. You always try to learn from your mistakes. However, what you learn might not be enough; you need to put into practice what you have learned. Otherwise, it will not do you any good. Some people's retirement plans are neat and aggressive. For example, they build a home in a place of their choice, and their home is ambitious and something they love dearly. While I write this, I am thinking of my assistant director from Forest Products Lab, where I retired from. About two or three years into her retirement, she started building a house in Florida, where she planned to retire. I did not stay there long enough to see how it all panned out for her. Some other people follow the same line of thought also. It makes sense that you are working and getting regular checks; therefore, you can finance the project you are after. When I was in California for an assignment, somebody was selling a cottage for a reasonable price. I thought this was an opportunity for me to buy something in California. However, there were some conditions regarding the employee being from a different region or something, so I could not buy it. I regretted that. Within a couple of years after that, I retired from the service. I had an opportunity to buy something in Florida also. I was serious, but it did not materialize for reasons beyond my control. The same property is more than double in price now. Opportunity comes in life only once. I believe that. A survey was taken a long time back at Great Lakes Steel, asking retirees what they would do if given a chance to start their life again. Several people replied that they would get a much better education. The value of education can never be underestimated.

Anyway, at this time, for the information of the young people, I want to jump to the tragedy that happened in New York on September 11, 2001. US soil had never experienced such a severe tragedy. The Twin Towers of the World Trade Center collapsed on that day, when they were struck by two jet airliners hijacked by terrorists affiliated with al-Qaeda. There were actually four hijacked airplanes that day. Two crashed into the Twin Towers, one into the North Tower and the other into the South Tower. The collapse destroyed the complex, which included some adjacent buildings. The debris from the collapsing towers damaged the other buildings and structures. Both the North and South Towers collapsed. A total of 2,763 people died, of which 2,192 were civilians, 343 were firefighters, 71 were law enforcement officers, 147 were airline passengers, and 10 were hijackers. Due to the impact and fire, the steel-framed structures were heavily damaged, and that caused the collapse.

One airliner, flying at 440 miles per hour, flew directly into the North Tower at 8:46 a.m., impacting the ninety-third and ninety-ninth floors. I was working in my office that day, and I told my office mate that the World Trade Center was on fire. After about seventeen minutes, the South Tower was hit by another airplane. Ten thousand gallons of jet fuel burned for a few minutes. The contents of the building burned for about an hour and a half after that. A couple of people ran down through a stairwell that was not affected. Several people jumped from the windows, not being able to withstand the heat. The North Tower collapsed after burning for about 102 minutes. There were people trapped under the debris. Phones lines jammed with about 230 million calls. At first, we thought it was just a movie, and it could not happen for real. We at Forest Products Lab watched the tragedy in the fifth-floor conference room. We all watched with awe as the whole thing unfolded. Since we were a federal government organization, we were asked to go home right away. Oh, what a day it was. It is still instilled in my mind like a nightmare. We were all glued to the

TV for several days after that, trying to figure out what had happened and how it had happened. Some people thought it was an inside job. It does not make any sense, but that was what some people thought when George Bush took over as the president of the United States. Things were so much under control that Bush wanted to have something significant in his presidency. He could not think of anything else and thought of something drastic like this. He or somebody in the US government took some key people into his confidence and planned what to do and how to do it. All the evidence points to controlled demolition of the three buildings of the World Trade Center. Yes, three, not just two. The scale of the operation and the cover-up was so vast that nobody from outside this country or not in complete confidence and sharing secrets with this country would have been capable of carrying out something like that. The third building that collapsed, at about 5:20 p.m., was a forty-seven-story tower across from the North Tower. There is sufficient evidence that there were explosions in the building even before the two towers fell. All the research and studies point out that these were controlled demolitions. There is footage of burn victims who were involved in these explosions. It seems that the collapse of the third tower was purposely not publicized much.

Furthermore, there were supposed to be more than two hundred people from Israel in the building, but they were given time off on 9/11 and stayed away from the building. The steel from the collapsed buildings was quickly disposed of. There was a book published, in Wisconsin, saying that 9/11 was an inside job. The name of the book is *Truth Jihad: My Epic Struggle against the 9/11 Lie* by Kevin Barrett. The whole thing makes me wonder. Some people say the truth might yet come out someday.

I know you have been waiting eagerly for the answers to the quiz I gave in the last chapter. Please refer to the questions.

1. Extramarital affairs include those between Shatrughan Sinha and Reena Roy, Shah Rukh Khan and Priyanka Chopra, Rekha and Amitab Bachchan, and Boney Kapoor and Sridevi.
2. My cousin Akhil watched *Nagin* fourteen times.
3. Guru Dutt, Divya Bharati, and Jiya Khan. Guru Dutt was a renowned actor and director. Divya Bharati was a young actress

who climbed the ladder of fame and success very quickly. She fell off the Balcony of a building when she was drunk and died. Jiya Khan was brought up in England and acted in films in Bollywood, such as *Ghajni* and *Housefull*.

4. As a youth, Dharmendra walked several miles to watch Suraiya's film *Dilligi*, which he watched forty times.

5. My dad liked Suraiya so much that he named his second daughter from his second wife Suraiya.

In 2010, one day, Shakeera complained about pain in the jaw and I think chest pain also. We went to the doctor, and the symptoms indicated a heart attack. The doctors at the University of Wisconsin confirmed she'd had a heart attack. They took care of her immediately and told us that she needed open-heart surgery about six to eight weeks from that time. The reason for the wait was because the heart has to be strong enough for surgery. In the meantime, they prescribed her some new medicine. This waiting period was hard on the family.

Shakeera took everything positively. We devoted quite a bit of time in prayers and *duas* (supplications). The date was set after a while for her operation. It's needless to say how hard it was for us to face all this. However, there was no other choice. We were all praying and hoping to God that everything would be all right. The risk was evident. However, the procedure was being done to make her better. On the day of the surgery, we went to the appointed place and filled out the required forms, and she went into surgery. It is hard to describe how anxious the kids and I were. She was in the hands of God and the doctors. She, however, positively went in there. We all went into the waiting room, and the employee in there kept us updated on the progress of the surgery. Every minute felt like a year. I could only wait, be patient, and pray. Big help came from Sajida, Shariff Saheb, Asif and family, and our kids. They all supported me to the max. That was the only way I could get through that day.

I could not keep tabs on what was going on that day. I think the surgery was about four to five hours. The surgeon was Dr. Neelu Edwards. He is a well-known surgeon. The doctor was compassionate. The clerk in the waiting room kept us posted from time to time. You can't imagine what was going through my mind when the surgery was taking place. I was asking God to give me courage to be able to get through the day, and every minute, I was thinking of Shakeera and praying for the operation to be successful.

Finally, the clerk at the counter told me that the doctor was on the phone. He said, "Everything went well, and she will be brought to the recovery room shortly." I thanked Dr. Neelu Edwards from the bottom of my heart, and I felt like kissing his hands. I thanked God, and our joy knew no bounds after we heard the good news. I felt like jumping up and down with joy. Everyone's face exhibited a smile, and there was a sigh of relief from every well-wisher. Dr. Neelu Edwards said, "I have done my job, and she needs to do her job now."

In other words, she needed to follow the diet and exercise regimen. By God's grace, she is following the marching orders well and has been feeling good since. She goes for checkups regularly and to the heart specialist about twice a year. At the same time, she has to take care of other health problems, run the household, and take care of the grandchildren, especially Farah's kids, Lailu and Zaydu.

A few weeks later, I felt a dull pain in my chest. It was uncomfortable. It felt like heartburn. It was constant and would not go away. Hence, I made an appointment at the University of Wisconsin Hospital. They did a stress test on a treadmill and what is called a nuclear test, and I came out okay on the tests. Needless to say, I was thankful to God and came home. I have been particular with my food, and I like to exercise regularly. I feel that time spent on exercise is time well invested in your health. Therefore, I believe you should take time to do your workouts. I read an article that said one half hour of exercise about four or five days a week will be good. I asked some of the experts in this field, and they said, "This is the minimum." The idea is to increase the heart rate when you exercise. Shakeera and I joined gyms, such as Princeton Club and Gold Gym. Of course, it becomes a burden to go to the gym, but look at the positive aspects of the workouts. You can at least do this much for your fitness. Also, since I am volunteering at Meriter Hospital, I have been using the gym facility there. It is a small facility, but it is not crowded like the big clubs. You almost always find the machine you want to work on. One trick about exercise is you can treat it as a routine. Routines don't seem to burden us that much, right? I cannot stress to you the importance of exercise in our lives. Always warm up a little bit and cool off at the end. This will relax you a little bit. Don't overdo any exercise.

Let me turn our thoughts to another issue. In some schools of thought in Islam, making cartoons of God's messenger is not acceptable. In 2011, a French weekly newspaper featured a cartoon of Prophet Mohammad. The name of the newspaper is *Charlie Hebdo*, and it thus insulted the great Prophet Mohammad (PBUH). Freedom of speech and expression has to be such that it will not make fun of, degrade, or insult the prophets of God. Two brothers who claimed to belong to a branch of al-Qaeda broke into the French newspaper facility with assault rifles and killed eleven people and injured eleven others. The paper continued to publish and sell issues. Instead of the regular sixty thousand copies, the following issue print ran 7.95 million copies in several languages.

Over a period of time, there have been several incidences of printing cartoons of Prophet Mohammad (PBUH). Also, some time back, there was a movie called *The Messenger*, which I watched on VHS. In the movie, viewers could hear the prophet talk, but the movie did not show his image or face. This was okay for people, and no objections of any kind were raised. I watched this movie a couple of times to make sure they didn't show his face. I am sure they did not.

I ran into the following information on the *Wikipedia* page about this topic. In 2005, a Danish newspaper published cartoons that showed Prophet Mohammad. In a lot of people's views, these cartoons were objectionable, which led to protests around the world, including violent demonstrations and riots in many countries. In Islam, there is a strong belief about cartoons of the holy prophets. They are considered highly blasphemous in many Islamic traditions. It was generally believed that the newspaper insulted Prophet Mohammad and Islam. The protests across the world resulted in about two hundred deaths, attacks on Danish and other European diplomatic organizations, and attacks on churches and on Christians. However, some groups sided with the Danish policies. To put fuel on the fire, the cartoons were reprinted in newspapers around the world in an act of journalistic solidarity. This flared up the political and social tensions between the Muslim and Western countries. The supporters kept arguing that this was all in accordance with the law of freedom of speech.

What are the limitations of freedom of speech and freedom of expression? Blasphemy should obviously be avoided, as it is not politically or religiously right. These cartoons were blasphemous to Muslims. The cartoonists argued that they meant to treat Islam the same way as Christianity. But they don't understand that the beliefs are much more stringent in Islam than in Christianity. In Christianity, it seems it is okay to depict an image or animation of Jesus Christ. There are even discussions regarding whether Jesus was black or white. There are movies about Jesus that show his image clearly. These two are different beliefs. A boycott was organized in Saudi Arabia and Kuwait, urging all Muslims to boycott not only Denmark but also Norway, France, Germany, and any country that printed these cartoons. In the United States, a decision was made not to publish the cartoons. It seems a local teenager wrote a letter to the publication and threatened the lives of the cartoonists.

Danish imams and eleven ambassadors from Muslim-majority countries, such as Turkey, Saudi Arabia, Iran, Pakistan, Egypt, Indonesia, Algeria, Bosnia and Herzegovina, Libya, Morocco, and Palestine, asked for a meeting with the Danish prime minister. They wanted to discuss the ongoing campaign of the Danish people and the media to harm the reputation of Islam and Muslims. The ambassadors' resolution was to take those responsible to task for the expression of a blasphemous attitude. The prime minister argued that it was not in his jurisdiction to take them to task. He said it was best to take them to court and let the court decide.

Peaceful protests were held in Copenhagen and attracted about 3,500 demonstrators in 2005. The Danish prime minister, even if he couldn't do anything with the publishers, should have at least disassociated from the publishing organization. Muslim countries continued to work diplomatically to try to resolve the issue. Islam and the prophet were ridiculed and insulted under the guise of free speech. It feels disgusting even to talk about it, but one of the cartoons portrayed a Muslim person being mounted by a dog while he was in prayer. What a gutter-filled thought to ever imagine. Freedom of expression cannot be used to defame religions. Large demonstrations were held in countries including Nigeria, Canada, India, and the United States. Also, peaceful demonstrations were held in support of the cartoonists in the name of freedom of speech. In India, Haji Yakoob Qureshi, a state minister in the Uttar Pradesh government, announced a cash reward for anyone who would behead the Danish cartoonists. There were some cases of Quran burning also. There are all kinds of crazy people in the world.

Did I tell you about my job at Coventry Village, the assisted living facility in Madison? It is a comparatively small facility with several elderly residents. My job was a weekend job. I used to take the residents to various churches in Madison. Different people went to different churches, as you can imagine. I had a set route, and the masses started at different times at different churches. Some riders were in wheelchairs, and some used walkers and canes. The wide-base vans were equipped with hydraulic lifts. The pre-trip inspections involved checking everything mechanical as well as the operation of the hydraulic lift. In case the hydraulic lift did not work automatically, there was a manual override. Sometimes an insurance underwriter rode with me to see if everything was working fine. Sometimes I was supposed to take some residents on a trip to nearby places, such as Baraboo and historical and exclusive shopping places. These trips were a challenge for me, as I was not always sure where to go. I had no GPS at that time. I was responsible for the safety of the residents who came along in the van. It was a good job. Sometimes I brought food home from the nursing home. Shakeera liked it because it was fresh and balanced food. The wheelchairs were on the back part of the van and needed to be secured properly to the wall and floor of the vehicle. I still had to drive carefully in order to keep the wheelchairs from tipping over. Also, I needed to make sure the wheels of the wheelchairs were locked.

In those days, even though I was careful, I still got some speeding tickets. The cops hide their cars in such a way that you cannot easily spot them. I might have been going just a few miles over the speed limit. That was enough for these cunning cops to nail me. Surprisingly enough, I got caught several times and had some points written against me. The rule is that if you accumulate so many points in a particular year, your license could get suspended. All these mishaps were in my own vehicle. However, one conniving guy who was a fellow employee somehow researched my driving record by himself or with the boss at Coventry Village. They called me into a meeting and brought this up. I could not defend myself much. They had my official driving report in front of me. I sensed that I was in trouble. They promoted this fellow employee of mine and gave me the choice to resign from my present position, and they gave me some other job choices. One of them was to work at the front desk during the night shift and also attend to any light maintenance calls during that shift. I thought this offer was just a setup to throw me out. I walked out of the job angrily and called their office in Chicago, which did not help me. I learned quite a bit in that job, and I enjoyed it while I was at it.

Now I would like to jump to another important story in world events. This time, it is in Pakistan. You have heard about the politics of Pakistan since it gained independence from British rule in 1947, when India also gained independence. There always has been a power struggle. India and Pakistan were one country for a long time. The split came when the struggle for independence resulted in Muslim Pakistan and Hindu India. The situation regarding Kashmir is still unresolved after many years. Each country has claimed a portion of it, and there is a portion that is Independent Kashmir. This is one of the biggest political conflicts that has been going on between the two countries.

The issue that I want to cover here is that of the struggle between Pervez Musharraf, former military general, and the prime minister. In 1999, Prime Minister Nawaz Sharif denied the landing of General Pervez Musharraf's plane in Karachi, directing it to land in an airport in Sindh Province. Musharraf responded by arranging to try Nawaz Sharif in an antiterrorism court with the attempted charge of plane hijacking. He said there was not enough fuel in the plane to fly farther than Karachi. It was planned to make the plane crash by exhausting its fuel in the air. Pervez Musharraf said it was sinisterly planned by Nawaz Sharif. In the meantime, Pervez Musharraf snatched power by a coup d'état. The courts sentenced Sharif to life imprisonment, and he was barred from holding any government posts or contesting in any elections. The rivalry and power struggle between the two men went back and forth.

Eventually, Pakistan's Supreme Court granted relief to the former Pakistani prime minister and chief of Pakistan Muslim League by relaxing the ban on his right to contest in elections. The sequence of events changed fast in Pakistan during that era. In 2007, Musharraf won the presidential election, but the Supreme Court disapproved it. He declared emergency rule, dismissed Chief Justice Chaudhry, and appointed a new Supreme Court, which, of course, confirmed his election. About a year after that, President Musharraf resigned after the political parties launched impeachment proceedings against him. In 2009, the reinstatement of the judges who were dismissed by Musharraf took place. Various other political games happened after that. About three years before the time of this writing, the parliament approved Nawaz Sharif as the prime minister after his Muslim League-N party won the parliamentary election. Nawaz Sharif had been a prime minister twice before, in 1990–93 and 1997–99. Pervez Musharraf became a close ally to the United States. He helped President George Bush in fighting terrorism. Some sources nicknamed Pervez Musharraf as Busharraf.

Now I will turn to another important personality in Pakistan. Her name is Benazir Bhutto. Bhutto was the eleventh and thirteenth prime minister of Pakistan. Her terms were 1988–90 and then 1993–96. She was the eldest daughter of Zulfikar Ali Bhutto, a former prime minister and founder of the Pakistan Peoples Party. She was the first woman to be elected head of a majority Islamic nation, and she is the only female prime minister of that country. Her ruling period was tarnished by issues like recession, corruption allegations, and high unemployment. However, due to her reforms, she earned the nickname Iron Lady. Her government had to be dismissed again by the president. She went into exile in Dubai in 1998. Nine years later, in 2007, she reached an understanding with President Musharraf and returned to Pakistan. All her corruption charges were dropped. Bhutto aspired to serve the country again. She took part in active campaigning and attended rallies. Unfortunately, Bhutto was assassinated in 2007, just two weeks before the general election. She was the leading candidate and projected winner in that election. She is buried next to her father in the Bhutto family's graveyard.

Asif Ali Zardari was born in 1955. He is a Pakistani politician and the current co-chairperson of the Pakistan Peoples Party. He served as the ninth president of Pakistan from 2008 to 2013. A landowner from Sindh Province, Zardari became famous when he married Benazir Bhutto. He became the first gentleman when his wife became the prime minister in 1988. Increasing tensions developed between Bhutto's brother, Murtuza, and Zardari. They always seemed to have differences of opinion about the principles of the party. Murtuza was killed in a police encounter in Karachi in 1996. The Bhutto government was dissolved a month later by the then-president, Leghari, and Zardari was arrested and indicted for Murtuza's death as well as corruption charges. He was released from jail in 2004 and went into exile in Dubai. He returned to Pakistan when Bhutto was assassinated. Zardari's party won the general election in 2008. Military ruler Musharraf was forced to resign, and Asif Zardari became the elected president in the fall of 2008. He was also pardoned and acquitted of various criminal charges in the same year.

His life took a big turn when he married Benazir Bhutto. The marriage was an arranged marriage according to the traditions. The lavish wedding ceremony was followed by luxurious evening parties with thousands of friends attending. The marriage enhanced Bhutto's political position, as she earned respect as a married woman. Zardari was involved in huge corruption cases as well as misuse of public funds. Both Bhutto and Zardari were in and out of jail several times for various crimes, including money laundering. Once, he was hospitalized for attempting to kill himself. In his opinion, it was an attempt by police to murder him.

When Benazir Bhutto was assassinated, officials asked his permission for an autopsy, which he did not allow, per Islamic beliefs. The funeral took place the next day. Zardari asked for an international inquiry into her death, and he made a statement that if Musharraf's government had adequate security, this tragedy could have been avoided, and she would still be alive today.

In Bhutto's political will, Asif was named the successor to the chairmanship of the party, but it was decided that Bilawal, Bhutto's son, should take over the chairmanship. Zardari would be co-chair, at least until the nineteen-year-old Bilawal completed his studies overseas.

I want to give a brief note here about the birth of Pakistan. Prior to independence in 1947, the territory of modern Pakistan was part of British India. In the nineteenth century, the land was incorporated with British India. The history of Pakistan began with the birth of a political party named the All-India Muslim League in 1906.

In 1930, one of the greatest poets and philosophers of all time, Sir Mohammad Iqbal, envisioned and called for an independent new state exclusively for Muslims in the northwestern part of India. In 1930, a barrister named Mohammad Ali Jinnah formulated a two-nation model. This called for formation of independent states on both the east and west sides of British India. This notion resulted in the partition of India, which was opposed by some of the political leaders at that time. The country became independent from British rule on August 14, 1947. The first prime minister of Pakistan, Liaquat Ali Khan, proclaimed that the future constitution of Pakistan would be based on the ideologies and democratic principles of Islam. A military leader named Ayub Khan became the enforcer of martial law in the country. Pakistan and India had a few wars between them. Pakistan's defeat in one of the wars ultimately led to the formation of East Pakistan and the birth of Bangladesh. Democracy was restored in Pakistan again in 1972–77 with Zulfikar ali Bhutto as the prime minister. He was ousted by Zia-ul-Haq, who became the country's third military president. A victory of the Peoples Party of Pakistan, led by Benazir Bhutto, made Bhutto the first female prime minister of Pakistan.

Over the next decade, she went back and forth on holding power with the Pakistan Muslim League, led by Nawaz Sharif. But in a 1999 coup, General Pervez Musharraf assumed power. He appointed himself as the president. The administration arranged to have a nationwide general election in 2002 and elected a new prime minister named Zafarullah Khan. In 2004, Shaukat Aziz was elected prime minister. Benazir was assassinated in 2007. The election of 2013 brought in Nawaz Sharif as a third-time prime minister. Sorry if this all sounds confusing, but that's the way it happened in Pakistan during the period covered. It has been very unstable. The countries of India and Pakistan have been blaming each other for any terrorist activities in their countries.

In 1947, quite a few Muslim families migrated to Pakistan from India. Our elders, including Dada Saab and my dad, made a decision to stay in Bangalore, India. Even though we did not have our own home or any big commitments, we decided not to migrate to Pakistan. My siblings and I, as kids, loved Pakistan. We liked the slogan "Pakistan Zindabad," which means "Long live Pakistan." I think the pride of having something of our own played a big part in our sentiments. I have given an account of all this elsewhere in the book. It would have been a different kind of life if we had migrated to Pakistan. Who knows what changes that move would have brought for us? I've heard different stories from the immigrants, and it makes sense to me that the best decision for my dadaji was not to migrate. There were quite a few Hindus who expected Muslims to migrate to Pakistan. For several years after that, I grew up with a strong feeling for Pakistan. I used to draw pictures of a crescent and a star, which depicted the symbol on the flag of Pakistan.

Now let's talk a little bit about Saddam Hussein. Saddam Hussein (1937–2006) was the fifth president of Iraq, serving in that capacity from July 1979 to April 2003. He belonged to a political party called the Ba'ath Party, which is a combination of Arab nationalism and socialism. He played an important role in a 1968 coup that brought his party to power in Iraq. He served as a vice president under Ahmed Hassan al-Bakr. In the seventies, he was instrumental in nationalizing oil and other industries. All state-owned banks were put under his control. Soon after, the oil money made the economy grow at a fast rate. The war with Iran made the system insolvent. There were other reasons for the insolvency too. The Sunni sect of Arabs made up only one-fifth of the population of Iraq. The positions of power were mainly filled by Sunnis. Saddam came into power in 1979. He suppressed several movements, particularly Shia and Kurdish movements. He managed to maintain power during the Iran-Iraq War and the Gulf War. He showed opposition to the United States and was condemned for attacking Israel. Iraq was also condemned throughout the West for its dictatorship. The total number of Iraqis killed by the security forces of Saddam's government is estimated to be 250,000.

Iraq has attacked two Israeli cities with scud missiles. Both Tel Aviv and Haifa were hit in attacks that began at 3:00 a.m. their local time, while most of the people were asleep. Initial reports mentioned that one of the missiles had a chemical warhead, which proved to be untrue. Israel has the strongest military force of any of the Middle Eastern countries. It was presumed that any attack by Iraq would be answered with massive retaliation. American president George Bush made an appeal to Israel to hold back on retaliation. The allied forces planned to destroy Iraqi missile sites and mobile launchers, which would prove dangerous to the security of Israel. Bush was determined to protect Israel from any further attacks. Israeli prime minister Yitzhak Shamir called a meeting to make a decision regarding the Israeli response. A day-long meeting did not bring any substantial result regarding what course of action to take. They declared to the media, "Israel reserves the right to retaliate in the manner they choose and with the scale they decide on."

Israel decided to leave the retaliation decision in the hands of allied forces. Iraq fired the scud missiles on the Israeli cities again the next day, but the retaliation did not come.

I want to give one note about the missiles Iraq produced. Al-Samoud was a liquid-propellant rocket ballistic missile developed by Iraq in the years between the Gulf War and the 2003 invasion of Israel. The production of these missiles started in 2001. While all this was happening, I was busy planning my retirement from Forest Products Laboratory. During that time, I took an assignment to work in another region for a short time. The assignment was in Goleta, California. I went there in May, and the weather was beautiful in Southern California. I have given an account of this elsewhere in the book.

The al-Samoud missiles were banned by the UN, as their range was higher than the permissible limit. Iraq was asked to destroy these missiles. A number of them were destroyed by Iraq. A number of the missiles were fired at Kuwait during the 2003 conflict.

After a month of intensive air attacks, the allied forces launched a ground attack. They took a big risk that Saddam might use the weapons of mass destruction that the West believed he had. Even though Iraq was supposed to have a good army to defend itself, they started retreating. Four days later, US president George Bush announced a victory. Kuwait was liberated, but Saddam's regime was still in power. The United States and Britain launched a second war against Iraq in 2003.

All this news was disturbing to me. I was going through an emotional time in my life. I had announced at Forest Products Lab that I planned to retire in a few months. I was winding down on my projects. Somehow, there was not anything pressing that I was doing at the time. On our campus, there were some University of Wisconsin buildings. I was charged with the responsibility of looking into a central air-conditioning system for their buildings. We held a meeting with the officials in there. That's as far as I went on that project, as soon after, my last day at work approached, and I had to leave. It was an emotional departure for me. I was satisfied that in my tenure at the lab, I had made a good impact as an engineer in the department. Retirement is a time of lots of planning as well as lots of emotional thoughts, as you can imagine. Some of my colleagues were in their early seventies and still working. My belief is that you should retire while you can still enjoy life, while you are healthy. Anyway, I had a lot of flashbacks of my career, and I retired in March of 2003. At the time of this writing, by the good grace of Allah, I am in my thirteenth year of retirement, and I am volunteering a little bit here and there and working part-time wherever possible.

Now let's go back to Saddam's story. He was overthrown and captured to be subjected to trial for war crimes. In 2003, Pope John Paul II and other top officials of the Vatican released a series of condemnations against a possible military strike on Iraq, calling it immoral, not without risk, and a crime against peace. Even supporters of the US-led war, including the prime ministers of Britain, Spain, and Italy, were leery about the unilateral strike. The orders of the United Nations were brutally ignored. President Bush received advice from Pope John Paul II not to proceed with the air strikes. Concerns surfaced about the impact of the war on the relationship between Muslims and Christians of the world. There were statements from the Vatican saying that war is a "defeat of humanity" and that a preemptive strike on a sovereign nation was not justified legally or morally. A unilateral military action would be a crime against peace. There were no grounds for self-defense either. They did not threaten us in any way whatsoever. An American attack on an Arab country would give rise to horrific political issues. A top Vatican official said, "We want to ask America: Is it worth it to you [to start this war]? Because of this, don't you envision decades of unrest and hostility in the world?"

The pope sent an envoy to meet Iraqi leader Saddam Hussein. In the West, all the discussions gravitated toward a war against Iraq. It has also been said that younger George Bush wanted to take revenge against Saddam Hussein for not yielding to his father's efforts of removing him from his dictatorship. He believed he had some unfinished business on his hands, and he felt obligated by his own conscience to finish it off. His prime goal became defeating Saddam and removing him from power.

Fareed Zakaria, on his *Global Public Square* program, examined the question "Why do they hate us?" I think "they" means the Muslims or radical Islam. I will try to highlight some of the things he talked about in that presentation. I won't cover the entire show here, as you can get it from the Internet. Per the show, today's radical Islamic movement started when there was a dance party at a church in Colorado back in 1949. An old gramophone (a machine that played 78-rpm and other records) played the song "Baby, It's Cold Outside." A Muslim student walked in, and he described later on what he experienced. He noticed a horrifying mixing of the sexes, with chests touching chests, people kissing each other, and the outlines of women's breasts showing in their tight dresses or sweaters. Of course, in those days, things were a little more conservative than at the time of this writing. Anyway, the young Muslim student had a bad impression of American society. Some of the Muslim clerics also do not have a good opinion of the policies of the United States regarding Muslims. America helped Bosnia during the early nineties and, thus, tried to protect Islam. In Afghanistan also, the United States protected the cause of Islam. This was Fareed's answer for some of the questions or complaints from radical Islamic representatives.

To the question of whether there will be seventy-two virgins offered to the martyrs who died in the cause of Islam, Irshad Manji replied that there is nothing like that in the Quran. She said the word has been misinterpreted by some people. Actually, seventy-two raisins are presented to the martyrs, not virgins, as it is talked about. Some imams in America have preached that their followers should ban the Constitution, ban the American flag, and start supporting Islamic State of Iraq and Syria. It is believed that the United States has determined that the actions of ISIS against Christians and other minority groups in Iraq and Syria constitute an act of genocide. ISIS has been committing crimes against humanity in general, and they have directed ethnic cleansing of the above groups of people and also, in some cases, Sunni Muslims, Kurds, and other minorities.

CHAPTER 13

Concluding Remarks

When my dad reached a certain advanced age, I always recommended he exercise. At any age, exercise is important, and we all should continue it in our old age as much as possible. I am a big proponent of working out and of keeping busy. When I was working at the steel mill in Detroit, some of my fellow employees used to say, "A busy man is a happy man." Nothing could be truer than this. When God doesn't like somebody, he makes the person bored with nothing to do. My slogan to myself and younger people has been to never run out of projects. Always do something that will be useful to you for your future. You have to be accountable for every hour you spend on this earth. One engineer from a consulting company that we hired used to say, "I have to sell every hour that I work for my company." In other words, we need to justify how productively we make use of our work time. Time budgeting is of prime importance in planning out a workday. Most people like a challenge. They like to accomplish more in less time. To achieve this, you need to work smart as well as hard. The more responsibilities you have, the harder you have to work. You might have heard the statement "Work smart, not hard." That certainly makes sense. If you work smarter, you can avoid working hard. Spinning your wheels and not moving forward makes the whole thing less productive. We have to concentrate on the outcome and not only on the output.

Pandit Jawaharlal Nehru, the first prime minister of India, used say, "I am not interested in the excuses for delay, but I am interested in the results." I will now copy here some of the quotes I try to live by.

> We must go vigorously forward, apply whatever knowledge
> and common sense we have to the task ahead, and
> everywhere and always prefer results to routine.
>
> —Gifford Pinchot

> The rung of a ladder was never meant to rest upon,
> but only to hold a person's foot long enough to enable
> them to put the other somewhat higher.
>
> —Unknown

> I helped raise two daughters (nineteen and twenty-three). They are bright, aggressive, fiercely competitive go-getters who aim for a goal and keep at it. We never told them they were different or they needed some special favor or rule to compete academically or any other way. We expected them to compete in whatever arena they chose on their merits. If they hit a road bump, go around it or over it, and they do!
>
> ------------Fred Green

> Go confidently in the direction of your dreams.
> Live the life you have imagined.
>
> —Henry David Thoreau

I made a mission statement for my career enhancement:

> I am committed to providing the finest and best (engineering) services for my employer with zero defects. It is my prime duty to deliver results for these services in such a manner that my customers seek me out to render the services over and over again and recommend me to their associates.

Whenever you work with a team on a project, you have to establish criteria for success. You have to lay it out for everybody's understanding right at the beginning. As you progress through the various facets of the project, you need to evaluate and assess where you are going and whether you are meeting the milestone deadlines. Before you start the project, you need to justify completion of the project. If there are environmental or regulatory constraints, that will be the biggest justification, and there will not be any alternatives as such. In other cases, you need to chart out the alternatives. Could one of the alternatives be doing nothing and continuing as is? Normally, there will be few areas where you can do that.

A couple methods used to evaluate projects are the program evaluation and review technique (PERT) and the critical path method (CPM). I always reviewed the milestone chart and assessed projects that way. Different projects will be at different stages of the game. It is a challenge to keep everything going at the same time. You need to keep the projects' expectations in mind. The end result should be in your mind all the time. Regular meetings should be held to check the progress of each team member. Each project team member should have a specific responsibility. Finger pointing and blame games are not part of the process. A logbook should be kept to record all important factors of the project. A conversation record of telephone calls is also of importance. If there is one thing everybody dislikes, it is an unpleasant surprise. If you have good communication going, there should be no surprises. A team member might need to act like a detective and investigate how the project is doing on the way toward its goal of success. A project is normally sponsored by another department. You are handling other people's money. The completed project has to meet the needs of that department. There should be clarity at both the technical and personal levels, especially if you want to avoid any unpleasant surprises. The excitement of planning how to succeed and the vision of future success provide a form of motivation. This can make things happen and help you proceed in the right direction. Luck also plays a helpful part.

You cannot finish a book without closing its chapters. You should understand why God blessed you with another morning to wake up. It is to forget the pains of yesterday and see the opportunity the new day has brought. Always do something that will not diminish your dignity and honor in any manner. Make up for the wrong things you might have done. See your family, and extend your love again. Make others feel happy, needed, and loved. You see, life is more than just a long day ahead. Love it, cherish it and make every moment count to the fullest extent.

For most of my career, I have been involved with project management. That's the natural reason why I have been expounding on it so much. The relationship between the project team and the sponsoring department should be encouraged and developed by the project leader. Both parties should realize the mutual interdependence and the stakes in the project. The mutual goal is project success. In fact, the whole project can be considered a process of contracting. It is about exploring and arriving at a mutual agreement that is communicated right at the start. Dr. A. P. J. Abdul Kalam, in his book *Wings of Fire*, talks about a technique called PACE, which stands for program analysis, control, and evaluation. Almost every week, the project team and the sponsor department formally have a meeting to check out where everything stands. Is everything on target? Are they on track to achieve the goal they have set? The project leader has to have good supervisory skills. He has to be assertive, not too aggressive, and never too passive. The leader should know how to deal with people, especially the people who are working for him. When a new supervisor or manager comes on board, the department's employees start judging him in various aspects. They want to find out the traits of the new supervisor. What are his operation methods? How will he deal with the shortcomings of his subordinates? How does he deal with the supervisors in other departments? How does he handle the day-to-day operations of the department? They explore him until they form an opinion about him. Some close friends might even talk about the new guy among themselves privately. This is how humans are, and we cannot change.

Shakeeb and I have discussed the various styles of supervision. Some of them are dictatorial, supportive, consultative, and authoritative. Please look into the details in your resources, and you will find an explanation for each. It is not within the scope of this treatise to go into it. Also, you have to find your own style of supervision, one that best suits your purpose and works for you. You can also adopt a combination of styles. In anything you venture to do, it's not about what you do; it's about why you do it.

You need to rise to the occasion and the challenge and discover your own strengths, even though you might feel alone at times. It is a well-known fact that dealing with people is the most difficult thing a supervisor can face. Ask yourself once in a while what you've got to show for the time you have put in on something. People believe in tangible evidence of what you have accomplished. Lack of planning on somebody's part should not give rise to an emergency and chaos on somebody else's part.

There never will be a second chance to make a good first impression. Out of pain and problems have come the sweetest songs and most gripping stories. No matter what happens, some memories can never be replaced. There comes a time when you have to choose between turning the page and closing the book.

Now, I want to say to the young readers, please take some time to read about Maslow's law of the hierarchy of needs on the Internet or via some other source. People have different needs levels. The highest-priority needs for everybody are physiological needs. These are the basic human needs, such as food, sleep, and shelter. Once these needs are met, the circle becomes bigger. Therefore, in the outer circle, we have security and safety needs. These are the second level of needs. Once we are satisfied with these needs, the third level of needs consists of the needs of love and belonging. After we have accomplished these, the fourth and fifth levels of needs are self-esteem needs and self-actualization needs. The highest level of needs, or the outermost circle, are longed for only after the other basic needs have been achieved. By God's grace, I have fulfilled even the highest level of needs in my life, and I thank God for it.

I have always strived to do things perfectly. Am I a perfectionist? Maybe, or maybe not. It is challenging. I believe in networking with people; exploring all resources; and working with time schedules, budget constraints, and so on. In brief, I did not do too badly. I tried to put the customer at the center of business activity. Going to engineering college on a bicycle about six or seven miles one way; studying under a shade tree in a park, sometimes out loud; writing out whatever subject I was studying on the mosaic floor of my room with a piece of chalk; trying to block out the loud noise of a flour mill in front of my room while studying; having a roommate (Akhil, my cousin); and studying all night at times paid off. I successfully passed the BE exam in 1964. It took me about six years for a four-year degree course, as some courses I had to repeat and redo the exam again. You don't have to repeat the subjects you pass. It makes sense.

What you have read in this book is a bird's-eye view of my life with some historic background attached. Let's move on. It's just a chapter in your entire eternal life That's how I want to take it. As A. P. J. Abdul Kalam says, there comes a time when you have to choose between turning the page and closing the book.

Again quoting from A. P. J. Abdul Kalam, "today I close the door to the past, open the door to the future, take a deep breath, try to gather new strength, step up to new heights, and start a new chapter of my life."

In the end, others will judge me according to their own scale anyway. However, I believe in the words of one of Doris Day's songs: "Que sera, sera. Whatever will be, will be. The future is not ours to see. Whatever will be, will be. Whatever will be, will be."

The will of God is the one that will prevail always.

EPILOGUE

This book was written with the sense that readers will learn something from the experiences of my life. As much as we would like to engineer them, the circumstances around us are the forces that truly dictate our life courses. From my childhood, I longed to be creative and to be able to contribute something to the world. Yet, this may simply be something misremembered by myself in the present time. Still, as the child I remember now, I would often take on projects and seek to acquire skills, all for the satisfying feeling of accomplishment that I might get at the end of my learning journey. For example, I remember the pride I felt once, in the early 40s, after having made a kite from scratch and then having learned to fly it. Similarly, I would make my own toys, based on the designs of other toys that I had or that I had seen. I improved on the designs and found my creations useful. Along with my brothers, I designed and constructed a number of shacks or small huts with sticks and palm tree branches. We had no practical reason for doing this. We made them for the sake of making and saying that we built it. This was all very prophetic, I think. After all, I would later on in my life, become an engineer. In fact, I originally wanted to become a doctor, despite all of my building experience. Yet, circumstances dictated that I would not pursue medicine. When I was 16, my father was transferred to a town where a pre-medical education (chemistry, botany, and zoology classes) was not available. In our new town, courses in physics, chemistry, and math were my only choices. In my course of study, in high school, I was a very good student. My friends often sought me to tutor them. I passed high school without a hitch, though I failed to earn the highest honor, distinction as a "first class" student by only 11 marks.

My marriage was an arranged marriage. And on the marriage market, as the engineer, I was very valuable. My hand was sought by a number of rich and distinguished families. Engineers were very much respected in those days. My desire to go abroad would help me make my decision as one family, Shakeera's family, had offered to pay for my trip and the tuition fee etc. At the age of 29, a bit too late, I think, I went to America on a "Father In-Law" Scholarship, as they called it. I struggled in my studies in the beginning. I was classified as a special student at the University of Wisconsin. I could not obtain high enough grade at this university and got accepted instead at Marquette University, Milwaukee, Wisconsin, USA where I secured my Master's in Engineering. I am so very proud of my accomplishment there. I happened to work for Dr. A.F. Elkouh who was considered one of the top researchers in the fields of Energetics. Also I had professor Bush for Thermodynamics. I had the opportunity of being a student of Glen Myers for Heat Transfer who is a well-respected researcher in the field. I have to mention Professor Abdullah Shariff from Bangalore who also enriched my interest in Mechanical engineering. My career as a Mechanical Project Engineer spans over a period of 40 years. After retirement, I became a tutor in Math and worked in miscellaneous jobs. I am blessed and fortunate to have retired from the Government of United States service. I have the hobby of writing and publishing Urdu poetry books of which I have two so far.

I hope to contribute to the society as much as possible in future. May Allah help and fulfil my dreams.

"دارالسلام"
بحرام راج پت
سنگلہ ورکشپ

مستاج سے سلامت باشند

بعد اسلام علیک کہ واضح ہووے کہ تمہارا خط مجھے ملیریم ہی میں پہرست ہوکر قریب ایک ماہ کا اوپر گذر گیا ۔ جب سے شاید رہ تمہیں فرصت ہی نہ ہوگی ۔ اِس اثناء ہی میں تمہارا رہا اجازت سے یہاں بھی آئی تھی ۔ پہلے دیکرے روز ہی تمہیں ایک خط لکھی تھی ۔ نہ تمہیں پہرست ہوا اور نہ اس کا پتہ ہی مجھے معلوم ہوا ۔ نہ اُسکا جواب آیا ۔ جب سے دونوں بچوں کی طبیعت بھی کچھ ناساز ہیں ۔ چھوٹے بچہ کو کھٹرا بخار آتا رہتا ہے ۔ بڑے بچہ کو باندں کا انگو ٹھا ٹوٹ گیا کلنے سے ہیسے وغیرہ جاری ہے ۔ دونوں بچوں کا ہاسپیٹال سے علاج جاری ہے ۔ ابھی والدہ کی طبیعت ویسی ہی ہے ۔

میں ملیریم میں پہرست سامان ضروت کا چھوٹر کر آئی تھی ۔ میں یہاں آنے سے ایک ہفتہ بعد نوکرے ہمراہ منگوا بھیجی تو بھلے دئیے نہیں ۔ بعد تکرار ے پورا پورا سب سامان دوازے پر بھیجوا دئیے سرکے بہار کے ۔ نوکری زبانی معلوم ہوا ۔ دیکھئے حسن اخلاق ۔ اور اُسی سے پہلا بھیسے ہی کہ دور وز کیلئے جاؤ ۔ اتنے دن کرنا اچھا بنی صباں آنا ہی افضل ہے وغیرہ

233

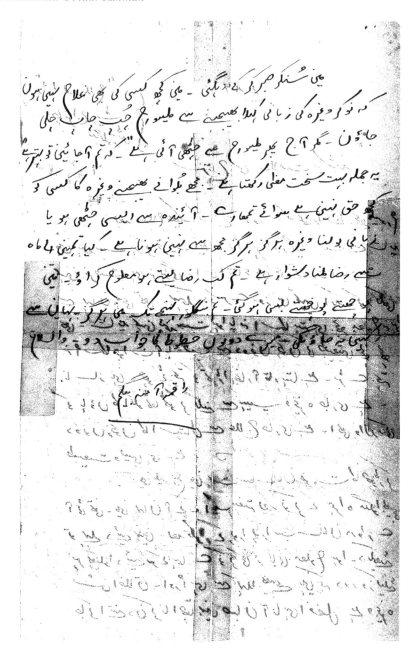

Letter dated 4-7-1937 from the Author's Mother to Author's Father

Note: This is an English translation. The original letter (seen elsewhere in the book) was written In Urdu.

My Crown Jewel, May God keep you well,

I got your letter in Malleshwaram [my grandpa's place] more than a month ago. It seems you did not get any time since then. In the meantime, after taking your permission I came to my Mom's house. As soon as I reached here, I had sent you a letter. I am not sure you got it or not, as I did not get any reply. Both kids [my younger brother Asif and I] are not feeling well. Younger kid has fever on and off. Older kid has a wound in his big toe. Both kids are under treatment. My mother's health is still not good.

I had left quite a few personal belongings at the Mother-in-law's house. When I sent a servant to bring the same back, at first, they did not even care or pay attention to him. The servant told me after much pleading, they threw my belongings by the exit door. What kind of an attitude they have? Also they sent a message with the servant that I should return to Malleshwaram as soon as the next day etc. I was patient about it. I am not anybody's servant that as soon as I receive a message like this I will silently yield and obey.

But today I received a note from Malleshwaram again "You better come back right away." This was a very rude message. Nobody has a right to order me around like this except you. In future they better not send any written or verbal messages like this. By the way is it so hard for you to take a few days off which you have not done in four months. Let me know when you can do this. I am sick and tired of repeatedly asking you this question

I am telling you, until you are back to Bangalore, I am not going anywhere from my Mom's house.

Please reply to my letters.
Wassalam, Amina Begum

ABOUT THE AUTHOR

Mohammed Obedur Rahman has also been known as Arif Pasha since his childhood. He always has had a creative urge. As a young boy, he designed several toys and made them himself, improvising with whatever material he had on hand. He made a kite with paper and sticks and created a film projector with a cardboard box and a lens. Similarly, Mohammad made toy cars from cigarette cartons, and along with his brothers, he constructed small huts and shacks to play in. He was proud of these things, and as he grew, he continued to take pride in his creations. He was excited to learn any skills that would help him make things. This creative urge developed as he grew up, working with his brain as much as his hands. After high school, Mohammed wanted to be a doctor, but circumstances led him to become an engineer instead. Eventually, he enjoyed a forty-year career as a successful engineer. He started as a young junior engineer in India and worked for about forty years in the United States as an engineer. In engineering, he took pride in creating and implementing new ideas in the projects he worked on. Quite a few of Mohammed's projects, such as a herbarium building at Forest Products Research Lab in Madison, Wisconsin, are still there today. In addition to his master's thesis in engineering, Mohammed has published two books of poetry, one in 2010 and the other in 2015. Both books have been received well in Urdu-speaking circles. He also has recorded two albums of his selected poetry. Mohammed still gets invited to participate in Urdu poetry symposiums from time to time. He also fills his time by giving back to his community through volunteering at local hospitals and schools. He currently lives with his wife in Madison, Wisconsin, where he continues his passion of writing Urdu poetry. Mohammed wanted to publish this book to make a record of the events in his life for the benefit of young readers. His philosophy in life is to apply himself with high intensity to any project he takes on or any goal he sets up for himself. He states that he might fail; however, he will not fail due to a lack of effort.

ABOUT THE BOOK

This book captures the essence of life in this world, with all its whims, fancies, and dreams. It takes you through a virtual tour of a common man's life in his own words. Learn from these stories, and imagine them as if they are shared with you in warm conversation over a cup of tea. You will learn history, facts, trivia, and interesting tidbits that will make you appreciate things in general in this world—children playing, birds chirping, thunder clapping—and then a silence will set in, never to be broken, unless perhaps in the far pasture of the Milky Way.

I meant this book to be entertaining, relaxing armchair reading, and the stories are such that you can identify with them. In addition, I wanted to keep my memories alive. In reading them, you will find some factoids to chew on.

Printed in the United States
By Bookmasters